THE ARTS
OF THE
SIKH KINGDOMS

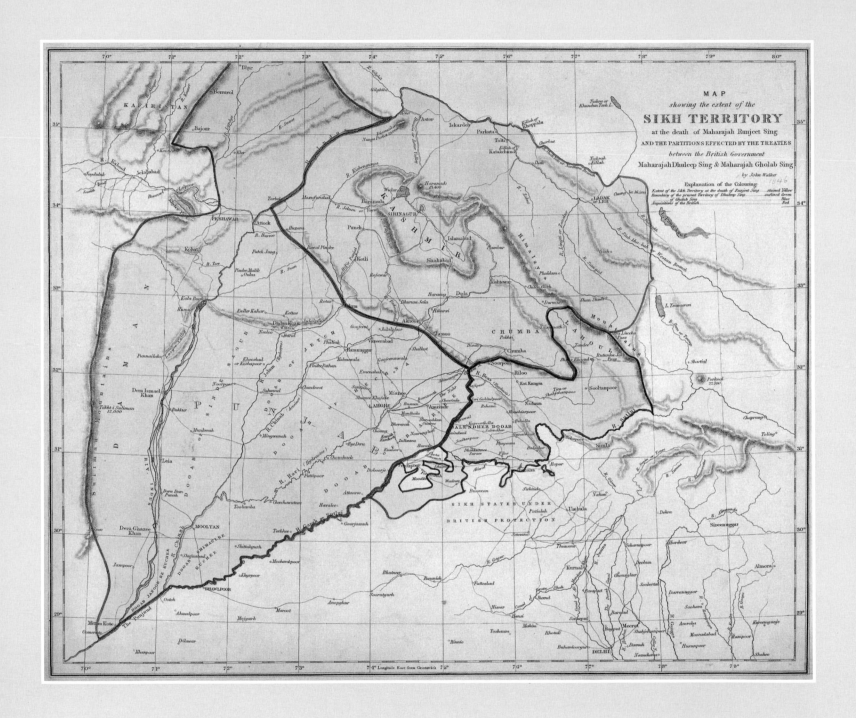

MAP
showing the extent of the
SIKH TERRITORY
at the death of Maharajah Runjeet Sing
AND THE PARTITIONS EFFECTED BY THE TREATIES
between the British Government
Maharajah Dhuleep Sing & Maharajah Gholab Sing.
by John Walker

Explanation of the Colouring

THE ARTS
OF THE
SIKH KINGDOMS

EDITED BY SUSAN STRONGE

First published by V&A Publications, 1999

V&A Publications
160 Brompton Road
London SW3 1HW

© The Board of Trustees of the
Victoria and Albert Museum 1999

Susan Stronge and all the contributors reserve their
moral right to be identified as the authors of this book

ISBN 1851772618

A catalogue record for this book is available
from the British Library

Designed by Harry Green
Photography by Mike Kitcatt, V&A Photographic Studio
Printed and bound in Great Britain
by Butler & Tanner Ltd, Frome

Every effort has been made to seek permission to
reproduce those images whose copyright does not reside
with the V&A, and we are grateful to the individuals and
institutions who have assisted in this task. Any omissions
are entirely unintentional, and the details should be
addressed to the publishers.

ILLUSTRATIONS

Jacket front: Detail of painting depicting Maharaja
Narinder Singh (see plate 200). Sheesh Mahal Museum
and Medal Gallery. Courtesy of the Department of
Cultural Affairs, Architecture and Museums, Punjab,
Chandigarh, India.

Jacket back: Marble floor beneath the
Guru Granth Sahib on the upper storey of
the Golden Temple (the Harmandir).
Courtesy of Guru Nanak Nishkam Sewak Jatha.

Frontispiece: Map depicting the Sikh territories
at the death of Maharaja Ranjit Singh (1839).
Courtesy of the British Library.

Contents

ACKNOWLEDGEMENTS

The idea of having a Sikh exhibition first came from Narinder Singh Kapany of the Sikh Foundation, Palo Alto, California. From the very beginning his inspiration and support have sustained the project, and our debt to him is enormous.

A great number of people have contributed to the success of the exhibition and book. At an early stage Professor B.N. Goswamy generously shared his knowledge and experience, drawing attention to important collections and paintings, notably the processional scene of Maharaja Narinder Singh of Patiala used for the cover of the book; his advice and information have been invaluable. A meeting with Harbinder Singh Rana and the Trustees of the Maharaja Duleep Singh Centenary Trust began a relationship between the V&A and the Trust which will certainly continue beyond the exhibition; their support, advice and cooperation have greatly enriched the project. Amandeep Singh Madra and Parmjit Singh offered to help in any way they could as soon as we met, and since then have unstintingly shared their knowledge, library and enthusiasm.

I was extremely privileged to meet Bhai Mohinder Singh; the subsequent generosity of the Guru Nanak Nishkam Sawak Jatha (UK) allowed us to include in the book the superb photographs of the Harmandir in Amritsar, including the extraordinary, unpublished inlaid marble roundel on the back cover, which we reproduce with enormous gratitude. Sandeep Virdee and his colleagues, particularly Nirmal Sidhu, made considerable efforts to provide these images and other information in time for specific deadlines.

A project on this scale requires substantial sponsorship and financial resources in addition to those provided from the Museum's own funds. In this context, we acknowledge the energetic and enthusiastic support of Mr and Mrs H. S. Narula, the committee and all those who supported the 'By the Five Rivers' Gala Evening, and Air India and others who have generously contributed. We are also grateful to Madame Krishna Riboud, who in addition to lending beautiful textiles from her Paris foundation, AEDTA, very kindly underwrote some of the borrowing costs; Gurshuran and Elvira Sidhu, Narinder Kapany, F.S. Aijazuddin and A.S. Melikian-Chirvani generously provided photographs without charge.

I would like to thank the following for their help in a variety of ways: F.S. Aijazuddin has been unstinting in his help, both personally and in his official capacity as Chairman of the Trustees of the Lahore Museum; A.S. Melikian-Chirvani read Persian inscriptions on many of the objects; W. Owen Cole read most of the text to check for major mistakes (any remaining errors must be the responsibility of the editor) and made significant contributions to the Glossary; Anne Colombe Launois-Sukanda (Sat Kaur) gave invaluable help over the two months she spent as an intern in the Indian and South-east Asian Department. The contributors to the book have been heroic in meeting tight deadlines. In addition, the following provided extremely useful advice or information at various stages in the planning of the exhibition: Richard Blurton, Sheila Canby, Neil Carleton, Christopher Cavey, Robert Del Bonta, Jeevan Deol, Elizabeth Errington, Eberhard Fischer, Mark Haworth-Booth, Alan Jobbins, Rochelle Kessler, Anthony North, Amina Okada, Venetia Porter, Thom Richardson, Fakir Seif ud-Din Bokhari, Shashi Sen, Patwant Singh, Stuart Cary Welch.

Lenders to the exhibition or their representatives, without exception, were very receptive to the idea of the exhibition from the first approaches and we are immensely grateful to them:

FRANCE: AEDTA, Paris: Madame Krishna Riboud, Madame Marie-Helene Guelton. Musée des Arts asiatiques-Guimet, Paris: Jean-François Jarrige and Pierre Cambon. Musée Jean de la Fontaine, Château Thierry: Madame C. Sinnig-Haas.

INDIA: The Government of India and R.V. Vaidyanatha Ayyar; the Government of Punjab and D.S. Jaspal; the Chandigarh Administration. National Museum of India, New Delhi: Smt Kasturi Gupta Menon, Anamika Pathak, Daljeet Khare, Rita Sharma. Government Museum and Art Gallery, Chandigarh: V.N. Singh, the late Suwarcha Paul, and Punam Khanna. Qila Mubarak Museum, Patiala: Jaswinder Singh. Sheesh Mahal Museum and Medal Gallery, Patiala. During my initial research visit, H.H. the Maharaja of Patiala allowed Narinder Kapany and myself to see his remarkable collection and later allowed photographs to be taken of the *hukmnama* and body armour of Guru Gobind Singh for reproduction in this book. Colin Perchard, Sushma Bahl and their colleagues have provided invaluable support.

IRELAND: Chester Beatty Library, Dublin: Michael Ryan and Clare Pollard.

PAKISTAN: The Government of Pakistan and Kindi Aslam, Senior Officer in the Ministry of Culture, Sports, Tourism and Youth Affairs in Islamabad, and by their museum colleagues: Lahore Fort: Ihsan Nadiem and Irshad Hussain. Lahore Museum: Anjum Rehmani, Nusrat Ali and the Board of Trustees. I would also like to thank Fakir Syed Aijazuddin for lending from his own collection, and Syeda Subohi Haider, who was typically generous in her hospitality during my research visit to Lahore.

UNITED STATES OF AMERICA: Narinder Singh Kapany lent objects from his collection which, by the time this book is published, will have been donated to the Asian Art Museum, San Francisco. Elvira and Gurshuran Sidhu, California. Harvard, Fogg Art Museum: Stuart Cary Welch, James Cuno and Rochelle Kessler. Metropolitan Museum of Art, New York: Philippe de Montebello, Stuart Pyrrh and Donald LaRocca – Arms and Armor Department; Daniel Walker, Stefano Carboni and Marie L. Swietochowski – Islamic Department.

UK: Her Majesty the Queen. Within the Royal Collection I thank Hugh Roberts, Caroline de Guithaut, and Alison Fairbank, and at the Royal Library and Archives: Oliver Everett, Lady Sheila de Bellaigue, Francis Dimond, Helen Grey. Royal Palaces Trust: Anna Keay. Royal Artillery Historical Trust: Brigadier K.A. Timbers. The British Library, London: Graham Shaw, Jeremiah P. Losty, Rod Hamilton and Linda Raymond. The British Museum, London: Robert Knox, Michael Willis, Rachel Ward – Oriental Antiquities; Joe Cribb and Elizabeth Errington – Coins and Medals. English Heritage: Rowena Shepherd. National Army Museum: Ian Robertson, Jenny Spencer-Smith. National Portrait Gallery: Charles Saumarez-Smith. Royal Armouries, Leeds: Guy Wilson, Thom Richardson and their colleagues.

THE SHIRVAN FOUNDATION: A.S. Melikian-Chirvani.

In the V&A, many colleagues have contributed to both the exhibition and the production of the book: Susan Lambert and Jan Van de Wateren; Linda Lloyd Jones and her colleagues, especially Anna Gustavsson and Howard Batho, whose patience in managing a range of exacting schedules has probably been tried to levels never experienced before; the conservation departments who took on this project at a difficult time and in particular Lynda Hillyer and her colleagues; Diana Heath, Simon Metcalf, Sophia Ward, Ingrid Barre, Pauline Webber and Mike Wheeler, all of whom have had a large share of the work; and Furniture and Ceramics conservation. Mike Kitcatt, of the Photographic Studio did a great deal of new photography for the book. From V&A Publications I am extremely grateful to Mary Butler, Miranda Harrison, and Celia Jones. Above all, I thank Deborah Swallow and all my colleagues in the Indian and South-East Asian department, without whose constant help and support this book would not have come out. SUSAN STRONGE, 1999

CHRONOLOGY OF SIKHISM, THE MUGHAL EMPIRE, AND THE BRITISH MONARCHY

SIKH GURUS (G = start date of guruship)		SIKH HISTORY AND RELATED HISTORICAL EVENTS IN INDIA	MUGHAL EMPERORS (start of reign)	BRITISH MONARCHS (start of reign)
1500 Guru Nanak (1469-1539)	G: 1507	1507: Nanak proclaims 'there is no Hindu, there is no Muslim' and Sikhism is founded		1509: Henry VIII
			1526: Babur	
Guru Angad Dev (1504-1552)	G: 1539		1530: Humayan	
			1556: Akbar	1547: Edward VI
1550 Guru Amar Das (1479-1574)	G: 1552			1553: Mary I 1559: Elizabeth I
		1565: Akbar visits Guru Amar Das		
Guru Ram Das (1534-1581)	G: 1574			
Guru Arjan Dev (1563-1606)	G: 1581	1598: Akbar visits Guru Arjan		
1600		1601: Completion of the Harmandir (Golden Temple) and the Adi Granth (sacred scripture)		1603: James I
Guru Har Gobind (1595-1644)	G: 1606	1604: Adi Granth installed in the Harmandir 1612: Guru Har Gobind imprisoned in Gwalior Fort	1605: Jahangir	
			1628: Shah Jahan	1625: Charles I
Guru Har Rai (1630-1661)	G: 1644			1649: Execution of Charles I
1650		1658: Mughal prince Dara Shikoh visits Guru Har Rai	1658: Aurangzeb	1653: Cromwell 1660: Charles II
Guru Hari Krishen (1656-1664)	G: 1661			
Guru Tegh Bahadur (1621-1675)	G: 1664	1666: Guru Tegh Bahadur founds the city of Amritsar		
Guru Gobind Singh (1666-1708)	G: 1675			
				1685: James II 1689: William III
		1699: Formation of the Khalsa		
1700 1708: Guru Gobind Singh ends the line of living Gurus by passing the guruship to the Granth Sahib			1707: Bahadur Shah	1702: Anne I
		1710: Banda Bahadur's Sikh forces take Sirhind from the Mughals	1712: Jahandar Shah	
		c.1715: Mughal emperor Farrukhsiyar puts a price on the head of every Sikh; Sikhs move into the Panjab forests and jungle	1713: Farrukhsiyar	1714: George I
		1716: Banda Bahadur and followers arrested, tortured and killed in Delhi	1719: Rafi ud-Darajat; Niku Siyar;	
			Muhammad Shah	1727: George II
		1738: Head priest of the Harmandir, Bhai Mani Singh, is tortured to death by Mughals		
		1738-9: Invasion of India by Nadir Shah of Iran		
		1748-68: Repeated Afghan invasions	1748: Ahmad Shah	
1750			1754: Alamgir II	
		1757: Battle of Plassey	1759: Shah Alam II	
		1761: Jassa Singh Ahluwalia takes Lahore		1760: George III
		1762: Harmandir destroyed by Ahmad Shah Abdali		
		1776: Reconstruction of the Harmandir's causeway		
		1780: Birth of Ranjit Singh		
		1783: Sikhs take Delhi for eight weeks		
		1799: Ranjit Singh occupies Lahore		

SIKH GURUS (G = start date of guruship)	SIKH HISTORY AND RELATED HISTORICAL EVENTS IN INDIA	MUGHAL EMPERORS (start of reign)	BRITISH MONARCHS (start of reign)
1800	1801: Ranjit Singh proclaimed Maharaja		
	1802: Ranjit Singh captures Amritsar		
	1809: Treaty of Amritsar between British and Ranjit Singh	1806: Akbar Shah II	
	1813: Ranjit Singh given Koh-i nur by Shah Shuja		
			1820: George IV
			1830: William IV
	1838: Birth of Dalip Singh	1837: Bahadur Shah II	1837: Victoria I
	1839: Death of Ranjit Singh		
	1840: Death of Maharaja Kharak Singh; Nau Nihal Singh dies next day		
	1843: Murder of Maharaja Sher Singh		
	1843: Dalip Singh proclaimed Maharaja		
	1845-6: First Anglo-Sikh War		
	1846: Treaty of Lahore		
	1846: Treaty of Bhyrowal		
	1848-9: Second Anglo-Sikh War		
	1849: Annexation of the Panjab		
1850	1850: HMS Medea sails to Britain with Koh-i nur diamond		
	1854: Maharaja Dalip Singh goes to Britain		
	1857: 'Indian Mutiny'		
	1858: India becomes part of the British Empire	1858: End of Mughal empire	
	1863: Rani Jindan Kaur dies in London		
	1864: Maharaja Dalip Singh visits India for cremation of his mother		
	1864: Dalip marries Bamba Muller in Cairo		
	1872: Namdhari Sikhs launch agitation against the British		
	1876: Prince of Wales' tour of India		
	1877: Queen Victoria made Empress of India		
	1882: Panjab University founded in Lahore		
	1886: Dalip Singh takes *amrit* in Aden, returning to Sikhism		
	1893: Death of Maharaja Dalip Singh		
	1897: First Sikh settlers move to Vancouver and California		
1900	1903: Delhi Durbar at which Edward VII was proclaimed Emperor of India		1901: Edward VII
	1911: Coronation Durbar in Delhi		1910: George V
	1913: Gadr Party founded in California by Sikh immigrants		
	1919: Jallianwala Bagh massacre: General Dyer's troops open fire on peaceful crowd in Amritsar		
	1925: Gurdwara Act passed: control of gurdwaras in India handed back to Sikhs		
			1936: George VI
	1947: Independence. Partition of India; huge casualties on both sides as masses cross the new border		
	1948: Mahatma Ghandi assassinated		
1950			1952: Elizabeth II
	1966: Panjab State split into three parts: Panjab, Haryana and Himachal Pradesh. Panjab becomes a Panjabi-speaking state		
	1971: East Pakistan becomes Bangladesh		
	1984: 'Operation Blue Star': storming of the Harmandir by Indian Army troops. Mrs Ghandi assassinated by Sikh bodyguards. Delhi riots, Sikhs targeted		
	1997: HM Queen Elizabeth II visits the Harmandir		
2000			

INTRODUCTION

This book and its accompanying exhibition mark the tercentenary of the Khalsa, an event of fundamental importance in Sikh religious history, by examining the little known but remarkable cultural history of the Sikh kingdoms of the Panjab in the 19th century.

When Ranjit Singh became Maharaja of the Panjab at Lahore in 1801, he created an atmosphere that allowed the cultural life of the entire region to flourish. Much of this has been forgotten, perhaps because aspects of his personality have defined the period so strongly that other characteristics have been overshadowed. Without exception, foreign visitors commented on his magnetism that combined with an acute military astuteness to allow him to unite the whole of the Panjab and conquer Kashmir. He brought peace to an area which had suffered from repeated invasions throughout most of the preceding century, and his tolerance allowed Hindus, Muslims and Sikhs to live and work together, following their own religious paths without interference.

This harmonious coexistence makes it almost impossible to define a recognisably 'Sikh' art, because there were no rigid restrictions where patronage was concerned. Ranjit Singh's Golden Throne, for example, was made by a Muslim, and court artists of all religious denominations worked for patrons equally without regard for their religion. Even commissions of a specifically Sikh nature, such as architectural decoration of the Golden Temple at Amritsar or paintings of the Ten Gurus, might be given to Muslim or Hindu practitioners as well as to Sikhs. Ranjit Singh's own religious devotion is not in question – far from being the result of negligence, his choices sprang from the quintessential egalitarianism of Sikhism.

All this has led the artistic life of the court to be seen almost exclusively in terms of painting and, within this, the art of portraiture, because the characters are immediately recognisable as belonging to a Sikh setting. This approach is all the more appealing because prominent figures of the court, such as the leading sardars like Lehna Singh Majithia, the three Faqir brothers, or the Hindu Dina Nath, were also intrinsically fascinating characters. However, it has meant that the arts of the book have tended to be neglected and the abundant but almost completely unrecorded evidence of wall paintings has been largely ignored, except by a small group of Indian art historians concentrating, inevitably, on monuments in Indian Panjab.

Ranjit Singh is dismissed as producing no significant architecture, though the most famous of all Sikh monuments, the Golden Temple, owes its present appearance to his transforming initiative: the fine work of the goldsmiths, the marble inlayers, wall painters and others all suggests the presence of strong local traditions combined with informed patronage of master craftsmen from other regions. The architecture produced under Sikh rule in 18th and 19th century Panjab is almost unknown – Patiala's Qila Mubarak, the most significant Sikh fort to have survived, was founded in 1765 and still stands, barely mentioned in guide books and a cause for concern as its wall paintings flake and its walls crumble. Gulab Singh's fort in Jammu, and the monuments of Pakistan (notably Ranjit Singh's palace, pavilion and tomb in Lahore, overshadowed by the Mughal fort, and the fort at Shaikapura) are similarly left out of the reckoning. Perhaps even more importantly, the modest structures found in many parts of the region now divided between Pakistan and India, with their painted walls and carved wooden details, are disappearing, unrecorded and unlamented, their contribution to our understanding of the cultural life of the Panjab under Sikh rule being lost for ever.

In certain fields, the Sikh court undoubtedly led the whole of the subcontinent: the British probably regretted providing Ranjit Singh with cannons that were copied with such skill by Sikh engineers, guided by the French generals astutely employed by the maharaja to reorganise his army. Many of these were made at the Lahore foundry where firearms of excellent quality were also produced, continuing the sophisticated metalworking traditions of the city, whose steelworkers made weapons that were at the same time ruthlessly effective and beautifully ornamented.

The Panjab had a well established tradition of textile production, many of its towns and cities trading their embroideries or woven silks over a wide area. The patronage of the Sikh courts must have ensured their survival. The histories and contemporary accounts of visitors to Ranjit Singh's court make it clear that Kashmir shawls were highly prized and abundantly used, and surviving shawls demonstrate their extremely fine quality. Yet a detailed study of the precise interaction of the court with the shawl industry has still to be written.

After Ranjit Singh's death, the Panjab suffered a decade of upheaval and war culminating in the annexation of the Sikh kingdom to the British crown. Despite all this, artists and metalworkers continued to be employed at Lahore, and the traditional industries carried on at their respective centres into the 20th century. This could not have happened without the cultural nurturing provided by the Sikh courts: after annexation the rulers of the kingdoms of Jind, Nabha, Kapurthala and, especially, Patiala followed the model that had been provided by the greatest of all the Sikh rulers, Maharaja Ranjit Singh.

CHAPTER ONE

THE SIKHS OF THE PANJAB

KHUSHWANT SINGH

1. Lotus flower with the Ten Gurus. Kashmir, *c.* 1840. Gouache and gold on paper, 44.5 × 44 cm. National Museum of India (59.155/2).

There are around 16 million Sikhs in the world. About 14 million are in India, largely concentrated in the north-west of the country on the borders separating it from Pakistan. Sizeable communities of Sikhs also exist in the United Kingdom, Canada, the United States and in smaller numbers in other countries. Almost all of these are of Panjabi origin.

Sikhism is barely five hundred years old. It was founded by Guru Nanak (1469–1539) and evolved in two phases roughly a hundred years apart. It was proclaimed around 1500 and the compilation of its sacred scripture, the Adi Granth or Guru Granth, was completed by the fifth Guru, Arjun, in 1604. In 1699 the last of the ten Gurus of Sikhism, Gobind Singh, turned a large section of his followers into a casteless community, the Khalsa, or 'the pure'.

Guru Nanak's family were Hindus, of the Bedi caste (those conversant with the Vedas, the sacred scriptures). He was born on 15 April 1469 in the Panjab, some 40 miles from Lahore. The boy received nominal education and was married by the age of 12. In accordance with his father's wishes, he tried his hand at different trades before realising that he had a more important mission in life. He sought the company of wandering hermits, both Hindu and Muslim, and engaged in discourses on spiritual matters with them. He visited places of pilgrimage in India and Arab countries, and composed hymns in praise of God and man's duty towards his fellow men and women. A Muslim minstrel, Mardana, became his closest companion and set Nanak's hymns to music. Wherever they went, people came to hear them sing and to listen to Nanak's sermons.

Nanak was a man of gentle ways, with a kindly sense of humour, and his crusade was without anger, violence or recrimination. He never made any claim to kinship with God, nor did he clothe his hymns in the garb of prophecy. He was against the fanaticism and intolerance prevalent under the rule of the Mughals, as well as the widespread discrimination against women and 'lower castes'. He was content to be teacher, or *guru*; people became his disciples, or *shishyas*, from which the word Sikh is derived. Their meeting places became *dharamsalas*, meaning the 'abode of faith'; later these were called *gurdwaras*, or 'doorways to the Guru'.

Guru Nanak's message was simple: there is only one God, who is unborn, eternal and indefinable, but the only reality. The only way to reach Him is to obey His ordinances (*hukum*) under the guidance of a Guru. Guru Nanak chose his closest disciple, Angad (Guru 1539–52), as his successor and he in turn chose his disciple Amar Das to be the third Guru (1552–74) of the fast-growing Sikh community. Guru Amar Das chose his son-in-law Ram Das to be his successor and thereafter the last six Gurus were drawn from the same family of Sodhis.

Guru Ram Das (1574–81) built a new township in which his son Arjun Mal dug a pool, in the middle of which was built a temple (plate 2). The town grew into the Panjab's centre of trade and commerce and came to be known as Amritsar (the pool of nectar) and the monument at its centre the Harmandir (temple of God), also called the Golden Temple.

Guru Arjun (1581–1606) compiled an anthology of hymns composed by the preceding Gurus and the religious writings of saints, both Hindu and Muslim. He was himself a

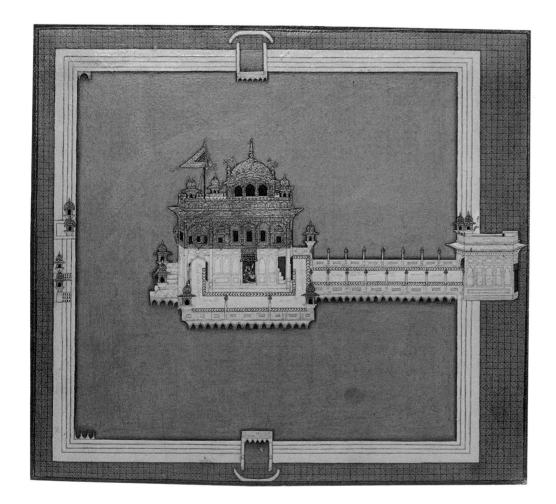

2. *The Golden Temple at Amritsar*, Panjab, *c.*1840. Watercolour and gold on paper, 25.1 × 27.5 cm. Kapany Collection.

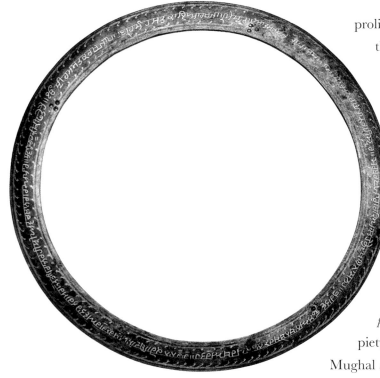

3. Quoit, 1775–1850. Steel inlaid with gold inscriptions, diam: 21 cm. Metropolitan Museum of Art, Bequest of George C. Stone, 1935 (36.25.2878).

prolific poet and over half of the compendium of more than six thousand hymns that form the Adi Granth were from his own pen. Thus, Guru Arjun gave the community a place of pilgrimage, Amritsar, and its own scripture. He also became its first martyr. Perturbed by the Guru's growing influence, the Mughal emperor Jahangir (r. 1605–27) ordered the Governor of Lahore to arrest him. The Guru was subjected to severe torture which resulted in his death.

Guru Arjun's martyrdom brought about a dramatic change in the development of Sikhism as his son and successor, Hargobind (Guru 1606–44), decided to arm his followers against Mughal persecution. Facing the Harmandir he raised a new building, the Akal Takht or 'Throne of the Timeless (God)', and girded himself with two swords, one representing *miri* or political command of the community, and the other *piri*, spiritual power. For this reason, he is known as *miri-piri da malik*, master of piety and power. Guru Hargobind fought neighbouring chieftains as well as the Mughal armies, which led to him being imprisoned for over a year in Gwalior Fort on the orders of Jahangir. He chose his grandson, Har Rai (Guru 1644–61), for his successor, who then chose his son, Hari Krishen. Guru Hari Krishen (Guru 1661–4) was in Delhi when he succumbed to an attack of smallpox, and his temporary residence in the capital, Bangla Sahib, is today the largest and most frequented *gurdwara*. Before he died, Guru Hari Krishen indicated that the next Guru should be his uncle Tegh Bahadur.

The ninth Guru, Tegh Bahadur (Guru 1664–75), had lived quietly in the village of Bakala since the death of his father Guru Hargobind in 1644. He now emerged from seclusion to renew contacts with his followers scattered across northern India. On his way to Assam he stopped for a while at Patna, where his son Gobind Rai was born. When he returned to the Panjab, Guru Tegh Bahadur attracted great crowds and financial support. His call to the people to stand firm against the religious persecution of the Mughal emperor Aurangzeb (r. 1658–1707) led to him being summoned to Delhi. Refusing to renounce his faith, he was sentenced to death and executed. The site of his incarceration and execution in Chandni Chowk, a quarter of old Delhi, is now the *gurdwara* Sis Ganj.

Guru Tegh Bahadur's son, Gobind Singh (Guru 1675–1708), succeeded to the guruship at the age of nine. He had spent his boyhood in Patna, where he was born, studying Persian and Sanskrit and learning the arts of war. He began to organise the Sikhs into a fighting force, describing his mission in life: 'To uphold right in every place and destroy sin and evil; that right may triumph, the good may live and tyranny be uprooted from the land.' He taught the peaceful followers of Guru Nanak the use of arms, but knew that to raise a body of warriors he also had to convince them of the morality of the use of force: 'When all other means have failed, it is righteous to draw the sword.'

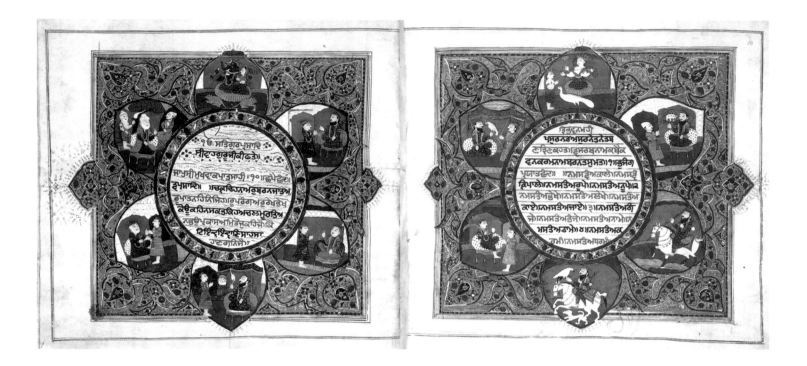

On the first day of the month of Baisakh (which then fell on 30 March) 1699, at Anandpur, he initiated a new order by sprinkling five of his followers (*panj piare*) with *amrit*, or nectar, which had been stirred by a double-edged dagger (*khanda*) to the chanting of hymns. The five then did the same to him. He changed his name from Gobind Rai to Gobind Singh and with a standard surname the Singhs (meaning lion) became one family; Sikh women were similarly initiated and given a common surname, Kaur (princess).

Guru Gobind Singh fought many skirmishes with neighbouring hill chieftains and built a chain of forts. These activities attracted the attention of the emperor Aurangzeb and in 1701 the Mughal governors of Sirhind and Lahore besieged the fort of Anandpur. After three years of bitter fighting, during which the Guru's two eldest sons were killed, the fort fell. Although the Guru escaped, his mother and two younger sons were captured, the boys then being executed. Guru Gobind Singh slipped through the Mughal lines and went south, eventually reaching the Deccan to join the new Mughal emperor Bahadur Shah, who had asked for help in the war of succession following the death of Aurangzeb in 1707. On the way, Guru Gobind Singh finalised the authentic version of the sacred book, incorporating hymns composed by his father, Tegh Bahadur. He declared that after him the Sikhs were to regard the sacred book (the Adi Granth, or Primal Book, also known as the Guru Granth) as their guide: it was the symbolic representative of all the ten Gurus. He kept his own compositions separate as the Dasam Granth (Tenth Book) (plate 4). While encamped at Nanded he was fatally wounded by two Pathans he had taken under his protection after their father had been slain in battle against the Sikhs, and died on 7 October 1708. A large *gurdwara* was built at Nanded and has become a place of pilgrimage.

4. Double-page frontispiece to a Dasam Granth manuscript depicting the Ten Gurus, Amritsar, 1850. Gouache and gold on paper. 35.4 × 33 cm. By permission of The British Library (Or. 6298).

5. *Lahore Life Guards 1838*, an illustration from *Panjabi Characters*. Bound volume, paintings perhaps by Kapur Singh, inscribed 1840–42, 27.1 × 21.5 cm. By permission of The British Library (Add. Or. 1347–96).

Before his death, Guru Gobind Singh empowered a hermit, Banda Bairagi, who had joined his entourage, to go to the Panjab and avenge the deaths of his four sons. Banda took a small group of Sikhs and planted the flag of rebellion against Mughal authority a few miles north-west of Delhi. As he moved northwards, the peasantry joined his forces, many Muslims and Hindus converting to Sikhism. By the time he captured the strategic city of Sirhind he was in virtual control of all the territory between the Jumna and the Sutlej and in 1710 made the old fort of Mukhlisgarh, in the safety of the Himalayas, his headquarters. He issued his own coins and, hearing that Bahadur Shah was unlikely to return to Delhi before the monsoons, decided to take the opportunity of destroying Mughal rule in Northern India. Banda embarked on a form of guerrilla warfare called *dhai phut* (hit and run), which proved highly successful against the heavily armed imperial forces. For five years, bands of Sikh horsemen ravaged the countryside between the Rivers Ravi and Ganges. Eventually, in 1716, the Mughal commanders led a huge army against Banda's forces, surrounding them and starving them into submission. Banda and several hundred of his followers were brought in chains to Delhi and paraded through the streets. The executions of his followers began on 5 March 1716 and continued for a week. Banda himself was tortured in the hope of discovering the whereabouts of the wealth he was reputed to have amassed but eventually, on 19 June, he too was executed with his infant son.

Mughal attempts to stamp out the Sikhs failed. On Baisakhi 1733, the Sikhs assembled in full strength at Amritsar and elected new leaders. The assemblage, which became a routine twice-yearly affair taking place at the festivals of Baisakhi in spring and Diwali in autumn, came to be known as the Sarbat Khalsa. Two remarkable men, Kapur Singh and Jassa Singh Ahluwalia, emerged as leaders and reorganised the disparate fighting units of the Sikhs into the Dal Khalsa, the army of the Khalsa. They were helped by the invasion of Nadir Shah of Iran (plate 6) in 1738, which dealt a mortal blow to the Mughal empire, which had already been weakened by the revolt of the Jat tribes around

Delhi and by the incursions of the Marathas from the south. The Iranian ruler swept across northern Panjab, routing the Mughal forces and occupying Delhi. The capital was plundered and its population massacred. Nadir Shah looted the imperial treasury and returned to Iran in the summer of 1739 laden with enormous booty including the Koh-i-nur diamond and the famed 'Peacock Throne' of Shah Jahan, made of gold and precious stones. Sikhs who had avoided fighting the Iranian forces on their way to Delhi closed in on the stragglers as they returned, plundering their camps every night and freeing many slaves. Nadir Shah's invasion utterly disrupted the Mughal administration of the Panjab.

The weakening of the Mughal empire, however, attracted the Afghan ruler, Ahmad Shah Abdali, who made no fewer than nine invasions between 1748 and 1768. The Sikhs realised that the nature of their operations against the Mughals and the Afghan invaders required the break-up of their forces into independent commands, each with its own sphere of operation but all meeting at the general assembly of the Sarbat Khalsa at Amritsar to discuss past successes and failures, and to make plans for the future. These twelve groupings, or *misls*, were led by Nawab Kapur Singh and, after his death, by Jassa Singh Ahluwalia, who took Lahore and made it his capital. Under him, Sikh power spread and coins were struck in the name of the *misl* confederacy.

When the Sikhs dispossessed the Mughals and became landowners themselves, leadership became hereditary. The Phulkian house, which later produced the ruling Sikh families of the Panjab was founded, and Jassa Singh Ahluwalia's descendants became rulers of Kapurthala. With the possession of lands and property, however, the *misls* began to fight among themselves. It was left to Ranjit Singh to abolish the *misl* system by absorbing them and forming a powerful and united Sikh kingdom.

6. *Nadir Shah*, Muhammad Panah, Mughal, mid-18th century. Gouache and gold on paper, 19.4 × 11.3 cm. IM 237–1921.

7. *Jamrud, the fort built by the Sikhs*, probably by Imam Bakhsh, Attock, *c.*1840. Watercolour on European paper, 19.3 × 28.7 cm. Musée national des Arts asiatiques-Guimet (39733/1). © Photo RMN – Thierry Ollivier.

8. Shield, Mughal, 1767. Buffalo hide, steel mounts overlaid with gold, diam. 43 cm. The Board of Trustees of the Armouries (XXIVA.236).

9. Shield, Lahore, c.1830–45. Steel overlaid with gold, lined with velvet embroidered with silver-wrapped silk, diam. 49.5 cm. The Board of Trustees of the Armouries (XXVIA.237).

10. *Ranjit Singh in Durbar*,
Imam Bakhsh, *c.*1838. Gouache
on paper, 25.7 × 17.6 cm.
Musée Jean de la Fontaine,
Château-Thierry.

11. Ranjit Singh's palace and tomb
between the Fort and the Great
Mosque in Lahore.
Photograph: Susan Stronge.

After the Gurus, Maharaja Ranjit Singh (1780–1839) is the man who commands the highest respect among Sikhs (plate 10). He was the only child of the head of the Sukerchakia *misl* based in Gujranwala and lost his father when he was only 12. In early infancy an attack of smallpox blinded his left eye and left his skin pockmarked; he was short and dark, a great horseman and a valiant fighter. Although illiterate, he was a shrewd judge of men. Despite the fact that he insisted on the exact observance of religious ritual, he was without religious prejudice and commanded the loyalties of Muslims and Hindus as well as Sikhs. At 15 he married Mehtab Kaur whose mother, the widow Sada Kaur, was the head of the powerful Kanahya *misl*. Under the tutelage of Sada Kaur, the young Ranjit Singh turned his attentions from the pleasures of the chase to bringing all the warring *misls* under his control.

In 1796 the Afghans, under their ruler Shah Zaman, again invaded the Panjab from Kabul. Many of the *misldars* fled; only Ranjit Singh stood his ground, urging the others to return and redeem their pledge to protect the peasantry from whom they had been collecting protection money. His boldness convinced them. Taking command of the Sikh militias, he forced the Afghans to withdraw and was acclaimed a saviour. With the assistance of Sada Kaur's forces he entered Lahore, and on Baisakhi (13 April) 1801 Ranjit Singh was proclaimed Maharaja of the Panjab, which he was to rule for almost forty years. His government, however, was not known after him but was known as the *sarkar khalsaji*, or Khalsa state.

One of his earliest campaigns, in 1802, was to recapture the sacred city of Amritsar, which was also the most important commercial city in the Panjab. It was divided between

12. *The Gateway of the Ram Bagh, The Cutcherry inside*, Felice Beato, Amritsar, *c.*1858–60. Albumen print, 23 × 28.7 cm. 80087.

13. *Kabul Infantryman*, probably Imam Bakhsh, Panjab, *c.*1835–40. Watercolour on European paper, 17.5 × 28.3 cm. Musée national des Arts asiatiques-Guimet (39743). © Photo RMN – Thierry Ollivier.

nearly a dozen families who owned different parts, but these were quickly overwhelmed and the fort, Gobindgarh, was surrendered to the maharaja. His domains gradually expanded across the region between the Indus and the Sutlej, but his plans to bring the remaining Sikh states beyond the Sutlej under his control were thwarted by the British, by this time the major threat in the region due to their military superiority. In 1806 Ranjit Singh decided to enter into a treaty with the East India Company in order to keep the Maratha forces at bay, but in 1809 he was forced to sign a further treaty, the Treaty of Lahore, whereby he abjured claims to suzerainty over the *misls* across the Sutlej (the 'Cis-Sutlej' states), thereby abandoning his designs to expand eastwards.

14. *Durrani chieftain and his groom*, probably Imam Bakhsh, Panjab, *c.*1835–40. Watercolour on European paper, 18.4 × 29.5 cm. Musée national des Arts asiatiques-Guimet (41833). © Photo RMN – Thierry Ollivier

Ranjit Singh then turned his attention to other neighbouring states. When members of the Afghan royal family came to him for help, he rescued their deposed head, Shah Shuja, from captivity in return for the Koh-i-nur diamond, which was reluctantly handed over in 1813. Kashmir itself was annexed in 1819, the year after Multan was taken. Ranjit Singh took on the traditional conquerors of India, the Pathans and Afghans, and occupied Peshawar and the tribal areas. His success as a ruler was due to the fact that he did not discriminate between his subjects on the basis of religion. His ministers were Muslims (plate 15), Hindus and Sikhs; in the army the artillery were largely Muslim, the cavalry mainly Sikh, the infantry Dogra, Gurkha, Sikh and Muslim. He hired two hundred foreigners, including French, Italians, Americans and Anglo-Indians to train his troops in modern warfare. Ranjit Singh had the most powerful army in India after the British and their mercenaries.

After the death of Maharaja Ranjit Singh on 27 June 1839 (plates 16 and 17), the Sikh kingdom was without a strong ruler. None of his sons or grandsons was able to hold the state together; rebellion broke out and there was violence on the streets of Lahore. The army, which had not been paid for months, became the arbiter of the state's destiny. The British moved their troops to the Panjab border, and assembled a pontoon bridge made of boats on the banks of the River Sutlej. Four fiercely contested battles were

15. *Faqir Aziz ud-din*, Panjab, *c*.1825. Drawing and colours on paper, 20.8 × 13.5 cm. Government Museum and Art Gallery, Chandigarh (D-29).

16. *The Death of Ranjit Singh*, Lahore, 1839. Gouache on paper, 40.5 × 56 cm. © The British Museum (1925-4-6.2).

17. Sections from the tomb of
Ranjit Singh. Wood and watercolour,
42.5 × 63.2 × 6.1 cm (944:12);
41.7 × 34.1 × 7 cm (944:6);
42 × 33.9 × 6.8 cm (944:7).
944 (IS).

18. *The Signing of the Treaty of Bhairowal
on 26 December 1846: Henry Lawrence,
Lord Gough, Lord Hardinge, Sheik Imam
ud-Din, Ranbir Singh, Dalip Singh, Frederick
Currie*, Panjab, *c.*1846–7.
Gouache on paper, 39.5 × 53.9 cm.
© The British Museum
(1948.10-9.0109).

19. *Maharaja Dalip Singh*, Hasan al-din, *c.*1845–6. Gouache on paper, 19.7 × 23.6 cm. By permission of The British Library (Add. Or. 710).

fought in the winter of 1845–6: Mudki (19 December), Ferozedshahr (21 December), Buddowal (21 January) and Sabraon (10 February). The British and their Indian mercenaries finally triumphed and occupied Lahore. Under the Treaty of Bhairowal of December 1846 (plate 18), they annexed the eastern half of the Sikh kingdom and became custodians of the other half. They recognised Ranjit Singh's youngest son, the 11-year old Dalip Singh as the heir apparent (plate 19), with his mother Rani Jindan as the queen regent. Two years later an incident in Multan gave them the excuse to resume war against the Sikh kingdom. In the battles fought at Chillianwala (13 January 1849) and Gujerat (21 February 1849), the remnants of the Khalsa army were defeated. On 29 March 1849, in a *darbar* assembled at Lahore, a proclamation was read out announcing the annexation of the Panjab to the British Crown. Maharaja Dalip Singh handed over the Koh-i-nur and was separated from his mother, Rani Jindan, shortly afterwards. He was taken to Fatehgarh, a remote provincial town in India and in 1854 went to Britain, where his mother eventually joined him.

Lord Dalhousie, the Governor-General of India who had proclaimed the Annexation, had been deeply impressed by the fighting qualities of the Khalsa army and incorporated several units into the British Army, a policy that was to pay handsome dividends: when Indian sepoys of the British Army rebelled and captured Delhi in the Great Mutiny of 1857, the Sikhs stayed loyal to the British and helped them capture the Mughal capital.

20. Sikh portraits painted on ivory. Box 23 × 39.7 cm. By permission of The British Library (Add. Or. 2640-7).

With British occupation of the Panjab came Christian missionaries and, after them, Swami Dayanand Saraswati, the founder of the Arya Samaj movement, who asserted that Sikhs were a part of the Hindu community. The Sikh response to these challenges was vigorous. The Singh Sabha, a society whose first centres were in Amritsar and Lahore, had the support of the rich landed gentry and orthodox Sikhs, and reasserted the independence of the Sikh religion. This was stated in categorical terms by the Sikh scholar Bhai Kahan Singh of Nabha in a booklet entitled *Hum Hindu Nahin Hain* (We Are Not Hindus). A socio-political offshoot of the Singh Sabha was a body called the Chief Khalsa Diwan, which organised annual educational conferences in different districts and opened Khalsa schools wherever it met. Its most important figure was the poet-theologian Bhai Vir Singh. The Chief Khalsa Diwan affirmed its loyalty to the British, and in

21. Watch and
watch-chains presented
by the Maharaja of
Patiala to H.H. the
Prince of Wales in
1867, M. Grandjean
& Co. of Paris. Gold,
enamelled and jewelled,
8 × 5.6 × 2 cm.
Lent by Her Majesty
Queen Elizabeth II.
The Royal Collection
© Her Majesty Queen
Elizabeth II
(11476, 11477, 11478).

22. Imperial Mughal spinel presented to Edward VII for his coronation by the Maharaja of Nabha. Inscribed with the titles of the emperors Jahangir, Shah Jahan and Aurangzeb. 4.6 × 2.4 cm, wt. 123 carats. Lent by Her Majesty Queen Elizabeth II. The Royal Collection © Her Majesty Queen Elizabeth II (11526).

return the British helped them to set up educational institutions, notably their first and most important, Khalsa College in Amritsar.

British rule brought unprecedented peace and prosperity to the Panjab in the second half of the nineteenth century. British engineers built a network of canals and opened up large tracts of hitherto waste land to agriculture that was then sold to farmers at nominal prices. Thousands of Sikh families migrated to Western Punjab to reap bumper harvests of wheat, indigo and rice. While the British confiscated large *jagirs* (lands assigned to indi-

23. Pair of gold perfume holders presented by H. H. the Raja of Kapurthala to the Prince of Wales in 1876, Panjab, *c*.1875. 13.1 × 8.2 × 5.3 cm. Lent by Her Majesty Queen Elizabeth II. The Royal Collection © Her Majesty Queen Elizabeth II (11317.1 and 11317.2).

24. Address casket. Gold set with diamonds, rubies and emeralds, presented by the people of Amritsar to H.H. the Prince of Wales in 1876. 7.8 × 13 × 13.1 cm. Lent by Her Majesty Queen Elizabeth II. The Royal Collection © Her Majesty Queen Elizabeth II (11230).

viduals as a reward for services), they handed over the lands to the peasant-proprietors who had always been the backbone of the *misl* as well as the forces of Ranjit Singh. At the same time the leaders of the Phulkian States – Patiala, Nabha, Jind, Faridkot and Kapurthala – had their ruling powers confirmed on their estates. This enabled them to divert their revenues from defence to more constructive pursuits: they built schools, colleges and hospitals, and patronised musicians, artists and craftsmen. The survival of the cultural traditions of the Sikhs was assured, enabling a twentieth-century historian to observe: 'A remarkable people, the Sikhs, with their Ten Prophets, five distinguishing marks, and their traditional rite of water stirred with steel; a people who have made history and will make it again' (F. Yeats-Brown, *Martial India*, 1945).

25. *Sangat Singh, Ruler of Jind*, Panjab, 1870–99. Gouache on paper, 26.8 × 19.2 cm. Government Museum and Art Gallery, Chandigarh (3687).

26. *Raja Jaswant Singh of Nabha*, Panjab, 1850. Gouache on paper, 15.7 × 10.7 cm. By permission of The British Library (Add. Or. 2601).

THE SIKH RELIGION

NIKKY-GUNINDER KAUR SINGH

27. *Guru Nanak with a Kneeling Hindu Raja*. Folio 123 from a *Janam Sakhi*, Panjab, 1733, 25 × 14 cm. By permission of The British Library (MSS Panj B 40).

28. *Guru Nanak*, Lucknow, *c.*1770. Watercolour on paper, 16.7 × 15.5 cm. Kapany Collection.

The Sikh religion originates with the person and ideology of Guru Nanak (plate 27). Sikhs worldwide revere Guru Nanak as the founder of their faith. Their homes, places of business and sacred places resonate with verses of their Guru and reflect images of Guru Nanak dressed in combined elements of Hindu and Muslim garb: he is contemplating the Divine, and his right palm, imprinted with the symbol representing *Ikk Oan Kar* (One Being Is) is raised to the viewer.

Nanak was born on 15 April 1469, in a small village in the Panjab called Talvandi. His father was an accountant for the local Muslim landlord. His mother, Tripta, is remembered in Sikh history as a pious woman. Although Nanak's family were upper-caste Hindus, from an early age he refused to go through any of the traditional Hindu rituals. The substitution of ethical conduct for elaborate ceremonies was central to his worldview. *Janam Sakhis* (stories, or *sakhis*, pertaining to the life, or *janam*, of Guru Nanak) provide Sikhs with a literary introduction to their heritage that is also a visual introduction, as the stories are usually illustrated (plate 28). The narratives portray the divine dispensation of their founder and his concern for kindness, social cohesiveness and divine unity. They poignantly illustrate Guru Nanak's rejection of empty ritual. For example, when Nanak was asked to wear the customary sacred thread symbolic of the twice-born castes he urged that the sacred thread be replaced with compassion, contentment and truth. In another scene he is seen sprinkling water from a jug over the village (a reference to the sprinkling of water by priests for dead ancestors), suggesting that there was a greater need for the precious water in the village fields. These stories about their first Guru support Sikhs throughout their lives.

Nanak grew up in a milieu which was philosophically and culturally vibrant, in which he met and conversed freely with Hindus, Muslims, Buddhists and Jains. In this diverse and pluralistic context, Nanak had a revelation of the divine as One Reality. He articulated his experience of the infinite and singular reality as *Ikk Oan Kar*, which is the quintessential formula of Sikh metaphysics and ethics. *Ikk*, or I, is also the numeral one;

Oan, or *Om*, from the Sanskrit *Aum*, refers to the Ultimate Unity; and *Kar* celebrates the existence of the One. This insight into the divine marked the beginning of Guru Nanak's mission. Thereafter, for 24 years, Guru Nanak travelled throughout India and beyond, spreading his message of absolute unity, accompanied during most of his travels by his Muslim companion Mardana, who played on the rebec while the Guru sang songs of intense love addressing the Ultimate One. The rich but simple style of Guru Nanak's teaching attracted people from different religious, cultural and social backgrounds. Wherever he went, people began to follow him, calling themselves Sikhs, a Panjabi form of the Sanskrit *shishya* or the Pali *sekka*, meaning disciple. Bhai Gurdas (d.1629), the first Sikh historian and theologian, called Sikhism 'the grand highway', *gadiraha*, showing the path through moral precepts. He viewed this new faith as 'a needle that sews materials that are ripped asunder, bringing harmony to the torn and conflicting groups'.

At the end of his travels Guru Nanak settled in Kartarpur, a Panjabi village he founded on the banks of the River Ravi. The daily routine and the moral ideals fostered in this first Sikh community constitute the core of Sikh ethics. It was here that the Sikh institutions of *seva* (selfless service), *langar* (community meal), and *sangat* (congregation) had their genesis.

Before he died in 1539 Guru Nanak appointed his disciple Angad as his successor. Guru Nanak also bequeathed his poetry to the second Sikh Guru. Guru Angad continued the tradition of sacred poetry which, he felt, was important not only for the beauty it brought to human life, but also for the knowledge it transmitted. The transference of guruship from Nanak to Angad was repeated successively until the installation of Gobind Singh, the tenth Guru (plate 32), in 1675. For the Sikhs, the same spiritual light is reflected in ten different bodies, and the same voice speaks through all ten.

In 1699 Guru Gobind Singh inaugurated the Khalsa, or Order of the Pure, at Anandpur. This was a casteless and self-abnegating body of Sikhs ready to take up arms against injustice and tyranny. The Khalsa was to embody the ideal of a free and egalitarian society propounded by Guru Nanak. Chanting verses from the Adi Granth, Guru Gobind Singh began the new initiation into the Khalsa by churning water in a steel bowl with a double-edged sword, while his wife dropped sugar crystals into the vessel; sweetness through the feminine hand was thus mingled with the alchemy of iron. The event opened the way for a new consciousness. The resulting drink (*amrit*) was sipped by all from the same bowl, sealing the pledge of equality and faithfulness. The *amrit* initiation has always been open to both men and women. They wear the emblems of the Khalsa, popularly known as the 'Five Ks' (uncut hair, or *kesh*; comb, or *kangha*; steel bracelet, *kara*; a short sword, *kirpan*; and breeches, *kachda*). Men are given the surname of Singh, meaning lion, and women the surname Kaur, meaning princess; women thus do not have to

29. Guru Nanak visiting Bhai Lalo the Carpenter. From a *Janam Sakhi*, Panjab, mid-19th century. Gouache on paper, 6 × 6.5 cm. Kapany Collection.

30. *Guru Har Rai*,
Guler, *c.*1815.
22 × 16 cm.
Government
Museum and Art
Gallery,
Chandigarh (F 45).

31. *Bhai Veer Singh, a Highly Renowned and Charitable Man*, Panjab, *c.*1850–60. Watercolour on paper, 37 × 54.9 cm. Kapany Collection.

32. *Guru Gobind Singh on Horseback*, Guler, *c.*1830. Gouache on paper, 32.6 × 23.5 cm. Lent by Gurshuran and Elvira Sidhu.

trace their lineage to their father or adopt a husband's name after marriage. Rebirth into the Khalsa Order represents an annihilation of the initiate's family (caste) lineage, of their confinement to a hereditary occupation and of all their former beliefs and rituals. The emblem of the Khalsa is an upright double-edged sword set in a circle, which in turn is encircled by a curved sword on either side. Besides the *Ikk Oan Kar*, it is the most pervasive religious image in Sikh arts, crafts and buildings. These two symbols decorate walls, doors and windows in Sikh homes, shrines and shops, and are also embroidered on garments and set in earrings and necklaces.

Before his death in 1708 Guru Gobind Singh ended the line of personal Gurus by passing the succession not to another person but to the Guru Granth, the holy book of the Sikhs. He declared that the Word as embodied in the Granth would be the Guru after him. *Granth* means book, and since the death of Guru Gobind Singh the understanding and conviction of Sikhs has been that the Granth is the eternal Guru. The

message and mission begun by Guru Nanak culminated in the Guru Granth. The sacred text opens with *Ikk Oan Kar*, and its 1,430 pages can be read as a poetic and sublime commentary on Guru Nanak's statement. As the manifest body of the Guru, the book is treated with the highest respect and veneration. It rests on cushions or quilted mats, draped in silk and brocades, with a canopy hanging over it for protection. Sikhs bow to the Guru Granth and sit on the floor before it; they remove their shoes and cover their heads in its presence. The honorifics *sri* or *sahib* are often added to the title. The Guru Granth is also known as the Adi Granth, or the 'primal book', in order to distinguish it from the Dasam Granth, the book of the tenth Guru compiled some time after his death. Although the Guru Granth forms the centre of Sikh worship, the poetry of Guru Gobind Singh is highly esteemed and also forms part of daily prayers. Guru Nanak's moral ideas receive in Guru Gobind Singh's verse a heroic diction and energetic metre. Guru Gobind Singh composed heroic and martial poetry to inspire men and women to fight against social, political and economic exploitation. Within half a century of their tenth Guru's death, Sikhs became a major political force, and established a state of their

33. *Baba Atal's Temple – The Sacred Temple – East View*, Felice Beato, Amritsar, *c.*1858–60. Albumen print, 23.2 × 27.9 cm. 80093.

own. In 1799 Ranjit Singh, the 19-year old leader of a Khalsa band, seized power peacefully in the city of Lahore and was proclaimed maharaja two years later.

Harmandir, the Golden Temple, is regarded by Sikhs all over the world as their holiest shrine and foremost pilgrimage spot (plate 33). It rests on a platform in the middle of a sacred reflecting pool; with its four doors welcoming people of all four castes, this first Sikh shrine is the paradigm for Sikh shrines, or *gurdwaras* (the word means literally a door, *dwara*, to ultimate enlightenment, *guru*). The domes and minarets of the buildings lead the eye towards the infinite skies. Most traditional *gurdwaras* are white and have a large courtyard, which provides an immediate feeling of expansiveness. A path surrounds the pool and devotees are often seen bathing in the water, sitting on the edge saying prayers and circumambulating in contemplative mood. Abstraction, symmetry,

34. *The Great Square, Amritsar*, 1880s. Albumen print, 20.9 × 27.8 cm. By permission of The British Library (50/2 (55)).

rhythm and repetition are essential characteristics of Sikh architecture. Abstract patterns make possible a passage into another world beyond the senses. Symmetrical designs emerging from the multiplicity of intricate details add to the feeling of tranquillity: the black and white marble slabs upon which the devotees walk are repeated rhythmically, as are the stylised flowers, birds, arabesques and lattice-work on the surfaces.

The Guru Granth is set at the very centre of each *gurdwara* (plate 35). There are no images or sculptures incarnating deity in any way. Metaphysical poetry, with its sensuous imagery, is the sole visual and aural icon for Sikhs; the recitation of the intangible verses enables the worshipper to recognise the Infinite One. This tradition goes back to Guru Arjan, who compiled the holy text for his community and ceremoniously installed the first volume in the inner sanctuary of the Harmandir on 16 August 1604. The Guru Granth contains the poetry of the Sikh Gurus along with that of Hindu and Muslim saints, and is the treasury of the religious, social and literary ideals of the Sikhs. Most of it is in the form of 31 traditional *ragas* (Indian musical measures), each with its particular characteristic, timing and season.

35. The Guru Granth Sahib being recited inside the Harmandir. 17 August 1998. Courtesy of Guru Nanak Nishkam Sewak Jatha.

36. *Kirtan*, the singing of hymns from the Guru Granth Sahib, inside the Harmandir. 30 March 1998. Courtesy of Guru Nanak Nishkam Sewak Jatha.

The Guru Granth is written in the Gurmukhi script, a special alphabet used in Sikh scriptures. The name Gurmukhi literally means 'from the mouth of the Guru'. The script was invented in the sixteenth century by the second Guru, Angad. It has 35 letters and has now become the alphabet of the Panjabi language.

According to the Guru Granth 'paradise is where Your poetry is sung' (*taha baikunthu jaha kirtanu tera*: p. 749). Reading the sacred verse, hearing it, singing it, or sitting in its presence constitute the core of Sikh ritual. All rites of passage take place in the sound and sight of the Guru Granth: the new-born baby is named in its presence; the marriage

37. Letter from Guru Gobind Singh, written to the brothers Rama (ancestor of the Patiala family) and Tiloka (ancestor of the Nabha and Jind families), dated 2 August 1696. Courtesy of H.H. the Maharaja of Patiala.

38. Guru Nanak as a young man, disputing with Hindu holy men, illustration from a prayer book of Rani Jindan (the mother of Maharaja Dalip Singh), Panjab, 1830. Gouache and gold on paper, 31 × 31 cm. By permission of The British Library (Pan D4).

ceremony entails walking round it four times; death in a home is followed by a continuous reading of the entire collection. The daily devotional routine (*nit nem*) of the Sikh involves the recitation of several hymns; these may be recited or read alone, with the families or with the congregation in a *gurdwara*.

As in the community established by Guru Nanak at Kartarpur, every daily routine action is imbued with spiritual significance. A hymn by Guru Arjan states categorically 'liberation is attained while laughing, playing, dressing up, and eating' (*hasandian khelandian painandia khavandian vice hove mukti*: Guru Granth, p. 522). The artistic images that express union with the Divine in Sikh scripture therefore emerge from everyday chores. Dyeing fabrics and stitching them, acts of dressing and applying make-up, working in a smithy or churning butter at home – symbolise complete devotion and single-minded attachment to the One. The immutability of Truth may be perceived through a task as mundane as sewing: 'Truth is eternal; once sewn, It never gets ripped asunder' (Guru Granth, p. 955).

CHAPTER THREE

THE
GOLDEN TEMPLE

PATWANT SINGH

44. Devotees bathing in the pool of the Harmandir. 16 March 1998. Courtesy of Guru Nanak Nishkam Sewak Jatha.

In the sixteenth century the site of the Golden Temple, destined to inspire countless future generations of Sikhs, was a serene stretch of water in a forested terrain, discovered by Angad Dev, the second of Sikhism's ten founding Gurus. His successor, Amar Das, was attracted by the tranquillity of the setting and built a small hut by the side of the pool for contemplation and reflection. Here he also charted the future course of the faith that the first Guru, Nanak, had founded before he died in 1539.

Because he could visualize that one day its enlarged and calm expanse of clear water would reflect a shrine of rare beauty, Amar Das's successor Ram Das bought the pool and the surrounding land. The most significant contribution towards establishing the fountainhead of the Sikh faith there, and the city of Amritsar around it, was made during the stewardship of Arjun Dev, the fifth Guru, between 1581 and 1606. Convinced of the faith's need for permanency and self-renewal, he wanted the place to become more than a centre of pilgrimage. It had to be the rallying point of Sikhs everywhere: a repository of their religion and a symbol of its resoluteness.

Credit for conceiving a shrine in the centre of the pool, to be called the Harmandir, or the House of God, goes to Guru Arjun. He decided that the Harmandir's plan had to reflect the clarity, simplicity and logic of the new movement, and its location in the centre of the pool would symbolize the synthesis of *nirgun* and *sargun*, the spiritual and temporal realms of human existence. Unlike traditional temple architecture, which provided only one entrance, the Harmandir would have one on each side to show that its doors would always be open to all castes, for to Guru Arjun 'the four castes of Kshatriyas, Brahmins, Sudras and Vaisyas are equal partners in divine instruction'.

The principle of universal participation was extended to the execution of the project, so that all Sikhs in congregations everywhere could have a role in building it. Their participation would take two forms: voluntary labour, or *seva*, and a donation, *daswandh*, of 10 per cent of their income to support the construction. Both these practices have endured ever since. While clearly not all Sikhs give 10 per cent of their earnings towards

45. *The Golden Temple*, **Panjab**. Sent to the 1862 exhibition. Watercolour on paper, 25.5 × 41.9 cm. By permission of The British Library (Add. Or. 486).

46. *The Akal Boonga, Umritsar*, William Simpson, Lahore, 1860. Watercolour on paper, 28 × 44 cm. 1141-1869.

47. *The Golden Temple*, Capt. W. G. Stretton, *c*.1870s. Albumen print, 17.7 × 26.8 cm. 2466-1906.

48. *View of Causeway*, Felice Beato, Amritsar, *c*.1858–60. Albumen print, 23.7 × 28.5 cm. 80094.

58. The golden
upper storey of
the Harmandir.
15 December 1997.
Courtesy of Guru
Nanak Nishkam
Sewak Jatha.

CHAPTER FOUR

RANJIT SINGH AND
THE IMAGE OF THE PAST

A.S. MELIKIAN-CHIRVANI

59. Gold token of Guru Nanak,
19th century. Diam: 2 cm.
National Museum, New Delhi
(65.497).

60. *Maharaja Ranjit Singh*, probably
Lahore, *c*.1835–40, gouache on paper,
30 × 22.6 cm. IS 282-1955.

O f all the principalities that emerged in the Indian subcontinent, few are quite so rich in paradoxes as the Sikh kingdom of the Panjab. Its capital Lahore was home to the last of the great Persianate courts of India, with Persian as the language of most state symbols, of high literature, of polished social intercourse – and yet the state was founded by the followers of a religious movement steeped in the vernacular culture of Panjab.[1] It was established by staunch defenders of the Sikh faith but it was also profoundly respectful of all creeds which intermingled happily in accordance with the explicit wishes of Maharaja Ranjit Singh. Most remarkably, perhaps, while it sought its way towards modernity, it yearned to uphold the glorious past of Hindustan. In this pursuit of the past, the Iranian legacy played a central role.

This was largely due to the very circumstances in which the Sikh creed emerged. Its spiritual master Guru Nanak, and his successors down to Guru Gobind Singh, delivered their spiritual message in Panjabi. Their teachings were set down in the Gurmukhi script and yet in its metaphysical tenets, as in the wording in which these are conveyed, there was much about Sikh teaching that would contribute to make its adherents deeply receptive to Persian culture. Similarly, to an outsider coming from the Iranian world marked by the pervading influence of Sufi mysticism, the Sikh creeds must often have had a familiar ring. The opening statement of the Guru Granth Sahib, proclaiming 'One Being Is', and the emphasis on God as the sole living Reality, echoes the Sufi concept of *Haqq*, God the sole Reality, or Truth. The first Sikh theologian referred to Sikhism as *gadiraha*, 'the road', much as Sufis describe their own quest of knowledge as *rah*, the Persian for road; the Sufi is the *rahrow*, or *salik*, 'he who travels along the road' that leads to illumination.[2]

A central Sikh institution, the *langar*, or place where communal meals were prepared to signify the equality of all and the abolition of the Hindu caste system, was adapted from a Sufi model.[3] *Langar* means 'anchor' in Persian, hence an 'anchorage point' on the sea of existence for those embarked on its boats in search of knowledge, and as such it could also describe the *khanqah*, or Sufi communal house, where in seventeenth-century

Hindustan food would be served to those in need. Borhan Tabrizi, the author of the most comprehensive Persian dictionary, written in Hindustan in 1651–2, defines this link clearly.[4]

The many parallels with Sufism, whether the result of direct influence or a shared heritage, left an enduring mark on Sikh attitudes. In the Hindustan world, where Persian had become the modern language of cultivated elites regardless of religious allegiance since at least the fifteenth century, they added a further incentive to acquire a thorough understanding of the language of the Sufi poets – Nezami, Sa'adi, Amir Khosrow, Hafez – whose names or lines crop up in one of the main chronicles of Ranjit Singh's reign, the *Zafar-Nama* or Book of Triumphs.[5] Apparently Ranjit Singh himself, although described by most authors as 'illiterate', knew enough Persian to have documents in that language read out to him.[6] A practising Sikh, he was concerned to allow every creed to blossom.[7] The relativist approach of his court, the conviction that 'the religion of God' (*din Allah*, to use the Koranic expression) is one, rings throughout the *Zafar-Nama*. Characteristically, although written by a Hindu, the book includes quotations from the Koran, cites the occasional Sufi maxim and generally reflects concepts that fundamentally agree with Sufi thinking.[8]

This deep affinity with Iranian culture through Sufism makes it less surprising that

61 and 62. Sikh coins (obverse and reverse). Top row: Double *mohur* with Gobinshahi couplet. Amritsar mint, dated vs 1883, diam: 3.2 cm. 1874.10.1.1 (Guthrie Collection). *Mohur* with Gobinshahi couplet. Gold, Amritsar mint, dated vs 1885/AD 1828, issued vs 1893/AD 1836, diam: 2.1 cm. 1912.7.9.209 (Bleazby Collection). Bottom row: Special rupee issue depicting Guru Nanak and Ranjit Singh. Silver, dated vs 1885/AD (18)93, diam: 2.3 cm. 1936.10-17.1. Gurdwara *tanka* depicting Guru Nanak with devotees Bala and Mardana. Silver, diam: 2.7 cm. 1922.4.24.4348 (R.B. Whitehead Collection).
© The British Museum.

Persian should have retained a pre-eminent place in the kingdom. Most symptomatically Sikh state sovereignty was expressed in Persian, starting with currency. Coins of a higher order, whether the rarer gold *mohurs* or the standard silver rupees, were inscribed solely in Persian.[9] In a way, they signalled a break with centuries-old minting traditions of the Iranian world and of Hindustan. Instead of naming the ruler, the obverse was struck with a Persian couplet. However, the couplets themselves were a legacy of the past. One, which concisely conveys the concept of spiritual transmission from the first to the tenth Guru, is first found in written form on the seal of Banda Bahadur (1708–16) stamped on two of his own letters.[10] The seal is dated to the 'first year of the coronation [*jolus*]', suggesting that the couplet was composed on that occasion while the war leader was engaging Aurangzeb's troops.[11] The couplet reads: 'Guru Gobind Singh received without delay from Nanak / The pot and the sword, conquest and victory' (*deg-u tegh-u fath-u nusrat be-derang – Yaft[e] az Nanak Guru Gobind[e] Singh*). This is the direct transmission from the first to the tenth Guru of the fundamental symbols of Sikh life. *Deg*, 'the pot', to feed all and sundry on an egalitarian base, and *tegh*, the 'sword' of glorious resistance to oppression, are Sikh symbols reflected, amongst other things, in Sikh paintings showing Guru Nanak and Guru Gobind Singh engaged in conversation.[12]

A second couplet proclaims, in one of several variants: 'the mint struck on the two worlds [a Koranic phrase describing the world of contingency, this world, and transcendental reality, the world beyond] is the greatness of the Lord – The conquest is that of the sword of Gobind, King of Kings, the sword of Nanak is that which bestows it (*Sikkazan bar har do 'alam fazl-i Sachcha Sahib ast – Fath-i Gubind Shah-i Shahan tegh-e Nanak wahib ast*).[13] Significant variations occur in the formulation. In most, the second hemistich includes the old Persian title *Shah* (king) or, as here, 'Shah-i Shahan' (King of Kings).[14] The tenth Guru is thus given a title which, in the Persian tradition, is used solely for the emperors of Iran. This is a way of hailing Gobind Singh as King of the World.

More remarkably still, on the reverse, Sikh coinage maintained the Persian formulae of the Mughal empire, pointing to a sense of institutional continuity, religious persecutions notwithstanding. A typical inscription reads, 'Minted in the capital Lahore, the [...]th year of the blissful, humane reign' (*zarb-i dar ul-Saltanat-i Lahor, sana-yi [the year or number] jolus-i maymanat-i ma'nus*).[15] Lahore is designated as the seat of the 'Sultanate', and the year of the reign specified in accordance with Mughal practice.

If coinage points to continuity with some fundamental aspects of the Mughal tradition, so does court painting. The image that the first sovereign of the Sikh state took care to project of himself was that of the heir to Mughal kingship. Artists repeatedly portrayed him in the guise of a Mughal ruler. One of the most revealing paintings was commissioned some time in the 1830s (plate 60). Intended by Ranjit Singh as a present to Colonel Henry Charles Van Coortlandt, who spent eight years in his service, the

63. *Equestrian Portrait of Shah Jahan*, Mughal, *c*.1630. Gouache and gold on paper, 28.1 × 20.7 cm. The Metropolitan Museum of Art, Purchase, Roger's Fund and the Kevorkian Foundation Gift, 1955 (55.121.10.21v). Photograph © 1980 The Metropolitan Museum of Art

miniature represents the ruler riding a white horse amidst attendants in a hilly landscape. His head is framed by a halo of light with short golden rays emanating from the outer circle. This is the imperial glory (*farr-e shahenshahi* in Persian) sung by Ferdowsi in the tenth century Book of Kings,[16] and scrupulously represented by seventeenth-century Mughal artists when portraying their emperors.[17] Behind the maharaja, an attendant holds at an angle the 'majestic parasol' (*chatr-e homayuni*), the Iranian symbol of royalty since Achaemenid times.[18]

Ranjit Singh's pursuit of the Mughal image went far beyond mere iconography. He collected jewels that once belonged to Jahangir and Shah Jahan (plate 64). Was it the bittersweet satisfaction of possessing the regalia of the emperors that had been ruthless to the community? Or did Ranjit Singh give precedence to restoring the grandeur of the past? The latter certainly played a role.

So vivid was the awareness of the Mughal paraphernalia, costume included, that the artists of the Sikh court painted idealised likenesses of the Gurus in imperial costume, complete with regalia. Guru Gobind Singh was depicted on horseback as a royal hunter in the mural paintings decorating the Golden Temple, as well as in single leaf paintings.[19] A bow is slung over his left shoulder, and he clutches the perch of a white falcon in his right hand. An attendant holds the imperial parasol over his head framed by the halo of glory. Hunting dogs, indispensable to retrieve the prey when hawking, cavort alongside the horse.

64. The 'Timur Ruby' mounted on a necklace of gold, diamonds and spinels. Lent by Her Majesty Queen Elizabeth II. The Royal Collection © Her Majesty Queen Elizabeth II.

Another idealised portrait represents Guru Har Gobind seated on his heels inside a mansion.[20] He wears a royal turban complete with aigrette and here too holds up the perch of a white hawk with his right hand, which is protected by a leather gauntlet. The rendition of a seventeenth-century sword with a typical Mughal hilt, and of a dagger with a white jade hilt ending with a curving knop, points to a quasi-antiquarian interest

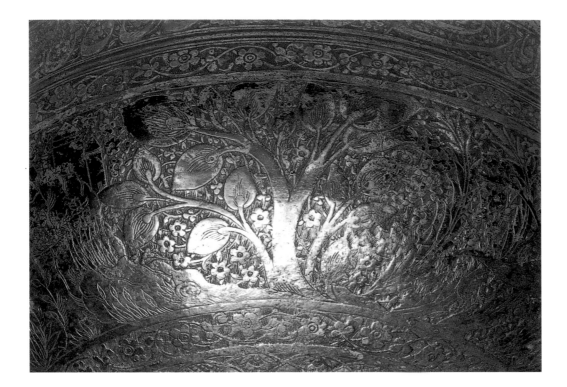

69. Detail of a large wine bowl (*jam*). Mughal, Jahangir period (1605–27). Tinned copper, silvered in the 19th century, diam. 32.5 cm, height 14 cm. Shirvan Foundation. Photograph: A.S. Melikian-Chirvani.

70. Candlestick (*sham'dan*), Mughal, inscribed to the name of (Mirza) Heydar al-Husayni, dated AH 1027/AD 1618. Brass with black overlay, diam. base 15.5 cm, height 23.5 cm. Shirvan Foundation. Photograph: A.S. Melikian-Chirvani.

71. Inkwell (*davat*), probably 16th century. Bronze, diam. 6.5 cm, height 8 cm. Shirvan Foundation. Photograph: A.S. Melikian-Chirvani.

72. Small wine bowl (*badiya*), Mughal, Jahangir period. Tinned copper. Private collection. Photograph: A.S. Melikian-Chirvani.

73. Decanter (*surahi*) with twisted flutes, 17th–18th century. Bronze, diam. 17.7 cm, height 30.2 cm. Shirvan Foundation. Photograph: A.S. Melikian-Chirvani.

Feroz-jang, the seventeenth-century warrior] – The "King of the World" [*Shah-i Jahan*, an allusion to Shah Jahan] Raja Ranjit Singh'.[34]

In his account of the circumstances in which he was invited to write the book, Diwan Amar Nath writes 'A commander [*sarhang*] came, saying: go, proceed to the court that has the magnificence of heaven. When the King of the World [*Shah-i Jahan*] remembers you your station is higher than high heaven' – again an allusion to Shah Jahan, who thus becomes the archetype for Ranjit Singh.[35]

This deep yearning for bygone glories found a striking visual expression in the architectural setting of court life and its artefacts. Ranjit Singh restored Mughal monuments. The bronze or tinned copper vessels displayed on banquet tables, the inkwells in which officials dipped their pens (plate 71), perpetuated the repertoire of Mughal forms. This can be verified in some of the objects represented in the 1820s. In a painting dealing with the perennial theme of the princely couple, a Sikh aristocrat is seated with his female companion.[36] He holds up a small wine bowl with high sinuous sides of a size and profile that can be matched from seventeenth-century vessels. Behind him, an attendant holds up a decanter (*surahi*) that is close in size, shape and proportion to a decanter that probably dates from the eighteenth century if not earlier (plate 73). Next to him, another attendant holds up a wine bowl (*badiya*) of sinuous profile (plate 72).

While paintings yield invaluable evidence about the continuity of form, they also raise questions that are not easily answered. Did the Lahore court actually have a predilection for vessels devoid of the intricate patterns and calligraphic panels so prominent in

CHAPTER FIVE

THE ARTS OF THE COURT OF MAHARAJA RANJIT SINGH

SUSAN STRONGE

79. *Ranjit Singh with Hira Singh*, Panjab, *c.*1835–9. Gouache and gold on paper, 28 × 22 cm. Kapany Collection.

80. Belt of Maharaja Sher Singh. Lahore, *c.*1840. Emerald set with diamonds and pearls, approx. length 83.5 × 15 cm. Lent by Her Majesty Queen Elizabeth II. The Royal Collection © Her Majesty Queen Elizabeth II (11291).

Early in February 1837 the chronicler of the court of Maharaja Ranjit Singh noted the activity taking place in Lahore in preparation for the marriage of Nau Nihal Singh, the Sikh ruler's son. A significant part of the preparations was for the reception of the British commander-in-chief, Sir Henry Fane and his entourage, and it is clear from the chronicle that these were meticulously planned, the shrewd maharaja being fully aware of the level of scrutiny to which all aspects of his court would be subjected.

He held a series of planning meetings with Colonel Wade, the British political agent posted in Ludhiana, at which they discussed plans for the rose garden in which one of the encounters was to be held, suitable sites for setting up the camp, and the kind of music and fireworks to be provided for the entertainments. The maharaja asked whether he should supply local wine or have it sent from Kashmir; Wade complimented him on the beauty of a garden which had already been prepared for the distinguished guests, with carpets and other floorcoverings laid out and water playing from the fountains.[1]

Out of Wade's sight, the maharaja double-checked everything with his officials and called the superintendent of his court workshops, Misr Beli Ram, to bring the presents being made for Fane and company to be inspected; some of these were 'huge special Persian guns set in gold cases, bejewelled ornaments, many garments and other things'.[2] The maharaja also ordered that when his chieftains appeared before the governor-general, they were to wear their best apparel, including the finest jewels; their horses were supplied with gold and jewelled harnesses and were also examined.[3]

The success of all this may be judged from the account of Fane's visit written by his

85. Part of carpet, probably Lahore, mid-17th century. Wool pile with cotton warps and cotton and silk wefts, 356 × 196 cm. IM 67-1930.

86. Carpet fragment, probably Kashmir, mid-17th century. Pashmina pile with cotton warps and silk wefts, 56 × 52 cm. IM 153-1926; Given by Mr V. Behar.

87. Mace, Panjab, made for Nawab Muhammad Bahawal, Khan-i Abbasi, AH 1186/AD 1772–3. Steel overlaid with gold, length 159 cm. © The British Museum (OA-10637).

Lahore had been the northernmost capital of the Mughal empire and was renowned for particular crafts and industries. Under Akbar (1556–1605), it had become an important centre of luxury carpet weaving and was a major metalworking centre: a family of astrolabists had produced astrological instruments for the Mughal emperors from the time of Humayun in the mid-sixteenth century, and Lahori armourers must have supplied the court with weapons from at least the late sixteenth century. Made of finely watered steel, these were chiselled with intricate designs and often decorated with gold and silver (plate 87).[6] Other towns in the Panjab had their own well-established specialities. Sialkot, for instance, produced paper of high quality, as well as weapons and a range of embroidered cloths; Gujrat also sold weapons, and Multan was known for its silk.[7]

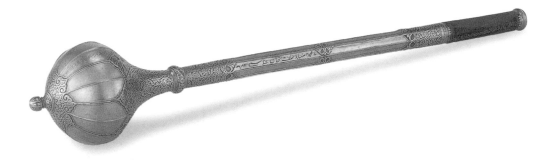

88. Tiles from Lahore monuments, Mughal, *c*.1600-50. Glazed earthenware. IM 251-1923; IS 68-1898; IM 271-1923.

89. Casket of Ranjit Singh, Mughal, 17th century. Wood inlaid with ivory and tortoiseshell, 30.7 × 39.5 × 28.5 cm. Kapany Collection.

The tiled Mughal monuments of Lahore were admired, Ranjit Singh apparently rescuing them from their neglected state, renovating them and adding his own buildings in similar style. His Baradari or pavilion at Lahore dating from 1818, for example, is discreetly inserted between the fort built by Akbar and his successors, and the enormous mosque of the Emperor Aurangzeb (1658–1707).[8] The Rambagh garden in Amritsar (completed 1831), with its fountains, pavilions and small palace, was made in imitation of Shah Jahan's Shalimar Gardens in Lahore (begun 1641), and was laid out under the supervision of the leading court figures Faqir Aziz ad-din, Desa Singh Majithia and Lehna Singh Majithia.[9] Ranjit Singh also built a palace next to the Mughal fort which still stands today.[10] Marble, inlaid with panels of *pietra dura* designs imported from the lapidaries of Agra (whose ancestors had decorated the Taj Mahal, and the Emperor Jahangir's tomb outside Lahore) was chosen for the decoration of the Golden Temple in Ranjit Singh's reign, and was used sparingly in other monuments. The designs are clearly distinct from their Mughal antecedents, although executed in the traditional style.[11]

These permanent reminders of Maharaja Ranjit Singh's patronage suggest a much greater level of innovative artistic activity than is usually acknowledged, and there is evidence to suggest that this was the case throughout the range of the arts.

At the centre of production in Lahore, supplying the daily needs of the court, was the *toshkhana*.[12] In it were housed the treasures of the court, its valuable goods, including presents received from foreign dignitaries, and cash receipts. A range of craftsmen was attached to it, working under the superintendence of Misr Beli Ram to produce jewellery worn at court, luxury goods and items for presentation. Distinguished visitors from Bukhara, Afghanistan, Iran, Nepal and India, as well as Europe, would all receive a *khil'at*, literally 'robe of honour' but often involving the addition of jewellery, gold coins, and richly caparisoned elephants or horses for the most important individuals. The components of the *khil'at* were either made in the *toshkhana* or were drawn from its stores of luxury goods, particularly textiles, imported from all over the kingdom and beyond its borders. Goldsmiths and jewellers from other parts of the Panjab might also be commissioned to supply particular items; Ranjit Singh, for example, ordered the Peshawar goldsmiths to supply a gold saddle on the occasion of Nau Nihal's wedding. Whatever their source, all purchases from beyond the *toshkhana* were carefully assessed and valued by Misr Beli Ram.

In 1838 the gifts assembled for the entourage of the new governor-general Lord Auckland demonstrate how closely rank determined the value of an individual's *khil'at*. When Misr Beli Ram laid them all out for the maharaja's approval, the court chronicler listed them. The most senior officer accompanying Auckland, Macnaughten, was to be given 15 garments, a pearl necklace, a jewelled armlet and a jewelled pair of gold bangles, an elephant with a silver seat, a horse with a golden saddle and a jewelled sword. The value and range of the presents descended the scale until the clerks of the various officers were reached; these were to receive small cash gifts or textiles of low value.[13] The governor-general and his most senior companions received no fewer than eleven *khil'ats* each, and his sisters were given ten each.[14]

Other presentations made by Ranjit Singh rewarded those carrying out religious duties. At Dussehra in 1835, for instance, the court chronicle notes:

> Guru Sadhoo Singh left for Kartarpur according to his old custom along with the Granth Sahib after receiving 11 fine garments consisting of *doshalas* [pairs of shawls], brocade, red silk, a turban and so on and two pieces of jewellery, one pearl necklace, one turban gem and one horse with a gold harness as a farewell gift, and an order to realise, as usual, entertainments for the Granth Sahib at Amritsar, Wirowal and other places.[15]

The same passage shows that the Holy Book itself was also honoured: the maharaja went to the Harmandir and 'a bejewelled gold umbrella, 500 ducats for gold work, a carpet, one handkerchief and many other things for Granth Sahib were presented by his men in his presence'.

The wealth of the Lahore court was clearly apparent on festive occasions. At the New Year festival of 1832, Shah Jahan's octagonal marble pavilion, the Musamman Burj, was decorated for an evening gathering. Golden candles lit the scene and gold chairs and stools were set out for Ranjit Singh's British visitors on brocades and embroidered floor coverings; the *qanats* (screens) were supported on gold- or silver-covered poles, and rose-water and wine were laid ready with gold utensils nearby.[16]

Given this profusion, recorded in page after page of the *Umdat ut-tavarikh* ('Pillar of History', the court chronicle), it is surprising that so little can now be linked with the court, and it is therefore impossible to judge the quality of the work done for it. However, one of the most spectacular artefacts to have survived does suggest a high level of skill. The 'Golden Throne' (plate 91) was made in the *toshkhana* for the maharaja by Hafez Muhammad Multani, according to the inventory of the Lahore crown property meticulously prepared by Dr John Login immediately after the annexation of the Panjab in 1849.[17] The throne was shipped to London in 1853 for the East India Company's museum and was eventually

91. The Golden Throne of Maharaja Ranjit Singh, by Hafez Muhammed Multani, Lahore, *c*.1818. Wood and resin core covered with sheets of embossed gold, 94 × 90 cm. 2518 (IS).

90. Order of Merit, presented to Lord Auckland by Maharaja Ranjit Singh in 1838. Enamelled gold, set with diamonds. Sheesh Mahal Museum and Medal Gallery, Patiala. Courtesy of the Department of Cultural Affairs, Architecture and Museums, Punjab, Chandigarh, India.

transferred to the South Kensington Museum, later renamed the Victoria and Albert Museum, where it has remained ever since.

All the European accounts mention Ranjit Singh's most valuable treasures, which he was always keen to show visitors, whether they were members of high-level embassies or individuals of more modest rank. All the writers single out the legendary diamond the Koh-i-nur.

An extraordinarily complicated history has come to be attributed to the diamond, many commentators claiming that it had been owned by Babur, the first Mughal emperor, who acquired it during his conquest of Hindustan in 1526 from the Raja of Gwalior, Vikramaditya. Before this, in the late thirteenth century, it is suggested that the diamond had been owned by the Khalji ruler of Delhi, Ala ad-din. It is supposed to have travelled to Iran in the mid-sixteenth century, when Babur's son temporarily lost the Mughal throne, and been given to Shah Tahmasp in return for his hospitality and military help. This 'history', however, depends on a great many leaps of logic, any reference to a very large diamond in historical texts often being taken to refer to one and the same diamond, regardless of any conflicting evidence.[18]

Whatever the earlier history of the stone, it does seem to have been owned by Shah Jahan, the renowned connoisseur and collector of gemstones. It stayed in Mughal possession until Nadir Shah's raid on the imperial treasury at Delhi in 1838, and was taken back to Iran the following year. At this time it may have been given the Persian name *kuh-i nur*, or 'Mountain of Light'.[19] After Nadir Shah's assassination in 1747, his general Ahmad Khan eventually took possession of the stone. Ahmad Khan became ruler of Afghanistan and took the title Ahmad Shah Abdali, and the diamond was inherited by various of his successors, until it came into the hands of Shah Shuja. Shah Shuja was ousted from the throne in 1812, and was imprisoned in Kashmir, where he was tortured. His wife then appealed to Ranjit Singh for help, promising him the diamond if he could free her husband. Ranjit Singh's army stormed the fort where the shah was held and Shah Shuja was released, but the maharaja showed considerable reluctance to relinquish the diamond. According to Dalip Singh's treasurer Misr Mekraj, Shah Shuja first sent a large topaz to Ranjit Singh, hoping that this would either fool or beguile him.[20] It did neither; Ranjit Singh kept the topaz, and a strategic withdrawal of food and water changed Shah Shuja's mind. On 1 June 1813 the Koh-i-nur entered the Sikh treasury.

The diamond was set into an armband (plate 92) with two other large diamonds

92. Original setting for the Koh-i-nur diamond, Lahore, *c.*1818. Enamelled gold, 10 × 15 cm. Lent by Her Majesty Queen Elizabeth II. The Royal Collection © Her Majesty Queen Elizabeth II (31734).

93. The 'Timur Ruby'. Lent by
Her Majesty Queen Elizabeth II.
The Royal Collection © Her Majesty
Queen Elizabeth II.

which, Ranjit Singh told Baron Hugel, a German visitor to the court, had been bought in Amritsar for 130,000 and 100,000 rupees respectively.[21] On the same occasion, Hugel was shown an emerald reportedly from the Jewelled Throne of Shah Jahan, although the circumstances of its acquisition are not recorded.

Other gemstones of superlative quality came from Shah Shuja, notably a huge, translucent, rose-pink spinel that had also belonged to Shah Jahan and had taken the same route through Iran and Afghanistan as the Koh-i-nur. This hereditary Mughal jewel bears its history on it in beautifully calligraphed Persian inscriptions which record its ownership by the emperors Jahangir, Shah Jahan, Aurangzeb and Farrukhsiyar, as well as Nadir Shah (who, the inscription notes, carried if off from Delhi) and Ahmad Shah. Despite this evidence, a spurious history also attached itself to this jewel until it had became transformed into the 'Timur Ruby' (plate 93), a historic stone associated with the Central Asian ruler known in the West as Tamberlaine.[22]

This time, Ranjit Singh had bought the stone from Shah Shuja as the court chronicle testifies. He suddenly showed a keen interest in Shah Shuja's possessions when one Mian Smad Joo came with items prepared for Lord Auckland's forthcoming visit: 'The Maharaja asked him whether Shah Shuja-al-Mulk was selling jewellery. He replied that the said Shah was maintaining himself only by that very means.'[23] The maharaja asked him to purchase the most valuable jewels, two spectacular rubies, on his behalf. On another occasion, a large turquoise which had been owned by Nadir Shah was also acquired from the hapless Afghan ruler and was seen by Baron Hugel.

In addition to jewels, the maharaja also collected jewelled swords, some of them of immense value. On 18 March 1837 Fane was invited to see Ranjit Singh's entire collection of treasures which, he noted, included some of the finest jewels in the world: 'The swords were many of them of great value, their blades alone being in some instances valued at £1,000, and the gold and jewels upon their hilts and scabbards at five times that sum. Many of them had been squeezed out of Shah Shuja, the ex-king of Caboul.'[24]

At Ranjit Singh's death in 1839 the treasury passed to his successors and, given the

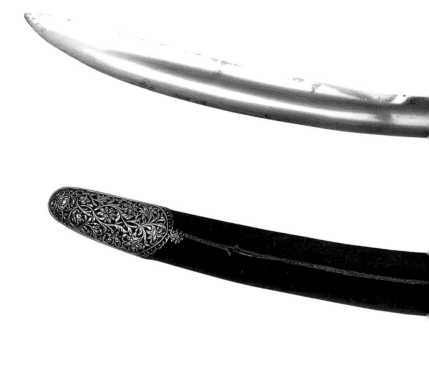

94. Arm defence, Panjab(?), said to be from the armoury of Shah Shuja, AH 1146/AD 1733–4. Steel overlaid with silver and gold, 36.2 × 18 cm. 190-1904.

massive upheavals that subsequently took place, seems to have remained surprisingly intact. The portrait of Sher Singh, Ranjit's son and eventual successor (see plate 220), shows with almost photographic realism the dazzling wealth of the treasury while the meticulous inventory made by Dr Login in 1849 indicates its range and quantity.[25]

The most spectacular gems of the treasury were sent to London where they were exhibited at the 1851 Great Exhibition. The Koh-i-nur disappointed the crowds in its poorly lit Chubb's 'patent diamond case' and was recut, losing nearly 43 per cent of its original weight.[26] It is now in the crown made for Her Majesty Queen Elizabeth the Queen Mother in 1937, and is worn on State occasions. The remainder of the collection was dispersed in a series of auctions at Lahore in the aftermath of annexation, although Dalip Singh was allowed to retain some of his personal jewels and valuables.[27]

In Lahore as elsewhere in the kingdom, the extremely sophisticated manufacture of arms and armour, and artillery, was nurtured by Ranjit Singh and his officers for obvious strategic reasons, but their patronage allowed a traditional skill of the region to continue to flourish.

The Annexation inventories of the armoury provide fascinating details about the collecting and manufacture of weapons from Ranjit Singh's reign to 1849. The most important swords, shields and sets of armour are classified by owner and their origin, as well as any embellishment carried out in the *toshkhana*, is noted. A set of mail and a helmet belonging to Maharaja Sher Singh, for instance, was 'Manufactured in Nurwarghur, polished and repaired in Lahore'. His shield was 'inlaid in Delhi and purchased from a mer-

95. Sword of Jahangir, presented to Queen Victoria by the widow of Lt Hodson of Hodson's Horse, length 85 cm. Lent by Her Majesty Queen Elizabeth II. The Royal Collection © Her Majesty Queen Elizabeth II. (67062)

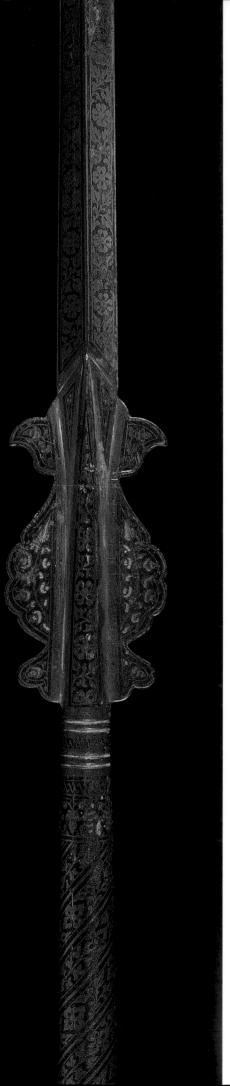

97. Casket, Sialkot, *c*.1880. Steel, blued and
overlaid with gold. H. 27.3 cm, diam. 20.3 cm.
IS 2411-1883.

96. Spear, Northern India, 18th century.
Steel, blued and overlaid with gold,
max. diam. *c*.20 cm, length *c*.200 cm.
Qila Mubarak Museum, Patiala (70/2).
Courtesy of the Department of Cultural
Affairs, Architecture and Museums, Punjab,
Chandigarh, India.

chant of the same place', while a quiver of Ranjit Singh was 'made to order in the Toshakhana', as was a powder horn, this time for a specific occasion, the marriage in 1838 of Khurak Singh, eldest son of Ranjit Singh.[28] Another list gives the names of the court servants who had examined particular pieces: 'Uzeemoollah' and 'Chowdry sekleegur' are among the armourers mentioned, and 'Banyaun' is a goldsmith giving a report on a small drum and saddle-axe made by his father.[29]

It has sometimes been suggested that after the Annexation the Panjab's *kuftkars*, or gold-inlayers, were diverted from their traditional work on weapons (plate 87). While it is clear that an industry grew up supplying European demand for gold-decorated steel cigar boxes and card-cases, this ignores the patronage of the later Sikh kingdoms. Patiala, in particular, continued to employ highly skilled workmen.

The manufacture of ordnance was transformed by Ranjit Singh's initiatives. In the early eighteenth century, the only artillery of the Sikhs had been captured from various enemies, but in 1807 Ranjit Singh established a foundry at Lahore for the repair and manufacture of guns. This produced firearms of high quality throughout the reign and probably also made artillery from the beginning; in 1808 some of the 35 to 40 'country' guns said to be in his possession must surely have been made there.[30] By 1831 a British officer observed that 'the guns were well cast and carriages in good repair; they had been made in Lahore and cost him [Ranjit Singh] Rs 1000 each.'[31]

The year 1831 was a landmark in the history of Sikh ordnance. In October Lord William Bentinck had come to Ropar to meet Ranjit Singh, and with surprising insouciance, presented him with British cannons. The maharaja was so impressed by the supe-

98. Nine-pounder howitzer, decorated with the Order of Merit, East India Company Foundry, G. Hutchinson, Cossipore, dated 1838. Bronze, length 127 cm. The Board of Trustees of the Armouries (XIX 247).

riority of British artillery that he decided to copy European models, using the technical skills of the Frenchman, General Court. The effects of Lord Bentinck's generosity were clearly apparent by 1838 when William Osborne saw the Sikh artillery: 'It consisted of a battery of fifty-three horse artillery, nine pounders, cast in brass in his own foundry at Lahore, from the patterns of those presented to him by Lord William Bentinck.'[32] He was struck by the proficiency of the gunners under Raja Dhian Singh's command, writing that their precision was 'extraordinary, when the short period of time since they have known of even the existence of such a thing is taken into consideration'.[33] No doubt further intelligence was provided by Lord Auckland's gift of two cannon from the British foundry at Cossipore, near Calcutta.[34] Court was assisted by Lehna Singh Majithia (plate 100), and the names of some of their gunmakers (Muhammad Hayat and Rai Singh) and foundry superintendents (Mian Qadar Bakhsh, Munshi Dil Bagh Rai and Jawahar Mal) are recorded in inscriptions on Lahore cannons.[35] Court's crucial role was acknowledged by Henry Fane: 'Court has brought his artillery and musketry to great perfection'.[36]

It is possible that the carriages for the guns still required improvement, however. One of the displays put on for Ranjit Singh by Fane's entourage related to a six-pounder field gun: 'It was thrown on the ground, dismounted from its carriage, taken all to pieces, remounted, men on their horses, and again in full gallop, in the space of five minutes.'[37] The maharaja was delighted and persuaded them to repeat the exercise claiming, genuinely or not, that he believed there had been some trick for them to perform such a complicated manoeuvre so quickly. They obliged; one can easily imagine the discussions that might have taken place afterwards about the lessons learned from the demonstration.

Artillery was the most effective section of the Khalsa army and was to inflict devastating blows on the British during the Anglo-Sikh wars of 1845–6 and 1848–9. However, once the guns fell into British hands, the conflict could not be sustained. The most spectacular cannon were shipped back to Britain; the firearms and other weapons of the Khalsa army which remained in Lahore became Dr Login's responsibility, and the finest were sent to London or sold in Lahore. The rest, the purely utilitarian pieces, were recycled. Login wrote to his wife:

> We are now working hard in the magazine, breaking up old arms as fast as we
> can . . . already I have supplied Napier with many tons of them for his work on
> the canals. I had the pleasure of having the first swords brought in converted into
> capital scythes for mowing the grass in the soldiers' gardens.

100. *Lehna Singh Majithia*, page from the *Crest-jewel of the Essence of All Systems of Astrology*, by Durgashankar Pathak, Benares, *c.*1833–9. 18 × 22 cm. By permission of The British Library (Or. 5259).

99. Order of Merit, Lahore, *c.*1837–9. Enamelled gold, set with emeralds, 9.1 × 4.8 cm. IS 92-1981 .

CHAPTER SIX

PAINTING IN THE PANJAB

B.N. GOSWAMY

101. *Descent from the Cross*, Mughal, Lahore, *c*.1598. Gouache and gold on paper, 19.4 × 11.3 cm. IS 133-1964 f. 79b.

It is time to reassess painting in the Panjab. Over the years it has aroused some interest, but has had no prominence in the histories of Indian painting, since it has been regarded as having no clear identity and its qualities are barely understood. Fixed notions have been formed relating to sources and influences, the amount and range of work done, the levels at which painting was patronised, the taste of the patrons – even the period it covers. Many of these ideas need to be rethought, for they are too narrow in scope, and some are rooted more in ignorance or prejudice than in fact.

Even though painting in the Panjab is thought of essentially as nineteenth-century work done in 'Sikh Panjab', there is little doubt that it goes back at least to the sixteenth century, when the *subah* (or province) of Lahore flourished under the Mughals (plate 101). Painters from the region were undoubtedly working in the imperial studios there, and illustrated manuscripts were being produced. In 1611, when William Finch, trading in indigo and other merchandise for the East India Company, came to Lahore, 'one of the greatest cities of the East', he saw a great deal of painting there and described it in vivid detail.[1] He took in the mural-covered walls inside the royal quarters of the Emperor Jahangir (1605–27), with their carved windows and the great 'devoncan', the *Diwan-khana*, or Hall of Private Audience. In his account there is an elaborate notice of a painted *darbar* scene depicting Jahangir 'sitting crosse-legged on a chaire of state' with his sons and leading court personages: 'Note also that in this gallery, as you enter, on the right hand of the King over the doore is the picture of our Saviour; opposite on this left-hand, of the Virgin Mary.'[2]

On the wall of another small gallery in the same royal quarters, Finch saw 'the picture of the Acabar [i.e the Emperor Akbar] sitting in his state, and before him Sha Selim [Shah Salim, later the emperor Jahangir] his sonne standing with a hawke on his fist . . . and by him his (other) three sonnes'. In the women's lodgings, 'where the King useth to sit', he notes, with some sympathy for the 'poore women' who had to endure these sights, that 'drawne overhead [are] many pictures of angels, with pictures of Banian dews, or

102. *The Dream of Vaux*, illustration
to the *Fables* of Jean de la Fontaine,
by Imam Bakhsh, Attock, *c*.1838-40.
Gouache and gold on paper,
25.5 × 17.7 cm. Musée Jean de la
Fontaine, Château-Thierry.

103. *Rama and his Brothers*, from a Mankot workshop, 18th century. Painting on cloth, 125 × 200 cm. Sheesh Mahal Museum and Medal Gallery. Courtesy of the Department of Cultural Affairs, Arch. and Museums, Punjab, Chandigarh, India.

rather divels, intermixt in most ugly shape with long hornes, staring eyes, shagge haires, great fangs, ugly pawes, long tailes . . .'

Finch's descriptions ring true because they conjure up images of work that is well known from the range of Mughal painting. It is safe to assume that work in the style associated with the Mughal court must have gone on here throughout the seventeenth and the eighteenth centuries, even if its scale is difficult to judge in the absence of clear documentation. It is of interest, however, that evidence is now beginning to surface, especially on work done in the eighteenth century in the late Mughal style in the Panjab plains. There is, for instance, a group of inscribed and dated paintings with clear 'Panjabi' themes such as Heer, heroine of one of the classics of Panjabi literature, and Puran Bhagat, a reclusive character from a well-loved Panjab legend, from which works seem to have been sold for specified sums by one Brijnath to Khudabaksh in 1748 in a small Panjab town.[3] It is also likely that several sets of 'portraits' of the great Sikh Gurus in a dry, late-Mughal style, which are scattered in different collections, were done in the Panjab plains (plate 104). It is difficult to think of the period as one of studied inactivity as far as painting is concerned.

All this while, not far from the plains of Panjab, in the belt of hill states stretching from Jammu in the west to Sirmur in the east, the great Pahari (literally 'of the hills') styles of painting were flourishing. Here, for some of the seventeenth century and throughout the eighteenth, work of great sensitivity – at once passionate and restrained, elegant and free of pretence – continued to be done in the family workshops of painters active at such centres as Basohli, Mankot, Nurpur, Chamba, Kangra, Guler and Mandi, under the patronage of Rajput chiefs. Pahari painting is so large and distinctive a chapter in the history of Indian art that it is usually treated quite separately from painting in the Panjab, but it is difficult to understand fully the development of painting in the plains without a clear reference to the powerful influence Pahari painting exercised.

The evidence of style had long suggested a strong connection but there is now a whole body of documents to which one can refer.[4] This includes not only the portraits of men of power and influence in the plains, such as the governors Adina Beg Khan and Mir Mannu, done by the great Pahari painter Nainsukh,[5] but also other evidence, such as

104. *Guru Hargobind Singh on a Terrace with an Attendant*, Panjab Plains, *c.*1750. Watercolour on paper, 10 × 7.25 cm. Kapany Collection.

the large and remarkable drawing showing the spread of the style of the distinguished family of painters to which Nainsukh belonged.[6] The drawing depicts the goddess Devi, her numerous spidery arms spread out around her, ending at points at which the names of several Pahari states and of three chiefs are inscribed within circles. All the three chiefs (or *sardars*) are Sikhs known to have been active in the second half of the eighteenth century: Jai Singh of the Kanhaiyal *misl*, his son Gurbaksh Singh and Jassa Singh Ramgarhia. They are mentioned by name apparently because they were masters of no known state or well-defined territory, but this leaves no doubt as to their connection with certain Pahari painters who must have worked for them. Further confirmation of this is provided by surviving portraits in Pahari hands of these chiefs, and by a fine group-picture showing Jai Singh Kanhaiya conferring with Pahari rulers including Raj Singh of Chamba, Prakash Chand of Guler and the young Sansar Chand of Kangra.[7] There is also an early reference to a 'picture of felicity', taken when a meeting took place between some Sikh chiefs, including a forebear of Ranjit Singh, in the environs of Batala. Clearly there was an interest in painting and, with Pahari painters close at hand, an opportunity. There

105 *Sassi Grieves for Punnu*, in the style of Nainsukh of Guler, *c.*1800. Gouache on paper, 16.5 × 26 cm. Rietberg Museum, Zurich.

is thus a case for revising some of W.G. Archer's conclusions in his fine early study of Sikh painting, among them the statement that it was 'the years 1810 to 1830 [that] saw the first approach by hill artists to Sikh patrons and the first expression of interest in painting by Sikhs themselves.'[8]

In addition to stray references, there is a large and uncommonly informative group of documents that establishes firmly the connection between at least one family of Pahari painters, based in Rajol, and the Sikh centre of power at Lahore.[9] Most of these, couched in the Persian current at that time at the Sikh court, are in the nature of *par-wanas*, or orders involving, or issued in favour of, members of Nainsukh's family, among them his son Nikka (plate 114) and Nikka's three sons Gokal, Harkhu and Chhajju. These *parwanas* deal with such topics as the terms on which a painter is engaged, the confirmation of an old grant of land, a summons to a painter asking him to present himself at the court, and even a letter to a hill functionary asking him to help the painter Chhajju who had been 'falsely implicated' in a case of murder. Many of the documents bear the seals of the powerful Sandhanwalia *sardars*, who were close relations of the maharaja, but

106. *Portrait of a Warrior*, ascribed to the Master at the Court of Mankot, *c.*1690. Gouache on paper, 22.7 × 16.8 cm. Government Museum and Art Gallery, Chandigarh (1236). Photograph by Brigitte Kammerer.

at least one was issued by the ruler of Lahore himself. This document, with its matter-of-fact tone and its references to past orders, captures perfectly the flavour of the times. Dated VS 1882/AD 1825, it is in favour of the painter Nikka and is addressed to the local Sikh functionary at Rihlu, near Kangra, a village in which the painter-family lived. The *parwana*, written in the *shikasteh* script and prefaced by the seals of Ranjit Singh, may be translated:

107. *Krishna kills Kansa the Demon King*, from the Bhagavata Purana series, ascribed to the Master at the Court of Mankot, *c.*1700. Gouache on paper, 21.5 × 31 cm. Government Museum and Art Gallery, Chandigarh (1282). Photography by Brigitte Kammerer.

May the Kardar of Rihlu be hereby informed.

The painter Nikka has been, from olden times, in possession of land valued at rupees one hundred and twenty-five (Rs. 125/–) per annum. This grant of land has been confirmed upon him on the recommendation of Sardar Budh Singh ji. It is ordered that the land should be left with him and without his being subject to render any [usual] service or *begar*. In this matter this should be treated as a strict injunction.

Written on the 31st of the month of Asuj, S. 1882. Under orders of the Huzur at Camp: Rambagh.

[In the margin] [Conveyed] verbally through Raja Sahib Jio.

Documents such as this, through their sheer routineness of text and phraseology, establish a great deal, for they convey the sense that a grant or an engagement of this kind was nothing unusual. Almost certainly in the *daftar-i mu'alla*, which is mentioned in one of the Rajol family documents, there must have been others. When Purkhu and Buddhu, the members of another prominent Pahari family of artists, establish contact in another surviving document, there is an almost casual reference to visits to Lahore from where one

108. *Vishnu as Kalki*,
from the *Gita Govinda* series
by Manaku, 1730.
Gouache and gold
on paper,
30.5 × 20.9 cm.
Lahore Museum (E 46).

109. *Vishnu as Vamana*,
from the *Gita Govinda* series
by Manaku, 1730.
Gouache and gold
on paper,
30.5 × 20.9 cm.
Lahore Museum (E 40).

of the brothers asks the other to get him some material.[10] The records kept by priests at centres of pilgrimage, which have yielded such information on Pahari artists, also contain names of artists who had come, at least temporarily, to live in Lahore, among them Deviditta of Basohli.[11] There is a sense of activity stirring within the kingdom, and this is not an account of the work of Pahari artists alone. There were, as we now know, many more. The sheer amount of work done in the Panjab must have been impressive.

In this connection, the evidence may be considered of Lieutenant William Barr, one of the many Englishmen who travelled through Sikh Panjab in the early years of the nineteenth century. An observant man, taking in and recording all that he was seeing, including the paintings that adorned walls at Lahore, Patti, Wazirabad, Gujranwala and Peshawar, Barr's descriptions are elaborate, though not free of wry comment:

> The gateway [of the maharaja's palace at Lahore] which consists of a tolerably lofty archway with a tower at each side, is covered from its summit to its base with paintings, the greater number taken from the history of Krishna as related in the Prem Sagar, though a few describe the habits and peculiarities of a wandering fakeer. The figures are almost all about one-third the size of life, but with proportions as ludicrous and absurd as they can well be. In some the eye occupies nearly the whole side of a face, and in others the head appears as massive as the body. Here fakeers may be seen with their hands clasped above their heads, and with finger-nails two or three inches long . . . In one compartment [Krishna] is portrayed with a milkmaid shampooing his great toe, in another, he is perched up in a tree, from the branches of which depend various articles of dress he has stolen from some fair damsels . . . Having satisfied our curiosity at these wonderful embellishments, we passed beneath the archway and came to the inner gate of the palace which we remarked is enriched with paintings of a similar character to those on the first, and though no doubt considered to be in good taste by the Punjabees to Englishmen they have a most ridiculous appearance.[12]

William Barr's Victorian views on the art do not have to be taken seriously, but the many similar passages in his account bear witness yet again to the fact of painting flourishing in the state.

It is difficult to imagine that all this could have happened without the encouragement or the approval of the maharaja himself. Far too much has been written about Ranjit Singh's alleged personal indifference to painting, or his holding the art in poor esteem. When he repeatedly put off the request of the British visitor, G.T. Vigne, that he be allowed to draw the maharaja's portrait, it has been seen as proof of Ranjit Singh being 'strongly averse to being painted', apparently because of his awareness of his own unprepossessing, pock-marked appearance.[13] When, in reply to the question about what he does, Vigne almost lightheartedly says, 'I can draw', the astonishment of the maharaja is

110. *Portrait of the Painter Manaku,* ascribed to Nainsukh, *c.*1740. Lightly tinted brushdrawing on uncoloured paper, 16.3 × 12.7 cm. Government Museum and Art Gallery, Chandigarh. Photography by Brigitte Kammerer.

111. *Mian Mukund Dev of Jasrota riding through a Meadow*, by Nainsukh, *c.*1754. Gouache and gold on paper, 30 × 45 cm. IS 7-1973.

interpreted as dismay that so lowly an art as painting could be regarded by a white *sahib* so highly.[14] This is hardly conclusive evidence. It certainly does not accord with other facts, such as confirming grants of land upon painters in royal service; having the royal quarters adorned with paintings covering wall after wall; visiting Europeans speaking of 'the state artist', and his portfolio of drawings, 'some of them very clever'; or the maharaja issuing orders from time to time to have reception chambers properly adorned with paintings. An entry in the court chronicle dated March 1834 mentions the Baradari (or pavilion) at Adinanagar, an unimportant little town that was sometimes used as a summer resort, being prepared under the maharaja's orders by Sardar Lehna Singh Majithia.[15] The *sardar* was instructed to carry out several improvements, among them 'to make the water run in large volume from the [River] Shahnahar [close to the Baradari]. It was further remarked that a painter for the purposes of making figures, pictures and

112. *A Sikh Ruler shooting Wild Boar from a Platform*, Pahari, possibly Nurpur, *c.*1820–30. Gouache on paper, 27.3 × 36.6 cm. Kapany Collection.

marks, pleasing to the sight, had been sent for and was to be given one rupee a day from the account of the maharaja'.

It seems from all this that the maharaja is often presented in an unfair light when it comes to his attitude towards the arts. The silence of the records in this respect, the sheer tumult and crowding of events during these years, the preoccupation of chroniclers and foreign visitors with capturing in their accounts the magnificence of his court, seem to obscure much from our view. We see remarkably little of the maharaja's private beliefs, his private and inner life. But on the rare occasions that we do, a very different feeling comes across as, for instance, when he personally takes an interest in the marble ordered from Jaipur for use in the *parikrama* of the Golden Temple, commissions silver doors with repoussé-work to be made for the shrine of the Goddess at Kangra, chooses the pashmina shawls to be sent for the *pandits* of Benares and Gaya, or retires in the night to listen quietly to Attar Khan playing upon the flute.[16]

113. *Raja Prakash Chand of Guler*, Pahari, *c*.1780–90. Gouache and gold on paper, 20 × 14 cm. Rietberg Museum, Zurich. Photograph by Wettstein & Kauf.

114. Drawing of the Artists Gaudhu and Nikka, Kangra, 1775, 14.6 × 10.8 cm. Lahore Museum (D 120 and 121).

Painting in the kingdom had patrons other than the maharaja. The Sandhanwalia *sardars*, mentioned frequently in the Rajol documents, were obviously fond of the art, as was Sher Singh, the maharaja's son who eventually succeeded him to the throne.[17] There is fair indication that another powerful family, the Majithias, also took an interest in painting. The redoubtable Dogra brothers – Gulab Singh (plate 117), Dhian Singh and Suchet Singh – so close to the maharaja, belonged to a branch of the Jammu royal family, which was associated with the patronage of painting for more than a hundred years. The European officers in the service of the maharaja – Claude Court, Jean-François Allard (plate 118), Paolo Avitabile, included – commissioned painters, for instance Imam Bakhsh of Lahore (plate 119), to produce illustrated manuscripts,[18] when they were not lost in contemplating the 'indecorous' pictures adorning the walls of their sprawling *havelis* (mansions), or puzzling out the Indian perspective used in painted scenes of battle.[19]

Whatever the nature and level of patronage, the area of the greatest confusion or

115. *Wedding Procession of Prince Anirudh Chand of Kangra*, ascribed to Purkhu of Kangra, *c*.1800–1805. Gouache on paper, 35 × 48 cm. Government Museum and Art Gallery, Chandigarh (353). Photography by Brigitte Kammerer.

116. *Parashurama leading Krishna and Balarama to Mount Gomanta*, from a *Harivamsa* series, by Purkhu of Kangra, *c*.1800–1815. Gouache on paper, 35.2 × 47.6 cm. Government Museum and Art Gallery, Chandigarh (3171). Photography by Brigitte Kammerer

misjudgement concerning painting in the Panjab seems to be in the range of themes treated. The view commonly taken is that it is synonymous with 'Sikh painting', and Sikh painting is in turn 'chiefly an art of portraiture'. In some ways this is a convenient formulation, for it sets crisp limits and helps establish a clear identity for the work. However, the more one sees and analyses the period, the greater one feels the need to question these statements. There is far more to painting in the Panjab than portraiture, or themes that are easily recognizable as 'Sikh'.

Easily recognised 'Sikh themes' undoubtedly include sets of idealised portraits of the ten great Gurus, and extensive series of paintings or drawings centring upon the *Janam Sakhi*, the traditional and much revered account of the life and travels of the founder of the faith, Guru Nanak. Certainly, a great deal of work was done on these themes and some splendid series were turned out, although they were not of interest to Sikhs alone. Idealised portraits of the great Gurus had already emerged in the Pahari tradition in the

118. *General Jean-François Allard and his Family*, Lahore, 1838. Gouache and gold on paper, 20.6 × 26.9 cm. Courtesy of the Arthur M. Sackler Museum, Harvard University Art Museums, Private Collection (443.1983).

117. *Maharaja Gulab Singh of Jammu and Kashmir*, Panjab, *c*.1846. Gouache on paper, 29.7 × 23.4 cm. IS 194-1951.

eighteenth century: Guru Nanak, as a recluse, for instance; Guru Hargobind with signs of worldly power surrounding him; Guru Harkishan as a young boy; Guru Gobind Singh as a plumed royal figure on horseback, with a hawk on his hand (plate 32). The itinerant groups of Kashmiri scribes and painters who produced countless manuscripts in the northern plains had, similarly, started illuminating the sacred text, and illustrating the *Janam Sakhis* at the same time, creating their own somewhat innovative variants upon the standard renderings.[20]

Portraiture, which has repeatedly been regarded as the most favoured theme of 'Sikh painting', was indeed produced on a considerable scale, and some very sensitive studies were turned out. The remarkably large number of informal painted sketches or drawings stand out from this period even more than the formal sets.[21] Notable among these informal works is the extensive series, now unfortunately scattered, featuring likenesses of courtiers and functionaries at the Lahore court by the painter Chhajju.[22] It is easy to understand this interest in portraits, for personal achievement needed to be celebrated in some way, and in a warring, unstable world ephemeral life was seen as worthy of commemoration.

Undoubtedly portraiture also received a fillip from the strong interest of Europeans then living in the Panjab or travelling through, with portraits being an obvious means of recording the characters they were living or dealing with. These then became objects of formal exchange between dignitaries. The most penetrating portraits of the times are those showing single individuals rather than groups of people, which tend to be somewhat dry and 'official'-looking. It is also striking that few scenes filled with authentic figures in *darbar* settings seem to have been done by the most competent of artists active at the Lahore court. There are of course those studies, done by not the most skilled of hands late in the nineteenth century, when the nostalgia for a fallen kingdom swept the Panjab;[23] or work done by visiting Europeans, some of it in oils as by the Hungarian painter August Schoefft (plate 220). But, surprisingly, in the time of the maharaja himself, little evokes the great splendour of the court – of which there is so much contemporary written description – as there is in Mughal painting, for instance.

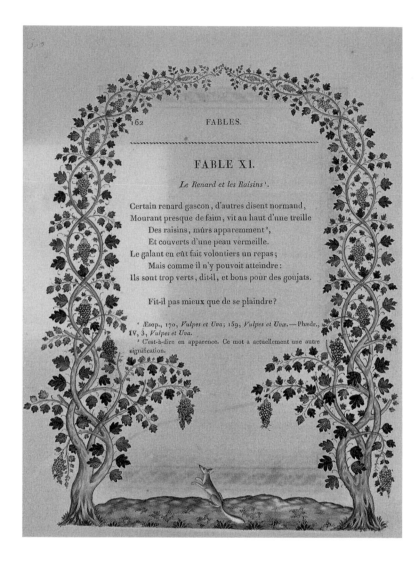

Despite the prevalent emphasis on Sikh paintings, there seems to be little doubt that what are rather loosely defined as 'Hindu themes', as distinct from Sikh, were widely produced throughout the period and the region. The sharp distinction between Hindu and Sikh themes that is sometimes made almost certainly belongs to a period much later than that of Maharaja Ranjit Singh. The evidence in this respect is considerable. One reads again and again about the widespread reverence paid to the Sikh Gurus and Sikh shrines by Hindus and Sikhs alike, about the maharaja and the Sikh nobility paying homage to Hindu shrines and texts (plate 124), the many devout pilgrimages to Haridwar,[24] the gifts made to the Brahmins of Kashi and Gaya,[25] the offering of silver doors at the shrine of the goddess, and so on. There is clear, visual extension of this in the lack of any sharp demarcation between Sikh and Hindu themes in the murals on the walls of Sikh royal palaces and other structures, whether in the first half of the nineteenth century or the second. The Hindu themes include scenes based on the *Prem Sagar*, the vernacular translation of the *Bhagavata Purana*, such as those described by Lieutenant Barr, as well as the

119. *The Horse and the Wolf*, illustration to the *Fables* of Jean de la Fontaine, by Imam Bakhsh, 25.3 × 17.7 cm. Musée Jean de la Fontaine, Château-Thierry.

120. *The Fox and the Grapes*, illustration to the *Fables* of Jean de la Fontaine, by Imam Bakhsh, 25.7 × 17.2 cm. Musée Jean de la Fontaine, Château-Thierry.

121. *Guru Nanak with Followers*. Detail.
Kashmir, *c.*1800. Gouache on paper.
Himachal State Museum (75.246).

panels on the walls of the Sheesh Mahal at Patiala which still survive, with their engaging renderings of the incarnations of Vishnu, the many deeds of Krishna, illustrations based on the *Satsai of Bihari*,[26] and so on.

When a view like this is taken, the whole issue opens up, and many things fall into place: the *Rasikapriya* series from the Kapurthala collection featuring Radha and Krishna so prominently; the famous 'Kangra' *Gita Govinda* with texts inscribed at the back not only in Sanskrit but also translated into Panjabi and written in Gurmukhi characters;[27] illustrated *nayaka-nayika* series;[28] 'Pahari'-looking erotic sets with Sikh figures. It would seem that, at least for a few decades, sets of portraits of the great Gurus and *Janam Sakhi* series were being produced in as many numbers, and with as much feeling, in the Pahari areas as works based on classical Sanskrit and Hindi texts were being made by painters active in the Panjab plains, and not for Hindu patrons alone.[29]

Later, things were to change. The availability of European models, the obvious attraction of 'realistic works', the appearance of such painters as Kehar Singh, Kapur Singh,

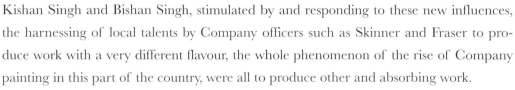

123. *Sikh Sardar*, Panjab, *c.*1830–40. Drawing on paper, 13 × 12 cm. IS 11-1957.

122. *A Sikh Youth dallying with his Consort*, 'Kangra style', *c.*1840. Gouache on paper, 18 × 13.8 cm. Reproduced by kind permission of the Trustees of The Chester Beatty Library, Dublin (MS 58.15).

124. *Ranjit Singh honouring Devi*, Panjab, *c.*1835. Gouache on paper, 26.5 × 21 cm. National Museum of India (72.313).

Kishan Singh and Bishan Singh, stimulated by and responding to these new influences, the harnessing of local talents by Company officers such as Skinner and Fraser to produce work with a very different flavour, the whole phenomenon of the rise of Company painting in this part of the country, were all to produce other and absorbing work.

113

CHAPTER SEVEN

TEXTILES IN THE PANJAB

ROSEMARY CRILL

125. Man's sash (*patka*), Kashmir, early 19th century. Pashmina, 110 × 48 cm. National Museum of India (64.458).

The court of Maharaja Ranjit Singh at Lahore left an impression of unrivalled splendour on all those who visited it, and it was particularly the lavish use of magnificent, brightly coloured silks, shawls and gold brocade textiles that impressed those who have left written accounts. One British visitor, Major-General W. G. Osborne, described the opulent setting for his first meeting with Ranjit Singh in 1838: 'The floor was covered with rich shawl carpets, and a gorgeous shawl canopy, embroidered with gold and precious stones, supported on golden pillars, covered three parts of the hall'.[1] The British commander-in-chief in India, Sir Henry Fane, remarked of the scene, 'The dresses and jewels of the Rajah's court were the most superb that can be conceived',[2] while Emily Eden, sister of the governor-general, Lord Auckland, wrote of the court, 'It reduces European magnificence to a very low pitch'.[3] Even the camp set up when the ruler was on the move was luxuriously furnished with tents and beds of shawlcloth. Fane describes Ranjit Singh's camp: 'The scarlet semi-anas [*shamianas*: awnings] and kanauts [*qanats*: screens] of Runjeet's pavilions looked beautiful from the opposite bank of the river, and when nearer, the illusion was not dispelled; for in addition to all the tents with shawl carpets and ceilings he had at Lahore, he had several new scarlet tents pitched, and the whole interior lined with Seikhs [Sikhs], in their picturesque and variegated dresses'.[4]

Dr (later Sir) John Login, the young Dalip Singh's guardian, writing in 1849, believed that 'for camp-equipage, old Runjeet's camp was the very finest and most sumptuous among all the Princes of India',[5] and painted a vivid picture of the twelve-year-old maharaja's travelling arrangements: 'Now when you are told the tents for the little man himself are all lined, some with rich Cashmere shawls, and some with satin embroidered with gold, *semianas*, carpets, *purdahs* [curtains], and floor-cloths to match, and that the tent-poles are encased in gold and silver . . . you may fancy that we shall look rather smart!'[6]

In contrast to the splendour of his surroundings, Ranjit Singh himself habitually dressed relatively simply, usually in a plain robe with only some choice pearls and

126. Man's sash (*patka*), Mughal, *c.*1725-50, pashmina, 317 × 67 cm. IS 12-1982.

127. Shawl, Kashmir, early 19th century, pashmina, 310 × 135 cm. IS 50-1967. Given by Mr R. Wyndham.

128. Silk fragment, Panjab, mid-19th century. Woven silk with gold, 138 (max.) × 78.5 (max.) cm. 7913 (IS).

diamonds for decoration.[7] The striking costumes of his courtiers and bodyguards, however, attracted the attention of many visitors, as Emily Eden wrote:

> One troop [of bodyguards] was dressed entirely in yellow satin, with gold scarfs and shawls; but the other half were in that cloth of gold which is called kincob – the *fond* [background] being gold and the pattern scarlet, or purple, or yellow . . . most of them had a silver or gold tissue drapery, which they bring over their heads and pass round their beards to keep them from the dust . . .[8]

Osborne was also impressed by these 'goorcherras' (bodyguards) 'handsomely dressed in chain armour and quilted jackets of either a bright yellow, green or scarlet colour'.[9] Courtiers such as Hira Singh favoured yellow silk for their garments,[10] and Raja Suchet Singh, also in a yellow quilted jacket, is described by Osborne as wearing 'three shawls of lilac, white and scarlet, twisted very round and tight' around the edge of his helmet.[11] Nineteenth-century paintings of Sikh *sardars* (chiefs) and courtiers by both Indian and European artists show them dressed mainly in close-fitting cotton robes with shawls draped around their shoulders, sometimes tied loosely at the waist, or with a loose-fitting

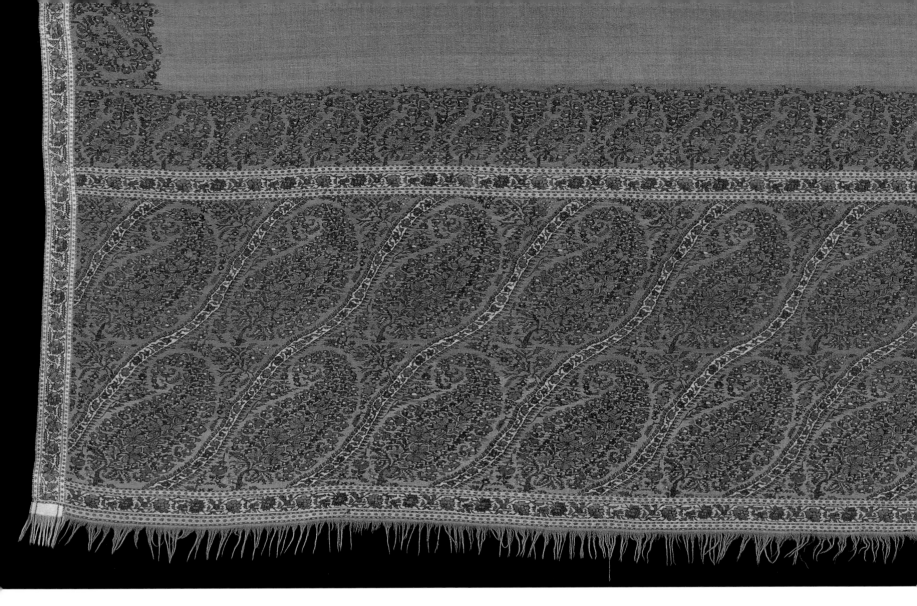

129. Shawl, Kashmir, c.1830–40.

Pashmina, 309 × 136 cm. IS 39-1970.

Given by Mr and Mrs G. H. G. Norman.

choga (outer robe) in place of the shawl as an outer garment. Most of the shawls in these paintings have plain fields with narrow patterned borders, while others have small repeating designs or, more rarely, wider floral end borders.

Ranjit Singh kept a huge store of textiles which were used in the court and also presented to visiting dignitaries as robes of honour or *khil'at*. Henry Fane's daughter Isabella describes the gifts lavished upon her father on one single occasion as 'very handsome, consisting of shawls, kincobs, silks, satins, horses with their trappings, a beautiful sword, jewellery, etc., etc.'[12] The store-rooms (*toshkhana*) of the palace in Lahore were packed with treasures, 'perhaps above all, the immense collection of magnificent Cashmere shawls, rooms full of them, laid out on shelves and heaped up in bales – it is not to be described!'[13] Kashmir had been under Sikh rule since Ranjit Singh's invasion in 1819 and a yearly tribute was sent to the court at Lahore, part of which was paid in shawls.[14] Lahore was a major centre of the shawl trade, and the admiring and acquiring of shawls plays a large part in the accounts of European visitors, male as well as female.

Shawls first began to attract the attention of Europeans as desirable items of dress during the last quarter of the eighteenth century, and they rapidly became extremely fashionable. By 1784 the governor-general, Warren Hastings, was commissioning shawls

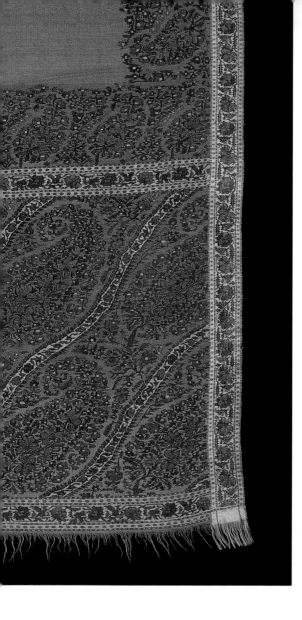

for his wife, and describes them in a letter to her as 'beautiful beyond imagination'.[15] The shawl's elegant simplicity and softness accorded very well with the 'Empire' style of the early nineteenth century, with its emphasis on drapery that flattered the natural contours of the body. They found favour with such fashionable figures as Lady Hamilton, who used them in her theatrical displays, and the Empress Josephine, who was painted on several occasions draped in elegant Kashmir shawls, of which she had a huge collection. The paintings by such early nineteenth-century French artists as Ingres and David are particularly useful for dating Kashmir shawls, which reached the peak of their popularity in France during the first half of the nineteenth century.[16]

Shawl production involved complex systems of manufacture and marketing, and much of our information about the production and trade in shawls in the early nineteenth century comes from the writings of William Moorcroft, a veterinary surgeon investigating the shawl industry for the British East India Company. By about 1820, when Moorcroft took up residence in Srinagar, there was already a strong presence there of merchants from China, Central Asia, Iran and Turkey, all concerned with purchasing the particular type of shawl that was appropriate to their local market.[17] Striped shawls known as *khatraz* or *jamawar*, for example, were particularly popular in Iran and Turkey (plate 131), where they were worn wrapped around the waist or head rather than as a draped garment. When shawls of this type appeared on the British market, they were often called 'Turkish shawls' on account of this connection. Both Britain and France were keen to

130. *Carpet weavers*, J. Lockwood Kipling, Amritsar, 1870. Charcoal, ink and watercolour on paper, 26.2 cm × 35.5 cm. 0929:33 (IS).

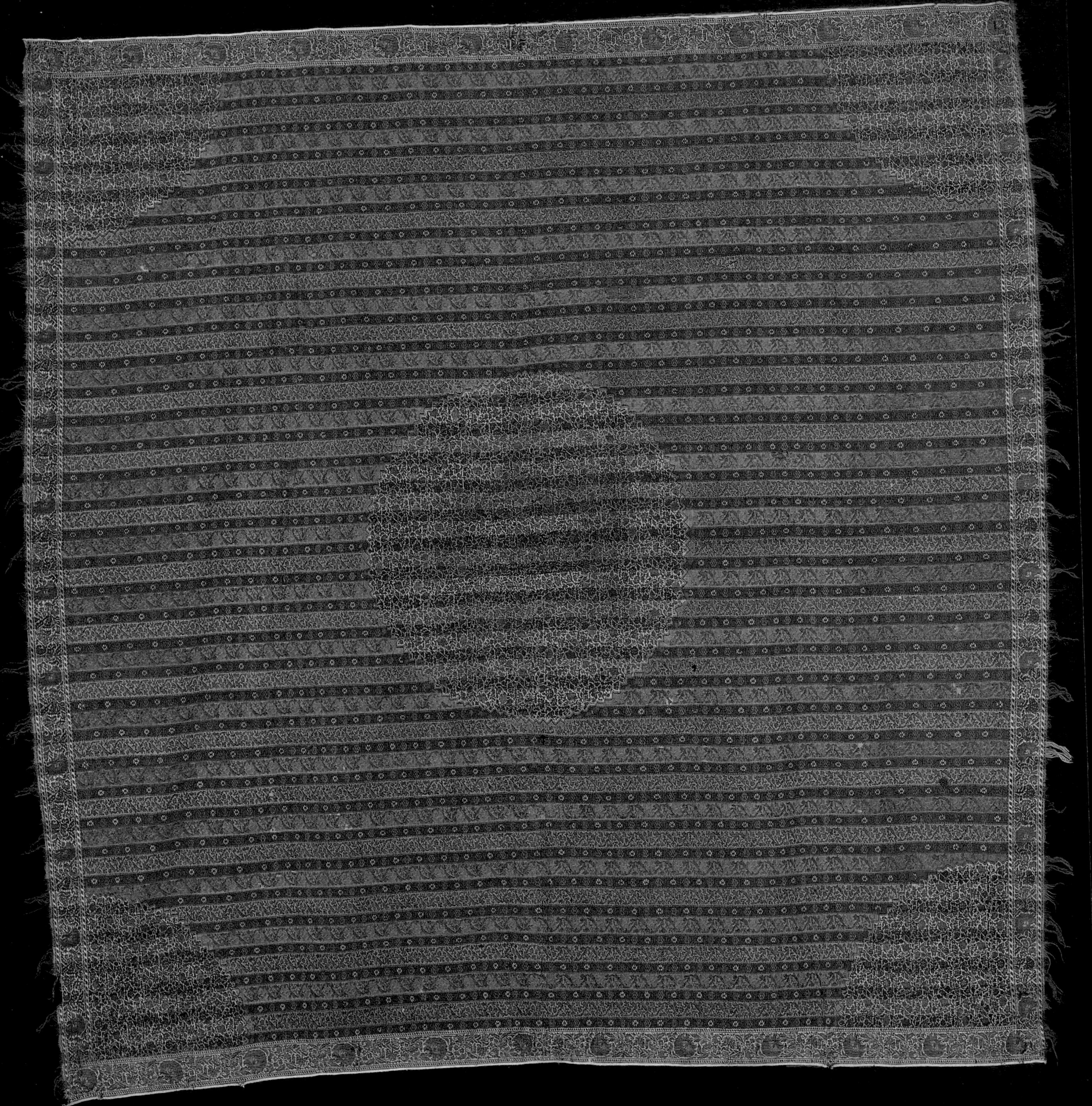

131. 'Moon' shawl, Kashmir,
*c.*1815–30. Pashmina,
160 × 160 cm. IS 5-1968.
Given by Miss Kathleen Whitehead.

develop their own shawl industries rather than dealing with local agents, but attempts to trade in the precious goat's wool (pashmina) in its raw state were unsuccessful, as were ambitious but doomed plans by Moorcroft and others to transport shawl-goats or weavers from Kashmir to Britain and France in order to establish local pashmina industries. As a result, finished shawls continued to form the basis of the trade, but European imitations were also produced from as early as the end of the eighteenth century.

132. *Raja Jai Singh of Guler with Prince Raghunath Singh and other courtiers*, by Muhammad Bakhsh, Guler, late 19th century. Gouache and gold on paper, 25.3 × 31.3 cm. Government Museum and Art Gallery, Chandigarh.

Outside Srinagar, the main trading centre for shawls was Lahore, and the presence there of Europeans working in Ranjit Singh's army was a major factor in the success of the trade, especially with France. Two of the key figures were the Napoleonic generals Jean-François Allard and Jean-Baptiste Ventura, although British and Italian soldiers and administrators were also to become involved. Allard and Ventura had been employed by Ranjit Singh since 1822 and, at least by 1835, were exporting to Paris shawls that incorporated design elements specially adapted for the French market. Allard's original involvement in the shawl trade may have been through necessity rather than choice: when the Calcutta bank in which he kept his savings collapsed in 1833, Ranjit Singh reputedly reimbursed him for his losses not in cash but in shawls, to the value of 30,000 rupees.[18] He would presumably have sold the shawls on his next visit to France, and returned with commissions from French buyers for more. Allard's activity as an agent for the shawl manufacturers is confirmed by the fact that Emily Eden commissioned some shawls directly from him when they met in Calcutta, and they were delivered to her in 1838 after 'a year and a half in the making'.[19] These included 'Four shawl dresses, four magnificent square shawls, and four long scarfs to match the dresses – but the fineness and the brightness of the whole concern is impossible to describe'.[20] In a painting of Allard and his family done in 1838 (plate 118), the general is shown dressed in European clothes but with a striped Kashmir *jamawar* robe (*choga*) draped over his shoulders. Allard died in 1839, but Ventura continued in the trade, staying on in the shawl business even after Ranjit Singh's death in the same year.

The decline of the shawl trade in the third quarter of the nineteenth century came

about for several reasons. The shawls in Indian style made by weavers in such European centres as Paisley, Lyon and Vienna had become immensely popular, and Indian weavers increased their output in competition. This inevitably led to a decline in standards which only accelerated their fall from favour. The whim of European fashion also played a part, as the introduction of the bustle in about 1869 emphasised the curve of the back, which a draped shawl would hide. The French defeat in the Franco-Prussian war of 1870–71 led to the collapse of the French market, and the final blow was dealt to the Kashmiri weavers by a terrible famine in 1877, in which many died. Kashmir shawls became relegated to furnishings in Victorian homes, often seen draping a piano or sideboard, but no longer considered fashionable wear. They continued to be given as wedding presents in conservative circles in France and Britain until the late nineteenth century.

The development of Kashmir shawl design from the simple floral motifs of the Mughal court in the seventeenth century to their overblown, European-influenced

133a and b. Shawl designs, Kashmir, c.1880. Watercolour and ink on paper, 57.6 × 25.7 cm and 57.6 × 25.2 cm. 06600&A (IS).

134. Shawl, Kashmir, c.1870. Pashmina, 350 × 144 cm. IS 119-1958. Given by the Dowager Marchioness of Reading, GBE.

135. Part of a shawl border, late 17th century. Pashmina, 18.5 × 68.5 cm. Collection AEDTA, Paris (2482A).

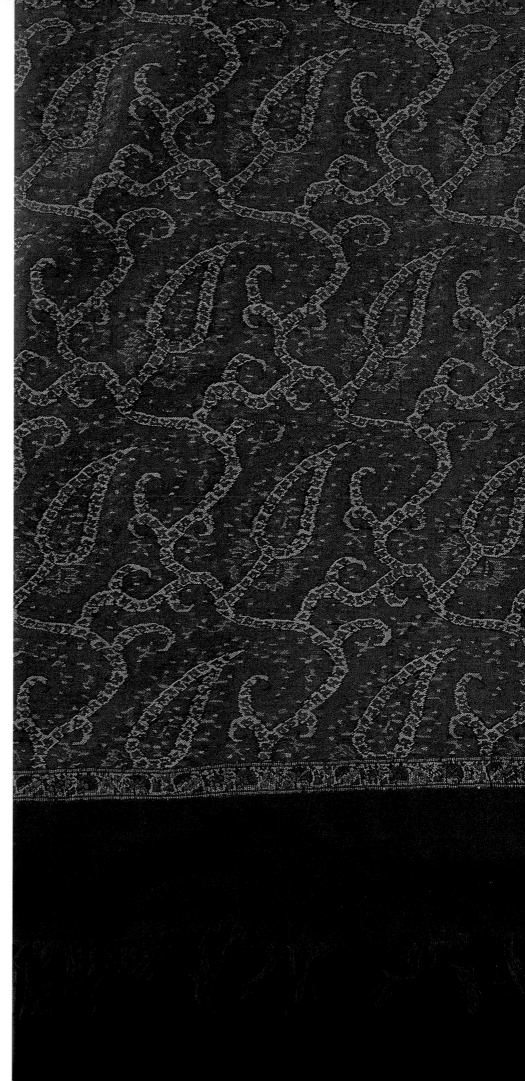

136. Shawl fragment, Kashmir, 18th century.
Pashmina, 15 × 20 cm. IS 139-1984.

137. Part of a shawl border, Kashmir, late
17th century. Pashmina, 25.5 × 68 cm.
Collection AEDTA, Paris (3211).

138. Shawl fragment, Kashmir,
late 17th century. Pashmina, 19.5 × 21 cm.
IS 13-1972. Given by H. M. the Queen.

139. Shawl, Kashmir, *c.*1840-50.
Pashmina, 254 × 248 cm.
National Museum of India (62.1877).

140. Man's sash (*patka*), Kashmir,
early 19th century. Pashmina,
61.6 × 65.5 cm.
National Museum of India (62.644).

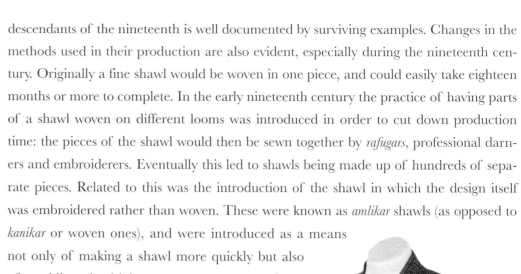

descendants of the nineteenth is well documented by surviving examples. Changes in the methods used in their production are also evident, especially during the nineteenth century. Originally a fine shawl would be woven in one piece, and could easily take eighteen months or more to complete. In the early nineteenth century the practice of having parts of a shawl woven on different looms was introduced in order to cut down production time: the pieces of the shawl would then be sewn together by *rafugars*, professional darners and embroiderers. Eventually this led to shawls being made up of hundreds of separate pieces. Related to this was the introduction of the shawl in which the design itself was embroidered rather than woven. These were known as *amlikar* shawls (as opposed to *kanikar* or woven ones), and were introduced as a means not only of making a shawl more quickly but also of avoiding the high taxes on woven goods. Embroidered designs at first imitated woven ones, but a new genre arose in about 1830 that incorporated new motifs with human figures and animals. This pictorial style was used mostly for *patkas* (sashes) (plate 141) and the edging of *chogas* (robes) (plate 142). The most elaborate examples of

141. Sash (*patka*), Kashmir, *c*.1835.
Pashmina embroidered with wool,
260 × 71 cm. 501-1907.
Bequeathed by Mrs Marian Lewis.

142. Man's robe (*choga*), Kashmir,
c.1850–70. Pashmina embroidered
with wool, length 135 cm. IS 1-1880.

143. Shawl of Gulab Singh, Kashmir, 1852.
Pashmina, 174 × 190 cm. Government Museum
and Art Gallery, Chandigarh.

this type of shawl are those embroidered with maps of Srinagar and the Kashmir valley,[21] and the densely embroidered shawl with dates corresponding to AD 1852 belonging to Gulab Singh, showing episodes from the *Sikandar Nama*, or Book of Alexander the Great (plate 143).[22] Ranjit Singh had earlier commissioned a pair of shawls depicting his own victories, which would almost certainly have been embroidered, for which he paid a staggering 50,000 rupees in advance. However, according to the traveller G. T. Vigne only one of the pair was ever completed, and this does not appear to have survived.[23]

The so-called 'reversible' or *dorukha* shawl appeared in about 1860: this did not involve any new weaving technique, but was a finely woven shawl in which all the loose threads on the reverse had been trimmed and secured by embroidery so that both sides appeared equally well finished. The design of the *dorukha* was often left incomplete at the weaving stage and was completed with embroidery.

Many woven textiles in Panjab were manufactured for domestic use and were of much less interest to an outside market than the Kashmir shawl. Silk and cotton fabrics like

144. Detail of plate 143.

145. Man's wrapped garment (*lungi*), Multan, Panjab, *c.*1855. Woven silk with gold-wrapped thread, 300 × 155 cm. 0782 (IS).

146. Silk fragment, Panjab, *c.*1850. Woven silk with gold-wrapped thread, 72 × 27 cm. 7247A (IS).

those worn by Ranjit Singh's troops were woven for furnishings as well as garments. There was a long tradition of silk-weaving in the Panjab, although little cultivation of silkworms actually took place there. Silk was imported from Bokhara, via Peshawar, and later from China, via Bombay. Silk yarn was spun, dyed and woven at several centres in Panjab, notably at Amritsar, Lahore, Patiala, Multan and Jallandhar. Much of the silk fabric produced in Panjab was woven in plain or two-coloured (*dhup-chan* or 'shot') lengths which would be made up into garments, especially trousers, or used for linings of robes. Other more decorative silk fabrics were striped *gulbadan* (literally 'rose body'), used for ladies' trousers (*shalwar*) and silk *khes* (woven double cloth), which, unlike its cotton equivalent, was often striped like a *jamawar* fabric.[24] Luxurious silk *lungis* (wrapped garments), either plain or in complex woven patterns, were worn wrapped around the waist or as turbans by men (plate 145). These splendid silks were specialities of several towns in the Panjab, especially Multan, Ludhiana, Shahpur and Bahawalpur.

The Hindu Rajput kingdoms of the Panjab Hills were the home of the distinctive embroidery style that has become known as the Chamba *rumal* (plate 147), although it seems likely that they were made in several of the Pahari (hill) courts and not only at Chamba. The most common form of Chamba *rumal* is a small coverlet of about one metre square or less, which would have been used as a cover for a tray of gifts or food at weddings and other ceremonials. The ground fabric is fine white cotton, and the design is embroidered in floss silk in a double darning stitch which means that the *rumal* is almost reversible. The designs may be sparse and simply drawn or much more complex: they often depict a courtly scene, usually a wedding,[25] or scenes from the life of Krishna, especially his dance with the milkmaids (the *rasamandala*), but they may also be embroidered with images of other deities such as Ganesh or Shiva and Parvati. Purely secular scenes such as hunts are less common, but *rumals* are also found depicting ladies in poses reminiscent of the local *nayika* paintings which portray the anguish of lovers.

The grander examples are large and elaborately decorated, one of the most magnificent being the V&A's superb depiction of the mythical Battle of Kurukshetra, which is 9.45 metres long. Reputedly embroidered in the palace at Chamba, it was presented to the South Kensington Museum (later the V&A) in 1883 by Gopal Singh, Raja of Chamba, and depicts the armies of the Kauravas and the Pandavas marching to face each other in a climactic confrontation in the centre of the hanging.[26] The figures and animals are bounded at top and bottom by rows of naturalistically drawn birds in various poses, and there is a conventional floral border running along both the top and bottom edges. Another very long Chamba *rumal* depicting a battle scene is in the Metropolitan Museum, New York, but here the figures are shown in two parallel registers, divided by a floral border.[27]

The fineness of the drawing in these and other high-quality *rumals*, and their similarity

147. Embroidered coverlet (*rumal*), Himachal Pradesh, probably Chamba, late 18th century. Cotton embroidered with floss silk, 95 × 95 cm. Collection AEDTA, Paris (2633).

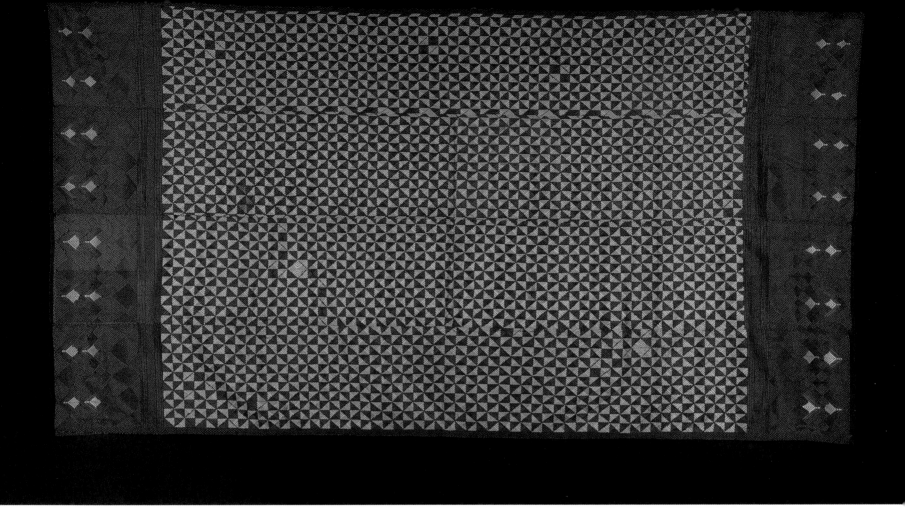

148. Woman's shawl (*phulkari*),
Panjab, early 20th century.
Cotton embroidered with floss silk,
264 × 140 cm.
Collection AEDTA, Paris (148).

to contemporary paintings, implies that the designs were drawn on to the cloth by court artists. It has been suggested that the embroidery would then be completed by 'the ladies of the court',[28] but there is no evidence for this and it is more likely that the work would have been done by professional, probably male, embroiderers. Closely comparable scenes, especially of musicians and weddings, are to be found in paintings from several centres in the Hills,[29] and in wall-paintings in Chamba palace itself (now displayed at the National Museum, New Delhi).

The dating of Chamba *rumals* is hard to establish firmly, as none is signed or dated. By relating the designs to paintings, however, it is possible to state with reasonable certainty that they were being made in at least the late eighteenth century.[30] They were still being produced in a coarser form during the twentieth century, using simpler designs in which the human figures had become stylised into abstract forms. These would have been made and used in a domestic context rather than being commissioned by a courtly patron. The later examples, as well as being more coarsely drawn and embroidered, tend to use much less fine cotton as the ground fabric.

One of the most familiar of all embroidery types from the sub-continent is the *phulkari* (literally 'flower work') of the Panjab. *Phulkaris* are made by village women (Muslim, Hindu and Sikh) for their own use as garments, usually head-covers or skirts, or on cere-

149. Woman's shawl (*phulkari*),
Panjab, early 20th century.
Cotton embroidered with floss silk,
264 × 127 cm.
Collection AEDTA, Paris (1558).

monial occasions as canopies or floorspreads, and also by professional embroiderers to commission from more affluent families. The *phulkari* is embroidered in a characteristic darning stitch in floss silk (*pat*), typically in yellow or white on a ground of locally made cotton cloth called *khaddar* which is dyed either a rusty brown or indigo blue. The most basic *phulkari* can be a combination of crudely embroidered flower motifs and coarse fabric, but the finer examples are among the most spectacular of Indian embroideries. The finest type of *phulkari* is called *bagh* ('garden') and has its surface entirely covered with geometric designs meticulously embroidered in a thread-counting technique from the reverse of the fabric (plates 148 and 149). Even in these expertly made pieces, the range of colours used for the embroidery is traditionally restricted to one or two, sometimes with the addition of a row of multicoloured motifs placed to frame the wearer's face when the *bagh* is in use. More modern *phulkaris* often incorporate brighter colours such as orange, purple and green.

A variety of *phulkari* embroidered with depictions of human figures and objects from everyday life comes from the eastern Panjab, particularly Rohtak, Hissar, Amritsar and Patiala. A third variety is known as *chope*: this is embroidered in a double-sided (i.e. reversible) running stitch, which gives a much sparser effect than the lavish *bagh*, but the *chope* is held in high regard and plays an important part in wedding rituals.

CHAPTER EIGHT

THE
MILITARY SIKHS

IAN KNIGHT

150. Six-pounder cannon, probably
Lahore, *c*.1825–40. Bronze,
L. of barrel 162.5 cm, calibre 8.3 cm.
Royal Artillery Historical Trust
(II.273).

On 27 November 1849 an anonymous British cavalry officer wrote a letter home from the camp at Ramnuggar, in central Panjab, describing the desperate nature of a battle in which he had fought just a few days earlier. It was full of praise for the enemy's performance under fire:

Nothing could exceed the accuracy of the enemy's fire; their range was beautifully taken for certain points, showing that they must have discovered them previous to our advance; and our artillery officers say they never saw anything finer than the way their Horse Artillery were brought up to the edge of the river, and formed up. No nation could exceed them in the rapidity of their fire . . . No men could act more bravely than the Sikhs. They faced us the moment we came on them, firing all the time, and, when we did come on them, some opened out and immediately after closed round us, while others threw themselves on their faces or turned their backs, protected by a shield from the stroke of the Dragoon sabre, and the moment that was given, turned round, hamstrung the horse, and shot the rider, while their individual acts of bravery were the admiration of all. Many stood before a charging squadron, and singled out a man, after killing or wounding whom they themselves were cut down immediately; while many, before their blows could take effect, received the point of a sabre, and fell in the act of making a cut . . .[1]

This professional admiration was typical of the views of many British soldiers who had found themselves, for the second time in just a few years, ranged against the might of the former Sikh kingdom of Lahore. As the British were quick to realise, the Sikh kingdom had provided them with the greatest military challenge of the conquest of India, and, indeed, only the Great Mutiny itself would involve the British army in bloodier and more brutal fighting. The Anglo-Sikh Wars left an indelible mark on British minds, creating an impression that the Sikhs were a race of natural warriors, whose martial qualities would later be exploited by their conquerors to form one of the most celebrated elements in the army of the British Raj.

The kingdom of Lahore had emerged as a political reality in the Panjab only under Maharaja Ranjit Singh in the first decades of the nineteenth century, but the Sikh faith had acquired a militant edge early in its history. Although Sikhism preached a creed which was essentially harmonious, arguing that both Hinduism and Islam confused and concealed a common true faith, it appeared heretical to the devoutly Muslim Mughal emperors, who drove the first converts out of central Panjab to take refuge in the inaccessible northern hills. As a reaction against this persecution, Sikhism developed a martial ethos that was enshrined by the tenth Guru, Gobind Singh, in the seventeenth century. He encouraged adherents to take the name Singh (Lion) and to carry arms at all times. Of the 'five K's', by which they were to demonstrate their

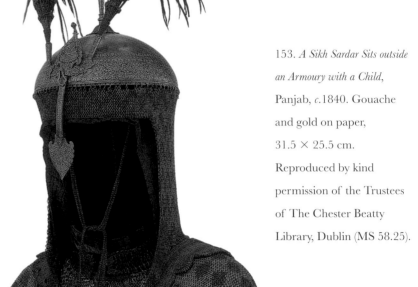

153. *A Sikh Sardar Sits outside an Armoury with a Child*, Panjab, *c.*1840. Gouache and gold on paper, 31.5 × 25.5 cm. Reproduced by kind permission of the Trustees of The Chester Beatty Library, Dublin (MS 58.25).

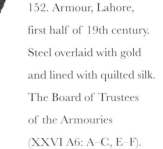

152. Armour, Lahore, first half of 19th century. Steel overlaid with gold and lined with quilted silk. The Board of Trustees of the Armouries (XXVI A6: A–C, E–F).

151. Pair of arm defences, Lahore, first half of 19th century. Steel overlaid with gold and lined with embroidered velvet. The Board of Trustees of the Armouries (XXVIA.36).

137

154. Turban helmet, Panjab,
*c.*1820–40. Gilt copper, diam. 13.7 cm,
width 18 cm, length 23.2 cm.
Kapany Collection.

155. Turban helmet, Panjab,
*c.*1820–40. Steel overlaid with gold.
Kapany Collection.

faith, four are suggestive of military prowess: *kes*, long, uncut hair, which when wound around the head provided protection against a sword blow; *kachcha*, short, loose trousers that were easier to fight in than long robes; *kara*, a steel bangle symbolising a traditional Panjabi throwing weapon, the sharpened steel quoit; and *kirpan*, a sword. The fifth is the *khanga*, a comb.

The essentially egalitarian creed of the Sikhs won the movement many converts and, as Mughal influence declined in the eighteenth century, Sikhism emerged as a significant

156. Punch dagger (*katar*), Panjab Hills, early 19th century.

Steel, chiselled and overlaid with gold, 32 cm.

The Board of Trustees of the Armouries (XXVI D 62).

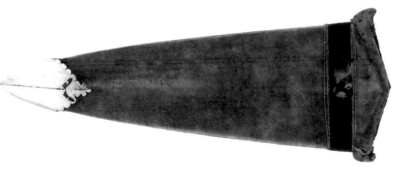

157. Punch dagger (*katar*) and scabbard,
Panjab Hills, early 19th century.
Steel chiselled and overlaid with gold,
32 cm. The Board of Trustees of
the Armouries (XXVI D 85).

political force, challenging both the administration of the Mughals and the dominance of raiding parties from Afghanistan. Unable to withstand an open battle against numerically superior forces, the Sikhs developed a highly effective guerrilla strategy. By striking at the economic base of Mughal administration – raiding villagers and landlords to deny tax income to the Mughals, and plundering merchants, who therefore came to avoid trade with the Panjab – the Sikhs undermined the essentially mercenary nature of Mughal power, making it difficult to pay and maintain occupying forces in the Panjab. Similarly, when Afghan armies passed through the Panjab on raiding expeditions, the Sikhs made the passage both uncomfortable and unprofitable by attacking baggage trains or ambushing stragglers. By the late eighteenth century, the Sikhs had already earned an enviable reputation as disciplined hit-and-run fighters, adept with both firearms and horses. As a result of their successes, the Sikhs gradually assumed administrative control over some parts of the Panjab, offering their protection in the vacuum which followed the decline of Mughal power. The Sikh forces were divided into proper administrative and military units, known as *misls*. The *misls* were the foundation upon which Ranjit Singh built the kingdom of Lahore.

Under Ranjit Singh, an astute, ambitious and occasionally ruthless chieftain born in

158. Matchlock musket (*toradar*), Lahore, early 19th century. Steel and wood, L. 153 cm, calibre 13 mm. The Board of Trustees of the Armouries (XXVI F 119).

159. Matchlock musket (*toradar*), Lahore, early 19th century. Steel and wood, L. 179 cm, calibre 15 mm. The Board of Trustees of the Armouries (XXVI F 42).

161. Primer, Lahore, late 18th or early 19th century. Horn with ivory head painted in colours, L. 24.1 cm. 2599 (IS).

160, below. Cartridge carrier, North India, early 19th century. Leather, velvet and ivory, 10 × 25 cm. The Board of Trustees of the Armouries (XXVI.F.106).

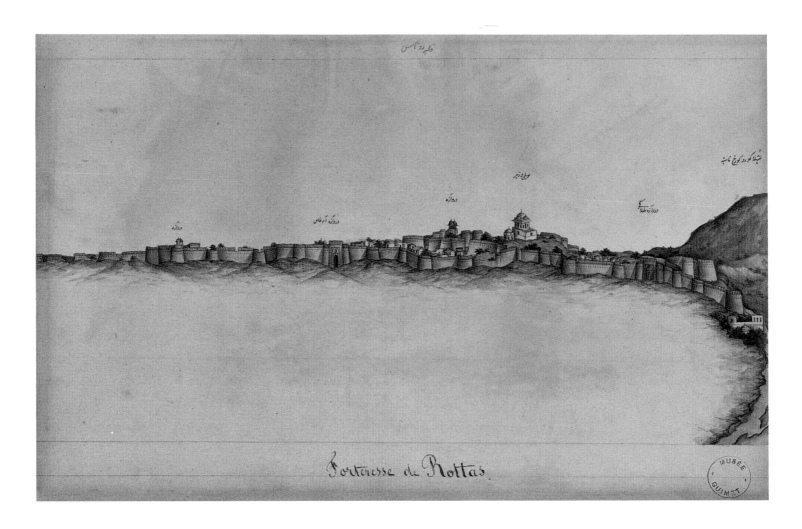

Forteresse de Rottas

164. *Rohtas Fort*, probably by Imam Bakhsh, Attock, *c.*1840. Watercolour on European paper, 19.5 × 30.4 cm. Musée national des Arts asiatiques-Guimet (39734). © Photo RMN – Thierry Ollivier

rulers around the world as professional advisers. Despite the fact that the British remained suspicious of any French military influence in their sphere of influence, a number of former French soldiers found work in India. In 1822 Ranjit Singh hired Jean-François Allard and Jean-Baptiste Ventura, the first of a number of ex-French army officers whom he employed to train his troops. Both Allard and Ventura had distinguished records: Ventura had been present during Napoleon's disastrous Russian campaign, while Allard had fought in Italy, Spain and France, and had remained loyal to Napoleon during the Hundred Days in 1815. As such, they commanded a wealth of professional expertise which was not otherwise available on the subcontinent, except to the Company.

Ranjit Singh's French advisers began by training small units of infantry and cavalry along French lines, but by the 1840s this had risen to a strong professional body known as the Fauj-i-Ain (regular army), numbering as many as 71,000 men. It consisted of infantry, cavalry and artillery. The infantry were organised along Napoleonic lines into battalions of 800 to 1,000 men, trained to perform the European manoeuvres of the day, advancing in line or column, or forming defensive squares. Curiously, their uniforms betrayed a strong British influence. They wore scarlet coatees (close-fitting coats with

165. *Mohammadan Artilleryman*, probably by Imam Bakhsh, Attock, *c.*1840. Watercolour on European paper, 18.5 × 28.3 cm. Musée national des Arts asiatiques-Guimet (39745). © Photo RMN - Thierry Ollivier

166. *Sikh Soldiers*, probably by Imam Bakhsh, Attock, *c.*1840. Watercolour on European paper, 18.5 × 28.5 cm. Musée national des Arts asiatiques-Guimet (39746).

short tails) and blue trousers, although in the hot summer months they had a more practical white uniform. Ranjit Singh lavished particular attention upon the artillery, organised into horse batteries, heavy siege guns drawn by bullocks, and light swivel guns mounted on camels. Following British precedent, the gunners wore braided blue jackets and striped trousers. French influence was more marked in the regular cavalry, with an exotic mixture of French hussar uniforms and more traditional Indian patterns.

Even British observers were prepared to admit that the Fauj-i-Ain was a competent force, one observer going so far as to suggest that its general proficiency rivalled that of the Company's Indian troops:

They are a fine looking body of men, dressed in white jackets and trowsers, with black belts and pouches, and wear the yellow Sikh turban. They submit willingly to the same discipline and regulations as our own Sipahis [sepoys], but have a prejudice against wearing the shako, and previous to their enlistment make an agreement that they shall not be required to do so, or to shave.

They work in three ranks, and do everything by the beat of the drum, according to the French fashion; are not what is called well set up, but beautifully steady on

parade, and fire with greater precision and regularity, both volleys and file firing, than any other troops I ever saw.[3]

That contest was to be put to the test following the death of Ranjit Singh. By that time the Company, driven by fear of a Russian threat to its Indian possessions, manifested in Russian influence in Afghanistan, had already begun to tighten its grip on its western borders. In 1839 the British had appealed to Ranjit to allow their armies passage through the Panjab, en route to Afghanistan. He had refused, and the British marched through Sind, to the south, instead. In the event, the Afghan campaign was a fiasco and the Company was chased out ignominiously within three years. To restore their flagging prestige and shore up their borders, the British conquered Sindh in 1843. The significance of this apparently haphazard policy and arbitrary use of force was not lost on Lahore, which had been in a state of flux since Ranjit's death. The maharaja Dalip Singh was a minor, and various factions within the royal court jockeyed for influence. Among these, the Khalsa emerged as one of the most powerful. Robbed of Ranjit Singh's strong central

167. *Bridge on the Sutlej. Feby 1846*, Henry Yule. Pen and wash on paper, 17.7 × 25.5 cm. By permission of The British Library (WD 1039).

146

168. *General Hugh Viscount Gough*, *c.*1850.
Painting on ivory, 15.2 × 12 cm.
Courtesy of the Director, National
Army Museum, London (7909-23).

169. Pair of pistols, Northern India,
first half of 19th century. Steel and
wood, length 37 cm.
The Board of Trustees of the
Armouries (XXVI F 217).

control, the Khalsa had become increasingly self-serving, its generals divided and dabbling in politics, while the men elected regimental committees to look after pay and provisions. This inevitably eroded the army's discipline and effectiveness. Suspicion of British interests, coupled with a sense of the Company's potential weakness, led some in the court to argue that the Khalsa needed a successful foreign campaign to occupy itself. In December 1845 the Khalsa, under the command of Lal Singh and Tej Singh, crossed the Sutlej into British territory (plate 167), and advanced on the British garrison at Ferozepore. It seems to have had no very clear objectives, and its aims have variously been described as a pre-emptive strike or a raid *en masse*.

The British hurriedly moved troops, a mixture of Company and Queen's (Imperial) regiments, to meet it, under the command of the British commander-in-chief in India, Sir Hugh Gough (plate 168). Gough, a veteran of the Napoleonic Wars, was a tough but unimaginative commander whose sole strategic aim was to keep up a constant pressure on the enemy. He believed that battles were won by the rigorous application of 'cold steel' – an approach that had proved successful in the past in India, but which was ill-suited to a disciplined force such as the Sikhs. Indeed, the following campaign had a number of characteristics in common with the Napoleonic wars, fought out instead in the exotic terrain and stifling heat of northern India. For the first time the British in India found themselves facing an enemy trained, armed and even dressed much as they were, and one that had been influenced by their old adversary Napoleon. The first battle of the war, outside the village at Mudki on 18 December, established the pattern for the conflict. Gough arrived to find the Sikhs already deployed in a strong position but, despite the fact that his men were tired and hungry,

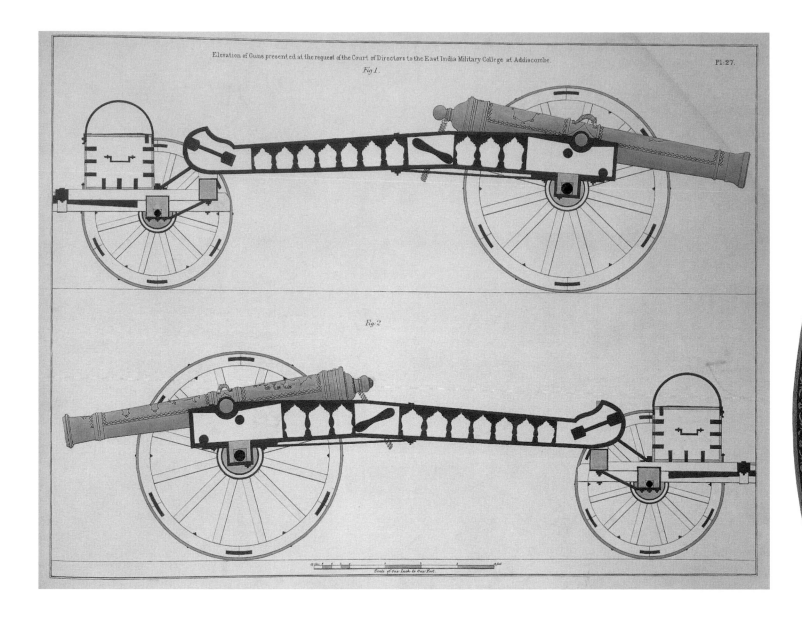

Elevation of Guns presented at the request of the Court of Directors to the East India Military College at Addiscombe.
Fig 1.

Pl. 27.

Fig. 2

Scale of One Inch to One Foot.

he immediately launched an attack. His infantry suffered horrendous casualties from Sikh artillery fire and musketry, but his cavalry easily routed the undisciplined Ghorchurras on either flank. Threatened on either side, the Sikh army fell back. Gough followed up with a rapid advance on the Sikh camp at Ferozeshahr, where another engagement took place. At a crucial point in the battle, Sikh reinforcements arrived and threatened to turn the battle against Gough, but they remained uncommitted and the main Sikh force withdrew.

The Khalsa lost the war not so much through tactical ineptitude or lack of courage as through the indecision and rivalry among its commanders. Hesitant, with its leaders often pursuing their own political aims, it soon lost the initiative to the British. When British reinforcements arrived with a siege train, a Sikh force attempted to intercept them, but was defeated at Aliwal in January 1846. The British were able to concentrate

170. *Plans of Ordnance captured by the Army of the Sutledge*, Captain Ralph Smyth, *c.*1848, 42.5 × 57 cm. By permission of The British Library (X 623).

171. Shield
of Lord Hardinge,
Lahore, 1847. Steel
overlaid with gold, diam. 60 cm.
The Board of Trustees of the
Armouries (XXVI A 79).

172. Sword of Lord Hardinge,
Lahore 1847. Steel overlaid with gold,
length 90 cm.
The Board of Trustees of the Armouries
(XXVI S 41).

their forces near the main Sikh position at Sobraon, and on 10 February took it by storm after a costly and bitter assault.

Sobraon effectively ended the Khalsa's capacity to resist and on 8 March 1846 the Kingdom of Lahore finally submitted to the Company. Britain was unwilling to annex the Panjab outright, although she did appropriate a particularly fertile stretch of border country, and settled instead for establishing a protectorate. While Dalip Singh's claim to the throne was recognised, a British resident (Henry Lawrence, plate 173) was established at Lahore and British administrators were distributed across the Panjab.

The country was not, however, reconciled to British rule, even indirect. Many officials at court worked to restore independence while, at a local level, many landowners and chiefs rejected British interference. Thousands of members of the Khalsa, particularly the regulars of the Fauj-i-Ain, found themselves unemployed and resented the loss of prestige and privileges which had previously been their right. Resistance to the British crystallised around the city of Multan, and in April 1848 two British officers were murdered in the city. There were too few Company troops available to contain the rising, while British indecision meant that the rebellion spread across a large area of northern Panjab. Many members of the Khalsa rallied to their old units. It was not until November that Gough once more entered the Panjab at the head of a British force. The fighting in the Second Anglo-Sikh War followed the pattern of the first, with much the same result. Although the Sikhs inflicted enormous casualties on the Company forces, the British regained the initiative, and Sikh resistance collapsed after Gough won a surprisingly adroit victory at Gujerat on 21 February 1849.

In the aftermath of this campaign, the British formally took control of the Panjab. The Khalsa was once more disbanded, but the British were keen to exploit the Sikhs' military skills, and soon raised Company units from among them. These were initially intended to police the unsettled border regions, but when the Indian 'Mutiny' broke out in 1857, the administrator of the Panjab, the energetic Sir John Lawrence, raised a Sikh contingent to support the beleaguered Company garrisons elsewhere in India. The Sikhs had not been exposed to the discontent which had caused many of the Company's Indian troops to rebel, and because they did not share the religious affiliations of the rebels, they proved a particularly effective force in suppressing the Mutiny.

Indeed, the performance of the Sikhs in the Anglo-Sikh Wars and in 1857 reinforced British preconceptions about Indian fighting qualities. The British tended to perceive Indian groups in terms of their military abilities, and developed the theory that some groups – the so-called 'martial races' – were inherently more suited to military service than others. Despite the fact that the Company's armies in the early years were recruited largely in southern India – and had a very successful record – the British believed that northern Indian groups were more aggressive. In particular, they came to see the Sikhs as natural soldiers and recruited a large number of Sikh units in the later part of the nineteenth century, encouraging their *esprit de corps* by drawing on the symbols of their supposedly separate identity. Sikh regiments wore distinctive uniforms and turbans, and often wore badges based on traditional Sikh devices, such as the quoit. In this way, the tradition of Sikh resistance was effectively subverted to the needs of the new administration. When the Indian Army was mobilised for service in the First World War, more than 35 per cent of its men were Sikhs.

173. *Henry Lawrence*. Painting on ivory, 14 × 24 cm. By permission of The British Library (Add. Or. 2409).

CHAPTER NINE

MAHARAJA DALIP SINGH

DAVID JONES

174. *Maharaja Dalip Singh*, George Beechey, Mussoorie, 1852. Oil on canvas, 91.5 × 74 cm. Private Collection. Photograph courtesey of Sotheby's.

175. *Rani Jindan*, George Richmond, London, June1863. Pencil drawing, 20 × 15.5 cm. Collection of F. S. Aijazuddin.

The complex and strange life of Dalip Singh, almost theatrical in the way that it subdivides into different scenes and acts, compresses into the life of a single individual all the tensions and violence brought about by the clash of two great cultures. It contains the sadness and dignity of human beings trying to act decently towards each other, despite being caught up in this clash and, on one side at least, an almost complete misunderstanding of the other's position.

Dalip Singh (1838–93), the last Sikh ruler of the Panjab, was the youngest son of Rani Jindan, a junior queen of Ranjit Singh, and came to the throne at the age of five in 1843 after a series of bloody coups and counter-coups left no other contenders. At first, the young boy catapulted on to the throne cannot have been aware of the struggles behind the scenes. The first years of his life were played out against the rich background of the court and the beautiful Mughal palaces of Lahore. He enjoyed falconry and had the best horses and elephants to ride. Every day costumes and trays of jewels were brought for him to choose from. He received a royal education with two tutors, one for the Persian of the court and the other for the Gurmukhi of the Guru Granth Sahib. He was taught to shoot with gun and bow, and trained in command by being given a troop of sixty boys.[1] The love of his mother and her brother Jawahir Singh, who played a particularly affectionate role in the boy's life, surrounded him.

It must have seemed a kind of heaven to the boy, but the brutalities of politics soon invaded. Jawahir Singh had been removing his rivals and following a pro-British line that alienated the Khalsa army, who summoned him before them on 21 September 1845. Although accompanied by Rani Jindan and Dalip Singh, he was killed before their eyes, despite the desperate pleas of his sister. The child was horror-struck and in later life often recalled his fear and shock, describing how he had been in his uncle's arms and realised he might be next.

The military history of the First Anglo-Sikh War which now broke out has often been told. The complex nature of politics at the court of Lahore is revealed by the peace

153

settlement, under which the Khalsa army was defeated but its nominal commander Tej Singh rewarded by the British. The other major figure in the Sikh government, Gulab Singh Dogra, had negotiated the peace and was made the independent Maharaja of Kashmir. The British had won because the Sikh state was divided. By the terms of the Treaty of Byrowal in December 1846,[2] a council of Regency (excluding Rani Jindan) was set up and a British Resident and garrison imposed as a temporary measure until Dalip came of age. At first sight the treaty seemed very generous, protecting the young maharaja until his state could be handed over to him intact, although reduced in size. In reality the British began to dismantle the Sikh state.[3]

Henry Lawrence (plate 173), who ruled the Panjab as resident, was charmed by the boy and personally kind to him, organising activities and magic lantern parties. However,

176. *Ranjit Singh*, Imam Bakhsh.
Gouache on paper, 19 × 24 cm.
Musée national des Arts
asiatiques-Guimet (39753).
© Photo RMN – Thierry Ollivier.

the maharaja's first recorded political act enraged Lawrence. At the annual Hindu festival Dussera in 1847 Dalip Singh publicly refused, despite British instructions, to mark Tej Sing as his commander-in-chief. Lawrence and Henry Hardinge, the governor-general, were convinced, probably correctly, that Rani Jindan had put him up to it. Lawrence acted swiftly. He asked the young prince to ride with him late at night; it was impossible to refuse and when Dalip asked to return to the palace, Lawrence told him that he was to spend the night in the Shalimar Gardens. The next day he learnt that his mother had been seized in his absence and placed under house arrest, and that he was forbidden to have any contact with her. Both mother and son were devastated, Rani writing to Lawrence:

> Restore my son to me, I cannot bear the pain of separation – my son is very young. He is incapable of doing anything. I have left the kingdom. I have no need of a kingdom – there is no one with my son. He has no sister, no brother. He has no uncle, senior or junior. His father he has lost. To whose care has he been entrusted?[4]

Although it is possible to conclude that the governor-general and Henry Lawrence, as well as his successor, his brother John Lawrence, took the Treaty of Byrowal seriously, it is clear Rani Jindan felt they had no intention of upholding it. In desperation she wrote, 'Why do you take possession of the kingdom by underhand means? Why do you not do it openly? On the one hand you make a show of friendship and on the other you have put us in prison. Do justice to me or I shall appeal to the London headquarters.'[5]

Lord Dalhousie (plate 177), the governor-general who replaced Hardinge, had absolutely no time for indirect rule,[6] and his new resident, Frederick Currie, was partially responsible for igniting the complex chain of events that led to the Second Anglo-Sikh War. While the rebels claimed to be fighting in Dalip Singh's name, no evidence was ever provided to show that he had any part in the revolt. Isolated in the palace, he can have had little idea of what was going on. Nevertheless, the rebellion gave Dalhousie the legal fig-leaf he needed and, despite the fact that the British had sworn to uphold Dalip's throne against rebellion, they now deposed him and the Panjab was formally annexed. The boy was sent into internal exile to a town called Fatehgarh in the care of a new guardian, Dr John Login. He left behind his throne, his palaces, much of his personal fortune and his country, never to return.

Fatehgarh was a remote provincial town near Kanpur and an admired centre of Christian missionary activity in North India, with churches, orphanages, schools, a carpet factory and a village of Indian Christian converts.[7] Dalip's extensive household was part-European and part-Indian, shared with his sister-in-law and her son.[8] He was allowed elephants and hawks, and had a guard of honour made up of Sikhs and Skinner's Horse. Rumours were spread by Dalhousie about Dalip's mother, who had fled to Kathmandu. It was said that an impotent Ranjit Singh had encouraged Rani Jindan

177. *Sir James Broun Ramsay, Marquess of Dalhousie*, Sir John Watson-Gordon, 1847. Oil on canvas, 242.5 × 151.5 cm. By courtesy of the National Portrait Gallery, London (188).

183. *Maharaja Dalip Singh*, Horne & Thornthwaite, London, *c*.1854. 14 × 11 cm. Ph. 192-1982.

184. *Cartes-de-visite* of Maharaja Dalip Singh and 'Maharanee Duleep Singh', Mayall. 2831-1934.

He could find nowhere to settle his mother, his own movements were curtailed by the government, and he was seriously worried that over-enthusiastic Sikhs would compromise him. The visit was an unhappy and painful experience.

Mother and son returned to London. The Rani made considerable attempts to adapt – attempting to wear British dress, going to church, encouraging him to take a British wife. And he was delighted to be reunited with her, commissioning portraits and sculptures of her hands in marble. Then, in 1863, she died. She had, however, made him remember the past. Following a return to India for her cremation, the maharaja was determined not to remain alone. Finding a wife was no easy matter. He had already alarmed Lady Login (Dr Login had been knighted in 1854) by telling her of his plans to propose to one of her relations, but finally chose, by correspondence from a Cairo mission school, a part-German, part-Ethiopian girl who spoke only Arabic. Her name was Bamba Muller.

He took her home to his newly acquired estate at Elveden, selected and purchased for him by the India Office. He transformed the run-down estate into an efficient, modern game preserve, and the house into a semi-oriental palace. With halls decorated with glass mosaic in the fashion of a *shish mahal* and dominated by the huge oil paintings of Ranjit Singh in *darbar* or at the Golden Temple and of his brother Sher Singh in regal splendour, and with sculptures of past glories and cases of jewels, the whole place was a pow-

185. *Royal Shooting Party, 8 December 1876, Elvedon Hall Suffolk*, J. W. Clarke. Lent by Her Majesty Queen Elizabeth II. Windsor Castle, Royal Photographic Collection © HM The Queen.

erful reminder of his former status. He lived with his wife and growing family, the sons wearing a variety of costumes but frequently photographed in Sikh clothes, and with uncut hair. He invited Edward, Prince of Wales to highly successful shoots; Sikh visitors would discreetly come and go. Dalip loved Elveden and rebuilt the church, cottages and a school. At the height of his troubles the threat of his leaving the village panicked the rector into describing the effect that this would have on 'the afflicted, the aged and the extreme poor', 'for the schools, clubs, and charities, hitherto entirely supported by His Highness, will be supported by him no more'.[18]

The new home had brought new expenses and, as the father of three boys and two daughters, he had to look to his future. His treaty pension was controlled by the India Office and at first all he wanted was an increase, a settlement of his existing debts and to see the fund's accounts.[19] The queen asked the India Office to look into the matter favourably. The maharaja agreed to his accounts being examined to see if he had been extravagant,[20] and all looked set for a reasonable compromise. The queen supported

CHAPTER TEN

CONTINUING TRADITIONS IN THE LATER SIKH KINGDOMS

B.N. GOSWAMY

187. Detail of plate 200b.

188. *Maharaja Karam Singh of Patiala and his Son*, Patiala, *c.*1840. Gouache on paper, 27.6 × 20 cm. Kapany Collection.

Great crashes drown out most other sounds. The fall of the powerful kingdom of Lahore, six years after Ranjit Singh's death, was sudden and complete. There was no long drawn out period of decline before the event, and the swift efficiency with which British power was established after the Annexation in 1849 is so fascinating that it tends to overshadow what followed, or what was happening around this time elsewhere in the Panjab, especially in respect of the arts. If the arts that flourished under the great maharaja are largely undervalued, or seen through distorting mirrors, those of the other Sikh kingdoms of the Panjab are barely considered.

The Phulkian states – members of the Sikh kingdoms that had by this time left memories of the marauding *misls* and their chaotic wars behind – did not all have Chaudhari Phul as their common ancestor as the name might suggest, even though the pre-eminent among them, Patiala, certainly descended from him.[1] Others were closely related, such as Nabha and Jind, and Kapurthala where the power of the Ahluwalia *misl* eventually came to be centred. Their emergence as kingdoms was slow. The energies of intrepid men, like Alla Singh ('gallant, and at the same time prudent', in the words of the nineteenth-century historian Lepel Griffin) and Jassa Singh Ahluwalia, had in the eighteenth century led to the formation of potentially powerful state units. It was, however, only early in the nineteenth century after they entered into a relationship with the British, then anxious to contain the growing power of Ranjit Singh across the River Sutlej, that true opportunity came their way for founding stable kingdoms. Given their new status as 'cis-Sutlej' states, their sovereign status may have become impaired as a paramount power kept a watchful eye on them, but the peace that ensued must have been a new experience. They could now, without having to look nervously over their shoulders and without being eyed by Lahore, garner resources, build, absorb, create systems of governance, and eventually develop their own style.

It is worth following developments in the area of the arts alone, especially at Patiala. After the dissolution of the great centre of power and artistic patronage at Lahore (plate 189),

189. *Dost Muhammad being received by Sher Singh in Lahore on his way to regain the throne of Kabul*, Panjab (Lahore or Amritsar), *c.*1845. Gouache on paper, 49.8 × 84 cm. Kapany Collection.

Patiala became the most important Sikh kingdom of the Panjab. Patiala was not always the court it came to be from the middle of the nineteenth century – the early period was marked by too much strife for sustained activity. It is therefore of interest to trace the beginnings of such artistic activity in the kingdom.

After a series of rulers (one of whom British historians described colourfully as 'a fine specimen of a barbarian – rude, courageous, impulsive, generous and ignorant'), the reign of Maharaja Karam Singh (1813–45) was a period of relative quiet. Fourth in descent from the founder of the state, he set out to establish a durable relationship with the British and to consolidate his hold on domestic affairs. But a true, intense burst of artistic activity came under his son and successor, Maharaja Narinder Singh (1845–62), 'the most enlightened ruler that Patiala has ever possessed', who acceded the throne at the age of 23.[2] Great new building enterprises were undertaken: the security of the Qila Mubarak, the great ancestral fort inside the city (plate 190), was abandoned for spacious new palaces and related structures outside the city walls, including the Moti Mahal, the Sheesh Mahal, the Banasar Bagh, a large man-made lake and well laid-out gardens. There was much literary activity, and poets from many centres in northern India settled in Patiala. Distinguished classical singers were invited to the court, the Patiala *gharana* ('family') of Hindustani music acquiring great fame, with the redoubtable Bade Ghulam Ali Khan becoming in recent times its best-known exponent. Murals were commissioned on a very considerable scale for palaces, religious establishments and forts. Miniature painting flourished and an impressive number of illustrated manuscripts of classical texts – including the *Janam Sakhi* of Guru Nanak, the *Sursagar*, the *Sudama Charit*, the *Rukmini Mangal*, the *Mahabharata*, the *Rasikapriya* – were produced. Patiala also emerged as a major centre of crafts, for some of which the city is still famous. Whole bazaars sprang up with row after row of specialist craftsmen plying the same trade, catering partly to princely needs: jewellers, embroiderers, dyers, makers of gold-worked footwear, tailors and drawstring makers. Suddenly, one is breathing the air of a court aiming at casting itself in the classical Indian mould: not merely a centre of power but a hub of cultural activity, of patronage extended to distant quarters. Many of the developments in the arts that took place during the reign of Maharaja Narinder Singh served as a model for his successors at Patiala and also influenced the rulers of other Sikh kingdoms – Kapurthala, Nabha, Jind, Faridkot, among them.

190. Qila Mubarak, the old fort at Patiala. Photograph: Susan Stronge

191. *A Tree Springs to Life*, possibly from a *Rasikapriya* series, Panjab Plains (Kapurthala?), *c*.1850. Gouache on paper, 28.5 × 23 cm. Government Museum and Art Gallery, Chandigarh (1777).

192. *Lady Watching a Heavenly Being Riding a Chariot*, Panjab Plains (Kapurthala?), *c*.1850, 28.5 × 23 cm. Government Museum and Art Galley, Chandigarh (1772).

As the century progressed there was a marked increase and gathering pace in the range of activity. There is evidence to suggest that, following the fall of the Lahore kingdom and the ensuing confusion, some of the artists decided to move elsewhere – 'we are like sunflowers', the artists of this area often said, 'seeking the warmth of patronage'. Some of the Pahari artists who had worked for Ranjit Singh and his nobles at Lahore returned to their native hills, but Patiala, with its considerable resources, its power intact and an emerging interest in the arts, must have been an obvious destination. An interesting case is that of the painter Deviditta, great-grandson of the celebrated Nainsukh of Guler (*c*.1710–1778), who had lived with his family at Basohli in the hills.[3] In the records of the priests at that great centre of pilgrimage, Haridwar, there are several entries relating to Deviditta. In 1856 (vs 1913), he describes himself as settled in the street of 'Kanhaiya Kapur, in the Machhihatta area' of Lahore; however, in 1866 and again in the following year, he is recorded as having come to Haridwar 'from Patiala', where he must obviously have been working. Another, earlier example of such migration is 'the painter Gohi, brother of Rodu and Bibru [Biba], and son of Hardayal, belonging to the town of Haripur-Guler in the hills' coming on a pilgrimage to Haridwar in 1843 from Patiala, where he was 'in the service of Maharaja Karam Singh'.[4] Nine years later Gohi's brother Biba also came to Haridwar 'from Patiala', where he was 'in the service of Maharaja Narinder Singh'.

193. *A King Consults his Minister about a Painting*, Pahari, *c*.1850. Gouache and gold on paper, 16.5 × 26 cm. Museum Rietberg, Zurich. Photograph by Wettstein & Kauf.

Names of other painters from the hills surface later: Ghathu Ram, Saudagar, Kehru. The evidence is brief, almost scrappy – such unfortunately is the case with all evidence on Indian painters of the past – but a pattern begins to emerge. There was work to be found in Patiala, perhaps even discerning patronage. Precise documentation is lacking but visual evidence raises the strong suggestion that painters also converged upon Patiala from other areas, especially from Alwar and Jaipur. Their hand is visible most clearly in the murals still extant in the glittering Sheesh Mahal, begun in 1847 for Maharaja Narinder Singh.[5] Panel after panel on those walls is executed in the recognisable style of Alwar-Jaipur, the painters seeming to carry on in Patiala where they had left off in their native Rajasthani setting. The range of themes, the treatment of individual episodes, the figuration, the line, the colouring, all leave no doubt about this. Unfortunately no names have survived of these Rajasthani artists. Oral evidence does, however, suggest that members of the extended family of a master-builder who was sent for by the court, Udai Ram Jaipuria – the one name that does seem to have stayed in local memory – might have been responsible at least for the rich floral embellishment in the Sheesh Mahal and other buildings in Patiala.[6] Other names, such as those of Ganga Baksh and Sheo Ram, float about in the air. The Rajasthani connection was obviously strong, for the records of the priests at Haridwar also speak of families of 'Rajaura Tarkhans' or 'Khatis' of Jaipur living in Patiala.[7] There is a long list of names, and some indication that the family was originally one of 'Jangir Brahmans', before it sank to the status of 'carpenter/mason-painters', much like some of the artisan families of the hills that are now so well known.

Apart from the Pahari and Rajasthani painters, at least one prominent family of Muslim artists, probably originally from Delhi, was active at Patiala. The name of Allah Ditta figures in oral evidence as the head of this family when it migrated. The names of his descendants Basharat Ullah and Muhammad Sharif are better documented, for paintings inscribed with their names have survived, including a fine equestrian study of Guru Gobind Singh, rendered by Muhammad Sharif for Bhai Gurmukh Singh, a member of the state's 'Honourable Council'.[8] Also travelling through the region, as in most of the other parts of northern India, were itinerant Kashmiri scribes and painters, copying and illustrating manuscripts to commission (plate 195). It would thus be natural for there to be exchanges of ideas between these different groups of painters. This convergence in Patiala of builders and painters, poets and musicians, from different directions must have produced a certain momentum.

What is striking in many of these later Sikh kingdoms is the fact that nearly all cultural

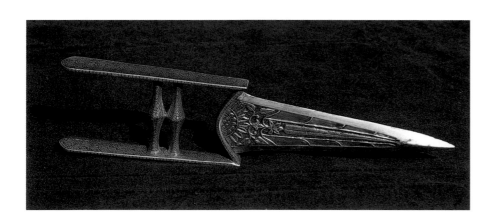

194. Punch dagger (*katar*). Patiala, 19th century. Steel overlaid with gold, length 31 cm. Qila Mubarak Museum, Patiala (73/13). Courtesy of the Department of Cultural Affairs, Arch. and Museums, Punjab, Chandigarh, India.

activity is marked by a catholicity of approach, a decided liberality of outlook. Taking Patiala as a case in point once again, during most of the period of growth there is a breadth of vision; there are no fissures along religious or sectarian lines, whether in matters of state or those of the arts. The rulers themselves were devout Sikhs, but the Prime Ministers of as many as four rulers were Muslims – Khalifa Muhammad Hassan whose family came from Samana being the most pre-eminent among them.[9] When building activity on a significant scale was undertaken under Maharaja Narinder Singh, *gurdwaras* were built besides palaces and forts, but there were also significant Hindu temples, among them Badrinath, Kedarnath, Tung Nath, Raj Rajeshwari. Obviously a text such as the *Janam Sakhi* of Guru Nanak remained a favourite for illustration, but the painters also spent much of their time illustrating classics of Hindu mythology or major literary works in Hindi. The murals of the Sheesh Mahal or the fort at Gobindgarh depict the same subjects as those of a Rajasthani palace: Krishna steals the milkmaids' clothes, Vishnu assumes his cosmic form, lovers collide

in the dark lanes as Bihari described in his *Satsai*, Sudama leaves his poor hut to go to Dwarka. Nothing comes as a surprise: neither the rich grants of land in the name of temples, nor the ruler's appearance at them for paying personal homage; neither the power wielded by able Muslim administrators nor the recitation of the *Ramayana* in the Qila Androon (the old fort at Patiala), or the state celebration of festivals associated with the different faiths. The sense one has is that all this is rooted in conviction, not policy. The parallels with Maharaja Ranjit Singh's kingdom come sharply to mind.

Finally, what is striking is the turn that painting takes when new challenges appear for painters in the form of European work at these courts. Work in the European mode, in oil or watercolour, was not unknown in the trans-Sutlej Panjab. There were European officers in the maharaja's service, professional artists and gifted amateurs passed through the region in such large numbers, and gifts were brought in by state visitors. Influences

195. *Vishwarupa with Arjuna and Donor Figure.* Page from a manuscript formerly appended to the Guru Granth Sahib. Gouache and gold on paper, 44.5 × 44 cm. National Museum of India (59.155/1).

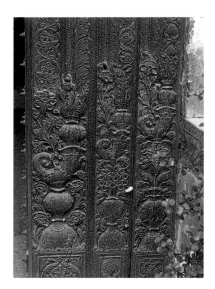

196. Carved wooden doorpost
at Qila Mubarak, Patiala.
Photograph: Susan Stronge.

197. *Raja Devinder Singh of Nabha*,
Panjab, 1840–60. Gouache on paper,
18 × 13 cm. By permission of
The British Library (Add. Or. 2602).

had thus started registering on the minds of the Indian painters then active, especially
when it came to rendering portraits, a genre already much in favour among Sikh patrons.
But in the second half of the nineteenth century at Patiala or at Kapurthala, Jind or
Nabha a range of painters seems consciously to have decided to take up the challenge,
meeting European art on its own terms – not working in the same medium but placing
the same marked emphasis on close observation. Such Sikh painters as Kapur Singh

(plate 199) and Kehar Singh, active in the third quarter of the nineteenth century, produced some fine studies;[10] Kehar Singh showed strong interest in endowing his figures with a marked sense of volume and Kapur Singh laid stress on capturing details of character. The names of these two artists crop up repeatedly. Some of Kapur Singh's studies, on machine-made paper, were inscribed with captions in English. Kehar Singh, 'possessed of . . . a darting, sure brush', seems to have moved around, certainly working first at Lahore and then at Kapurthala, turning out portrait studies, series of craftsmen at work, recording gifts of silverware with engraved messages, and even copying European-style coats of arms complete with inaccurately written legends in Latin.

Even more fascinating is the work done by painters from Rajasthan who had settled in Patiala. Obviously sensing a change in the air, aware of the impression that 'realistic' European-style portraits made upon their patrons and sensitive to new needs, these painters began to record appearances as never before. A prodigious number of portraits

198. *Group Portrait of Sikhs from Patiala*, Fraser Album, Delhi, *c.*1815–20. Watercolour on paper, 22.1 × 30.6 cm. © The British Museum (1988 10-20 01).

have survived, small-sized sketches often with the barest trace of colour in them, of everyday figures in their Patiala surroundings: warriors and petty nobles, performers and tutors, staff-bearers (*chobdars*) and torch-lighters (*farrashes*).[11] The drawings are done with brush on the usual hand-made paper of Sialkot, two or three sometimes on the same sheet and most of them inscribed in a spidery hand in Rajasthani *nagari* script identifying the subject. These works stand clearly apart from the dreary sets depicting trades and professions turned out in such large numbers in 'Company' India. The works of the Rajasthan artists are individual studies, sensitive and warm, produced not in fulfilment of some commission but as an artistic exercise. In the background of this kind of work is the rigour of a great tradition, and the desire to develop beyond it. The studies are sharp, authentic and remarkably fresh.

It is impossible to catalogue here all the work done in the states of the Panjab: the illustrated texts, rich murals, renderings of the great Gurus, series of royal portraits and sets showing professions, trades and castes. The true flavour of the work can however be caught by turning to a few examples. A truly representative work is that unusually large 'miniature' of a state procession now in the Moti Bagh palace collection (plates 187, 200a and b). This shows an enormous, dense phalanx of men – riders on horseback, accoutred soldiers, footmen in neat uniforms – moving in slow, measured steps from right to left, accompanying a group of exquisitely decorated elephants ridden by princes and men of rank. The dark, smoky forms of the elephants, barely relieved by gold-worked caparisons, rise like a cloud till the eye reaches the pre-eminent animal, support-ing a dazzling scalloped howdah in which may be discerned the figure of the maharaja, Narinder Singh: nimbate, grave and dignified, not oversized and oblivious to the panoply of power that surrounds him. A rank of men wearing blazing red turbans walks very close to the royal mount; a forest of lances held vertically, and differently inclined ensigns of royalty held aloft by another group of unseen soldiers, creates one more shield for the royal rider. The entourage is extremely detailed: the serried ranks, the individualised faces of men in the crowd, the glitter of the uniforms, the minutiae of weapons and saddlery and fly-whisks. There is, however, more to the scene than this, for at a slight distance, well ahead of the group around the maharaja, is yet another file of elephants. On the back of one of these, also under a domed howdah, is the sacred Sikh scripture, the Guru Granth Sahib, neatly covered by a textile and with a devout atten-dant waving a yak's-tail fly-whisk over it. It then becomes clear that the procession belongs to the Holy Book, not to the maharaja, who, despite all the rank and circum-stance, is meant to be seen as a humble follower, a devotee, bringing up the rear. The point made is sharp, the impact stunning. The work is packed with other details: the wall of the fortified city at the back, the European-style carriage in the distance, the ele-gantly carved palanquins carried on the shoulders of bearers. But all these add up to

199. Drawing of a hawk, Kapur Singh, 1880–99. Ink and watercolour on paper, 21.9 × 18.2 cm. Government Museum and Art Gallery, Chandigarh (L.80).

200a. Detail of plate 200b.

200b. *Maharaja Narinder Singh*, Patiala. Gouache and gold on paper, 100 × 110 cm. Sheesh Mahal Museum and Medal Gallery. Courtesy of the Department of Cultural Affairs, Arch. and Museums, Punjab, Chandigarh, India.

201. *Rain, Music and Mangoes*, Panjab Plains, mid-19th century, 25 × 21 cm. Sarabhai Foundation (KA 18).

202. *Portrait of an unknown man*, perhaps a peasant or artisan. Patiala. Private Collection.

little more than harmless diversions. The eye returns again and again to the elephant with the Holy Book. For that is where the spirit of the painting, with its fusion of Rajasthani and Pahari elements, clearly resides.

In another painting (plate 201), showing a Sikh chief enjoying music, rain and mangoes, the mood is entirely different and has a decisively Pahari feeling.[12] Quiet enjoyment is in the air. The comfortable-looking Sikh noble seated under a canopy is difficult to

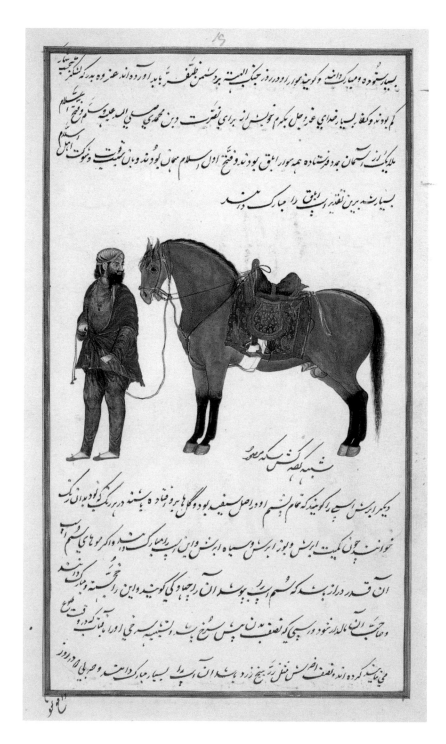

203. *Salhotar*, a treatise on farriery.
Kishan Singh, Kapurthala, 1851.
Gouache on paper, 32.5 × 20.5 cm.
By permission of The British Library
(Or. 6704).

identify. He could as easily be a figure from the hill states as from Lahore. There are no signs of royalty around him – no fly-whisk bearers, no parasols of the usual kind – but status is clearly established: he is the only one seated on a raised cushioned stool; musicians perform for him alone; an enormous basket of mangoes is placed directly in front of him as if he were the only one entitled to them. There are no hints here of the prowess of the *sardar*. He does not carry, even as a token, any weapon. All that engages him is the pleasure of the moment: the cooling rain of the monsoon months, luscious mangoes, perhaps great, soul-satisfying music. We see the chief more as a *rasika* than as a warrior. The painter establishes the atmosphere with skill. The garden in the background, with its plantain leaves and one of the mango trees laden with fruit, and the marble terrace, provide the perfect setting. Three musicians sing and play: the principal performer, the man with the greying beard carrying an orange-coloured *tanpura* (a stringed instrument), extends one hand forward as he sings; an accompanist sits next to him, long flowing hair barely covered by his small turban, and fingers perfectly poised to strike. The chief seems to be totally absorbed in the music, a small bunch of mangoes dangling idly from his right hand. There is informality and an endearing artlessness in the rendering. The work seems not to draw upon routine, or endlessly repeated pictorial clichés, instead it has a surprising directness.

Finally, there is the remarkably simple, unpretentious study of a man (plate 202).[13] The painter views him from very close, with a sense of engagement. This bearded man with uneven eyes and full lips, wearing a commoner's twisted turban, bears no mark of rank but is not devoid of dignity. He seems to look the viewer straight in the eye, not arrogantly but with honesty. The work is different from the delicate work done by Rajasthani artists. It goes well beyond those discreet, restrained studies, and takes one almost to the threshold of photography, as if anticipating it.

CHAPTER ELEVEN

EUROPEAN VIEWS OF THE PANJAB

F. S. AIJAZUDDIN

204. *Mountain Scene*, George Landseer, Kashmir, 1860. Pastel on paper, 25 × 35.2 cm. 41-1881 (2/3).

Istory often relies upon small persons to provide the true measure of man, leaving it to the naturally diminutive like Napoleon (1769–1821) or Ranjit Singh (1780–1839) to demonstrate how tall a person can stand amongst his contemporaries. Both these historical figures emerged within decades of each other in unconnected continents, both were commoners destined to create kingdoms through conquest, gradually expanding their empires until they reached borders their neighbours would not permit to be transgressed and, when they died within twenty years of each other, they left behind a parallel legacy of personal aura and public wealth. Either of them could have written 'My kingdom is a great kingdom; it was small, it is now large; it was scattered, broken and divided; it is now consolidated: it must increase in prosperity, and descend undivided to my posterity'.[1] In the end, their empires ended with them, leaving behind a residue of their baser elements.

If Napoleon and his France preoccupied the British in the west, Ranjit Singh and his

205. *Attok Fortress on the Indus*, probably by Imam Bakhsh, *c*.1835–40. Watercolour on European paper, 18.4 × 29.4 cm. Musée national des Arts asiatiques-Guimet (39731). © Photo RMN – Thierry Ollivier.

Panjab intrigued them in the east. The fascination of the Panjab was not limited to its geographical location and its historical role as a gateway into India. Unlike the other areas of mainland India which the British had been able to ingest or negotiate terms with, the emergent kingdom of the Sikhs in the Panjab demonstrated a self-confident vigour and vitality in sharp contrast to the decaying Mughal empire and its capital Delhi. They were intrigued by the young theocratic state they could see, as one of them put it, 'silently growing up under our eyes'.[2]

History may have been on the side of Ranjit Singh, but time was against him. His territories extended as far north as Kashmir, in the west to Afghanistan, in the south to Sindh and in the east to the River Sutlej; they were too widespread and too significant to be allowed to relapse after his departure into the internecine anarchy from which he had almost single-handedly rescued them. Even the inconsequential William Osborne (aide-de-camp and nephew of Lord Auckland, the Governor-General of India) who visited Ranjit Singh in May 1838, the year before the worn-out maharaja died, could foresee what eventually happened:

> The whole country between the Sutlege and the Indus must become the scene of a protracted and bloody war, only to be terminated by the interference of a third and stronger power, with an army and resources sufficiently strong to bid defiance to all hope of resistance, and that army must be the British army, and that power the British government, there can be little doubt.

He continued unabashedly, 'The East India Company has swallowed too many camels to strain at this gnat; and to judge from the appearance of the country, they will derive more nourishment from the smaller insect than they have done from many of the larger quadrupeds they have swallowed of late years'.[3]

By 1849, within ten years of his death, Ranjit Singh's 'enormous and splendid kingdom', as Queen Victoria enthusiastically described it, was annexed and incorporated into her own expanding empire. The Panjab remained etched in the memories of those who had seen its glory, witnessed its splendour and then tried to capture in their own words and images its unique persona. These European outsiders provided crucial material for later historians of the nineteenth-century Sikh kingdom of the Panjab, helping them to reconstruct it for us today, in however incomplete a way.

Early pictorial images of the Panjab are still very scarce. Occasionally one comes across works such as the eighteenth-century panorama recognisable as the distinctive skyline of the Lahore fort and its adjacent Badshahi mosque,[4] or the map of the environs of Lahore commissioned by Colonel J. B. Gentil,[5] or rarer still the miniature painting done in the 1770s of the tomb of the Mughal emperor Jahangir at Shahdara, near Lahore, which was purchased by Sir Claude Wade when he was the British political agent in Ludhiana between 1823 and 1839.[6] Topographical views of areas further afield or of towns

206. *The Attack on the Khyber*, probably by Imam Bakhsh, *c.*1840. Watercolour on European paper, 6.3 × 8 cm. Musée national des Arts asiatiques-Guimet (39733/2). © Photo RMN – Thierry Ollivier.

207. *A Group of Europeans*, Pahari, *c.*1810? Gouache on paper, 20.4 × 15 cm. Reproduced by kind permission of The Chester Beatty Library, Dublin (MS XIa 18).

208. Cover of *The Court and Camp of Runjeet Singh*, W. Osborne, London, 1840. H 22 × W 15 cm. Kapany Collection.

beyond Lahore dateable earlier than 1800 are virtually unknown. As the century progressed, however, the mists gradually lifted.

Various British diplomatic missions had visited the court of Ranjit Singh for negotiations, and provided first-hand opportunities for images to be assembled of the hitherto inaccessible kingdom and its physically unprepossessing ruler. A watercolour sketch, again of Lahore, by Thomas Longcroft, was most probably derived from notes provided by an observant member of the staff of Sir Charles Metcalfe (if not Metcalfe himself) when he

met Ranjit Singh in 1808.[7] A later mission yielded the first published portrait of Ranjit Singh, by a Delhi artist, Jewan Ram, and used by Prinsep in 1834 as the frontispiece to his book on the Sikhs.[8] Even though there was a relay of foreign visitors to Ranjit Singh's court between the years 1820 and 1838 – the British veterinarian William Moorcroft (1820), James Lewis, who published under the name of Charles Masson (1828), the Austrian Baron Charles Hugel and the proselytising Dr James Wolff (1836), all of whom published accounts of their visits – their observations were individualised, one-dimensional and written under often trying circumstances and from a cramped vantage point.

Ranjit Singh was not one to grant unrestricted access to his kingdom to those he did not trust. Those he did trust, such as his European mercenaries – the former Napoleonic generals Jean-François Allard and Claude Court, for example – knew better than to share

Illustrations to the *Fables* of Jean de la Fontaine, Imam Bakhsh, Lahore, c.1840. Gouache on paper. Musée Jean de la Fontaine, Château-Thierry:

209. *The Dream of a Dweller in 'Mogol'*; 25.7 × 17.6 cm.

210. *The Mouse changing into a Girl*; 25.5 × 17.5 cm.

211. *The Rat and the Elephant*; 25.5 × 17.5 cm.

212. *Maharaja Gulab Singh*, William Carpenter, *c*.1855. Watercolour on paper, 24.5 × 28 cm. IS 153-1882.

their information and interests outside their own immediate circle.[9] The maharaja realised only too well why the British authorities could never have enough material on the topography of his kingdom. It was of continuing interest to them, needed for translation into maps of the region, necessary to plan and determine future marching routes to the borders of Afghanistan.[10] In addition to fulfilling the official requirements of the British military forces, the published accounts of these unusually observant travellers also whetted the appetite of the European reading public. What the public sought and was soon able to obtain were accurate pictorial images, rather than pretty scenic views, to supplement the written description. Imperceptibly, topography *per se* receded into the background, becoming no more than a backdrop to the drama that unfolded as abrasive personalities jostled for supremacy at the Sikh court following Ranjit Singh's death in the summer of 1839.

The maharaja had been ill when Lord Auckland and his sisters Emily and Fanny Eden visited him in the winter of 1838. They were fortunate, however, in seeing Ranjit Singh and his court at their glittering best. Emily Eden, in particular, found herself captivated by what she saw. Her now famous sketches of the Sikhs and their ruler, published under the title *Portraits of the Princes and People of India*, did not appear until 1844 (the drawings by her less talented sister Fanny did not merit the same attention),[11] but the compositions, which placed her subjects full-length and centre-stage as if to emphasise their self-aggrandisement, established a norm (plates 213 and 214), which subsequent artists, for example Charles Hardinge, might have found difficult to improve upon. His portrait of the wily Raja Gulab Singh of Jammu (plate 216), shown in profile with face averted as if trying to avoid eye contact with the viewer, is close to Emily Eden's own distinctive style.[12] Hardinge recounted later how the raja gave him a history of all his campaigns and produced a sort of panorama painted by a native artist, portraying the events of his life: 'In one of these was a group of men pouring what was evidently molten lead down a prisoner's throat. We asked what they were doing, upon which he laughed heartily, and

213. *The Late Maha Raja Runjeet Singh*, after Emily Eden. From *Portraits of the Princes and People of India*, J. Dickinson & Son, London, 1844. Hand-tinted lithograph, 22 × 17.5 cm. Kapany Collection.

214. *Heera Singh*, after Emily Eden. From *Portraits of the Princes and People of India*, J. Dickinson & Son, London, 1844. Hand-tinted lithograph, 22 × 17.5 cm. Kapany Collection.

215. Order of Merit, Lahore, *c.*1838.
Enamelled gold set with emeralds and
diamonds. Lent by Gurshuran and
Elvira Sidhu.

216. *Maharaja Gulab Singh of Jammu
and Kashmir* (1792–1857), after an
original drawing by C.S. Hardinge,
Jammu, 1846. Lithograph.
Aijazuddin Collection.

217. *Entry into Lahore From the Parade
Ground*, plate from *Recollections of India*,
C. S. Hardinge, London, 1847.
67.5 × 51 cm. 102 L 6.

pointing to the cauldron said, "They are making tea!"[13] Understandably, the Prussian Prince Friedrich Waldemar, Hardinge's companion-in-arms and a fellow artist, preferred to keep his distance from the Dogra raja when doing his sketch of the same subject, and depicted him safely aloft on an elephant.[14]

Both Charles Hardinge and Prince Waldemar had come to the Panjab as part of the British forces which defeated but did not conquer the Sikh army in the First Anglo-Sikh War of 1845–6. Their drawings were sent home to London and Berlin, converted into lithographs and published in large portfolios, Hardinge's as *Recollections of India* in 1846 (plate 217) and Waldemar's in 1853 under the cumbersome title *Zur Erinnerung an die Reise den Prinzen Waldemar von Preussen nach Indien in den Jahren, 1844–1846*. By the time their portfolios had penetrated the market, however, their leisurely elegant form of pictorial journalism had been overtaken by a new journal, the *Illustrated London News*.

It began publication on 14 May 1842 and included in its December issue a view of the Bolan Pass in Baluchistan, adapted from one of G. Atkinson's lithographs published in his *Sketches of Afghaunistan* that same year. The following year the *Illustrated London News* covered the annexation of Sindh by Sir Charles Napier and, when the First Anglo-Sikh War broke out in the Panjab in 1845, the periodical augmented the written despatches received via the overland mail from India with woodcuts derived from sketches done almost ten years earlier by the traveller G. T. Vigne. Interestingly, the first set of woodcuts depicts General Ventura, one of Ranjit Singh's foreign mercenaries, and a view of his house at Lahore, close to the tomb of Anarkali.

Subsequent issues of the magazine were better co-ordinated and more topical. Officers in the field with a talent for drawing became a rich source, supplying many of the illustrations and thereby providing the distant readers with a feeling of immediacy and closeness to the actual battle action. By the time of the Multan campaign in 1848, the *Illustrated London News* no longer needed to draw upon previously published lithographs. The position was in fact reversed: sketches made on the spot in Multan by Dr John Dunlop (an assistant surgeon in the 32nd Regiment of the British Army) and published by the magazine in its reports on the campaign were artfully modified and released within a year in book form under the title *Mooltan, a Series of Sketches during and after the Siege* (plate 218).[15]

218. *The Capture of the Sikh Standards*, plate from *Mooltan*, John Dunlop, London, 1849.

37.8 × 28 cm. 59 D 15.

219. *Tomb of Runjeet Singh...*, plate from *Original Sketches in the Punjaub, by A Lady*, London, 1854. 28 × 37.5 cm. F 18 (39).

An unusual series of watercolours done slightly later by an anonymous but talented woman, the wife of an officer posted to Lahore, depicted the major monuments of Lahore, as well as the Golden Temple and other sacred buildings in the holy city of Amritsar, and the fort of Govindghur where Ranjit Singh maintained his treasury. These were published in 1854 under the title *Original Sketches of the Punjaub, by A Lady* (plate 219). Two other amateur watercolourists, Henry Oldfield (another assistant surgeon posted to Lahore in 1848) and Dr John McCosh (surgeon with the 2nd Bengal Europeans in 1849), also exercised their extra-medical skills. Dr McCosh was also a photographer, and it is to his ingenuity and skill in using the comparatively new process that we owe the first three surviving calotypes of Lahore, forerunners of a new approach perfected later by such professional photographers as William Baker, John Burke and Samuel Bourne.

Photography came too late to have been of significant use during the Second Anglo-Sikh War of 1848–9. That campaign culminated in the formal annexation of the Panjab, signed in the Sheesh Mahal of the Lahore fort. Ranjit Singh's empire was gradually dismantled, starting from its core. The young Maharaja Dalip Singh was weaned away from Lahore, and his mother, the irrepressible Rani Jindan, exiled from the Panjab. Loyalists and favoured retainers – Sikh, Hindu and Muslim alike – transferred their allegiance and positioned themselves into comfortable configurations in a new order. The Sikh Darbar slipped into memory, and then gradually subsided into legend.

Ranjit Singh's successors lacked the maharaja's self-confidence: if he had allowed himself to be portrayed it was because he knew that he would not be flattered. He did not need the trappings of power; he knew that he was its fount. His second son, Sher Singh, however, posed with an almost defiant vanity when playing host to the Hungarian portrait painter August Shoefft in 1840 (plate 220).[16] Ranjit Singh's favourite, Raja Hira Singh, modelled for the Russian Prince Alexis Saltykov in 1842 (plate 221), riding with his face covered in a thinly veiled attempt to remain incognito (or was it just to keep out the dust?).[17] The maharaja's youngest son, Dalip Singh, found himself dressing and acting the part of a rich oriental potentate, a role that fate, aided and abetted by Lord Dalhousie, ensured he would never fulfil.[18] It is perhaps significant that the largest collection of paintings extolling the Sikh Darbar, those done by Schoefft from drawings and sketches he had made during his visit to the Panjab in the 1840s, were completed more than ten years later – well after the annexation of the Panjab. These paintings were exhibited in 1855 at Vienna and were bought for, rather than by, Dalip Singh, then still in his teens. They hung in his various residences like colourful emblems of the heritage he had lost. His disinherited subjects had to rely upon miniature paintings or portraits on ivory to commemorate their Sikh heroes.

Dalip Singh's life in exile makes sad reading. He achieved nothing extraordinary and, if he was made to feel important, it was not because of anything he did; rather his importance lay in what others thought he symbolised. To many, and they were not all necessarily Sikhs, he was a living reminder of the past; to a loyal minority he represented the possibility, however unlikely, of its future revival.

Queen Victoria led the first group. Unwittingly, she elevated Dalip Singh to a position on canvas she could not, for reasons of state, sustain in real life. She had him painted by her favourite artist Winterhalter in 1854 (plate 182); she saw that he was included among her family of royals in William Frith's painting of the marriage of her son Albert Edward, Prince of Wales, to Princess Alexandra of Denmark in March 1863; and she commissioned a marble bust of him by the sculptor Baron Marochetti. Used to such exalted artistic circles, it was only natural that when Dalip Singh wanted a portrait of his mother Rani Jindan, who had joined him in London following her years of exile in Nepal, he should turn to the leading portraitist of the time, George Richmond (see plate 176).[19] Richmond succeeded in achieving a hat-trick of sorts by sketching three figures connected with the Sikh kingdom: Emily Eden, Rani Jindan and her nemesis, Lord Dalhousie.

220. *Maharaja Sher Singh*, August Schoefft, Vienna, *c*.1850. Oil on canvas, 110.7 × 920 cm. Princess Bamba Collection, Lahore Fort.

221. *Sikh Chieftains*, after an original
drawing by Prince A. Saltykov, Lahore,
1842. Lithograph.
Aijazuddin Collection.

The second group, the minority who nurtured the hope of a revival of the Sikh kingdom of the Panjab, was led by Dalip Singh himself. He fought for what he believed to be
his rights. But times had changed, and the restoration he hoped and planned for could
hardly be implemented from exile. Distanced from the Panjab, isolated and financially
distressed, Dalip Singh succumbed to the reality of his situation. Having been forced to
give up his kingdom in 1849, he surrendered all claims to it by dying far from the Panjab,
in Paris, the capital of Napoleon's French empire.

Napoleon, too, had died in exile. Yet years afterwards, the mere invocation of his
name could still attract the sympathies of dormant Bonapartists. Similarly, the images of
Maharaja Ranjit Singh and, to a lesser degree, those of his successors, could be relied
upon to revive passions amongst those loyalists who found solace in recalling the period
of Sikh rule in the Panjab. To them it remained and will continue to remain an apogee of
sorts, a golden period when, for the first and only time in its recorded history, the Panjab
was unified into a short-lived, but memorable nation.

CHAPTER TWELVE

PHOTOGRAPHY AND THE ROMANCE OF THE PANJAB

DIVIA PATEL

222. *Street inside the sacred tank area,*
Amritsar, Felice Beato, *c.*1857.
Albumen print, 28.4 × 23.7 cm.
80089.

223. *Sikh Sardar,* John McCosh,
1848–9. Calotype, 10 × 8.5 cm.
National Army Museum 6204/3 (242).

The Victorian age embraced photography with an enthusiasm and optimism that found one of its greatest outlets in British India. Amateur and professional photographers travelled through the country, taking pictures of architecture, landscape and people. Through the camera they fed the imagination of the Victorian public with images of empire, informing their curiosity and helping to shape their attitudes.

Photography arrived in India in the 1840s, at a time when the British were shifting their attention away from the established seats of power in Bengal, Bombay and Madras, towards the Panjab. The region formed the north-western gateway through which successive invaders had entered India and was therefore of considerable strategic importance. The Panjab also held a captivating romantic appeal: its territory stretched across the fertile lands of the Indus to sandy deserts and wild prairies of grass, to mountain ranges reaching up in the west to the Afghan border and in the north to the Himalayas. It was seen as the 'real' India, a vast untamed land peopled by wild tribes and sturdy peasants,[1] a perception reflected in the many novels written by the wives of officers stationed in the Panjab. It was this exotic ideal that early photographers helped to create.

The Second Anglo-Sikh War (1848–9) was the vehicle for introducing photography into the region. John McCosh, a surgeon in the Bengal establishment of the East India Company stationed in Ferozpore at this time, had taken up photography as an energetic amateur. He encouraged others to pursue the pastime: 'I strongly recommend every assistant-surgeon to make himself a master of the photograph . . . During the course of his service in India, he may make such a faithful collection of representations of man and animals, of architecture and landscape, that would be a welcome contribution to any museum' (plate 223).[2]

McCosh took two beautiful photographs of Lahore gate and Ranjit Singh's *samadh* using the calotype process. This was the first photographic process to enable a negative print to be taken on paper, from which many positive prints could be made. His main interest, however, was in recording people: army officers, officials and 'natives'. In a letter

193

to his wife dated 6 November 1849, Dr John Login, the guardian of Maharaja Dalip Singh, noted: 'Dr McCosh is anxious to take daguerreotypes here, and begs to be allowed to come tomorrow to take likenesses of all the notabilities collected here, myself included among the number, he says! I have told him he cannot take any of the prisoners!'[3]

One of these prisoners was Diwan Mulraj, the Governor of Multan. Whether McCosh was, after all, given access to the prisoner is not mentioned, but his personal album included calotypes of both Mulraj and Mr Vans Agnew.[4] The murder of Vans Agnew by Mulraj triggered the Second Anglo-Sikh War, and these images were therefore historically significant almost as soon as they were taken. The album also includes the earliest known photograph of the young Maharaja Dalip Singh.

McCosh was using a medium for which there was no established framework of practice, no rules on whom or what to photograph. The main concern of many photographers would have been to achieve a good likeness and a clear, even print. Unintentionally, however, the images reveal colonial attitudes that would powerfully influence photography in India for the next century. These colonial attitudes are most apparent in McCosh's photographs of the indigenous population. His subjects were to remain anonymous 'natives' and when assembled in his album were labelled collectively as 'Sikhs', while all Europeans were individually named. He noted in his book that 'the inhabitants of upper India are a race very superior to the Bengalis, being tall, stout and manly, very handsome in figure'.[5] Almost a decade later this recording of the racial types of India became an official project, and was one of the most important ways in which photography was used by the imperial powers.

McCosh gave up his hobby after returning to England in 1856 and, while he may not have been aware of the pioneering place of his images in the history of photography in India, he certainly recognised their importance as visual documents of the time: 'These photographs have no pretension to merit . . . Their fidelity will however make amends for their sorry imperfections. Like fragile remains of lost ages their value is enhanced because the originals are no longer forthcoming.'[6]

The Second Anglo-Sikh War led to the annexation of the Panjab in 1849. Under the leadership of John Lawrence, the chief commissioner, a unique relationship developed between the Sikh nation and the British. The Panjab came to be seen as an example of good governance and encouraged a sense of mutual respect, which was to prove highly advantageous to the British.

On 10 May 1857 a section of the Indian army rebelled at Meerut and the Indian

224. *View from the Causeway away from Harmandir*, Felice Beato, *c*.1857. Albumen print, 25 × 28.5 cm. 80088.

Mutiny, as the British called it, spread over the year as far as Peshawar, the northernmost part of the Panjab, to Chittagong in the east. The scale of the rebellion and the manner in which it was represented in words and pictures aroused Victorian emotions in a way unequalled in the history of British India. A year after covering the Crimean War (1854–6), the renowned *Times* correspondent W. H. Russell travelled to India to report on

225. *General View of Tank and Temple*, Felice Beato, *c*.1857. Albumen print, 23.3 × 28.0 cm. 80092.

the atrocities. Also following on from the Crimea was the Italian-born photographer Felice Beato. The age of the war reporter and the war photographer had arrived.

Beato had travelled to India intending to photograph the Mutiny, believing in the profitability of such images, but by the time he arrived the Mutiny was virtually over and he was left to record the aftermath. He is now known primarily for his photographs of Lucknow, in which destroyed buildings lie in ruins in the background and the remains of skeletons litter the foreground; his images of Amritsar are largely unknown. A catalogue advertising the sale of Beato's prints, however, includes 19 of Amritsar, including a panorama of the city and a series of images of the Golden Temple (plates 224 and 225).[7] It appears that he did not produce as many prints from these negatives as he did for the Mutiny sites, perhaps believing that his photographs of Amritsar, where Mutiny damage was minor, and the Golden Temple would not be of interest to a public that had been

226. *Hodson's Horse Regiment*,

Felice Beato, Lucknow, March 1858.

Albumen print, 30.2 × 23 cm.

National Army Museum, 5608-6-20.

reading about death and destruction. Nevertheless, they are beautiful images showing architectural details that do not exist today, and are probably the earliest photographs of the Harmandir.

Throughout the rebellion, the Panjab had remained largely loyal to the British, and much of the British success was attributed to regiments such as Brasyer's Sikhs.[8] Sikhs, along with Pathan soldiers recruited from the north-west frontier, were seen as possessing the 'cavalry spirit' and were admired for their 'dash, elan, swagger and readiness to engage the enemy without counting the cost'.[9] Beato captured something of this spirit in his portraits of soldiers and officers. Three of the most striking photographs were of members of Hodson's Horse Regiment. These were taken in March 1858 at Lucknow when it had been recaptured and victory in the rest of India was assured. In one photograph he positioned Panjab cavalrymen around two British officers in a composition that gives a sense of the respectful relationship that existed between them, but which draws attention to the gallant and defiant-looking soldier in the centre (plate 226). Beato took a separate photograph of this soldier, who was probably a Pathan, alone in front of the same background.[10] In this image, and in a further group portrait of three Sikh 'native officers' (plate 227), Beato captured the ideal which soldiers from the Panjab, and especially the Sikhs, epitomised for the British: courageous and honourable, yet fundamentally simple natives.[11] These images, along with newspaper reports and popular novels, all played their part in embellishing the tales of Sikh loyalty which continued to be requested for many years.

While travelling across India, Beato taught photography to a Captain Tytler and his wife Harriet. Tytler was commanding the 38th Regiment when it mutinied in Delhi in May 1857, and it is assumed that he learnt photography when he was given six months leave in May the following year. He took over three hundred photographs of Mutiny-associated sites and also included studies of the Golden Temple.[12] These large-format calotype prints were regarded as being of the finest quality and 'clearly showed the eye of an artist'. Credit was also given to his wife who, apparently fully recovered from the experience of having given birth in a two-wheeled cart during the Mutiny, 'not only selected most of the subjects but even developed the pictures herself'.[13]

Beato's own prints went on display in London at H. Herings, photographer, printseller and publisher to the queen, in 1859 and 1862. They may well have inspired Samuel Bourne, a young photographer, to practise in India (plate 228).[14] Although the Mutiny had been suppressed, images such as Beato's would heavily influence the way the public and photographers who travelled there came to think about the people and sites connected with the Mutiny.

227. *Three Sikh Native Officers*,
Felice Beato, Lucknow, March 1858.
Albumen print, 21 × 15.2 cm. India
Office Library and Records, 27 (20).

Over the next few years, the uses of photography began to be explored in other directions and with objectives that were more defined, far-reaching and fundamentally political in nature. Lord Canning, the Governor-General of India (1856–62), had requested amateurs and professionals to take likenesses of the people of India as a memento for himself and his wife. After the Mutiny this idea was developed into a formal system of categorisation and documentation in which photography played a key role.

In 1861 directives were sent out to local governments across India requesting co-operation in photographing the tribes, races and castes of India. Under the heading of 'The Punjab', and subheading of 'Sikhs', photographs were requested of 'Sikhs in ordinary costume. Under this head should be given specimens of the priestly sects of Bedee

228. *Hazuri Bagh and Lahore Fort*,
Bourne & Shepherd, Lahore, *c*.1866.
Albumen print, 23.4 × 29 cm. 52907.

(descendants of Gooroo Nanuk), and Sodhee (descendants of Guru Govind) also of Ukalees, and of one or two of the Grunthees at Umritsar, also Muzbee Sikhs'.[15] It was seen as desirable to have two prints of each 'as the collection when complete will be of much scientific value'.[16] One reason behind the growing interest in the inhabitants of other countries was the desire to prove scientifically the superiority of the European races; it was also part of the emergence of the new field of anthropological study and the inevitable consequence of the expansion of imperial powers across the globe.[17]

The photographs were sent to the India Museum in London where they were amalgamated into an eight-volume set, *The People of India*, published between 1868 and 1875.[18] The volumes were divided into the regions of India, and although the fourth and fifth volumes contain a section on the Panjab, entries for Sikhs are also found in other regions. Each photograph was accompanied by a letterpress containing extensive information

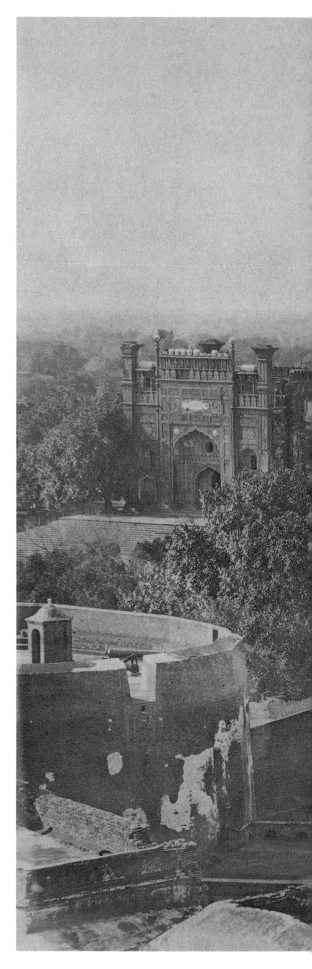

229. *Oodassee*, Shepherd & Robertson, *c*.1862.
Albumen print, 16.7 × 12 cm. 59.0.21.

230. *A Sikh*, from *The Costumes of the People of India*,
Captain W. W. Hooper and Surgeon G. Western,
1860–70. Albumen print, 18.6 × 12.2 cm. 0932:5.

about the physical appearance and the personal characteristics of each 'type', along with their relationship to other groups in Indian society, thus providing information for a greater understanding of the people – an invaluable aid to the preservation of British rule.

Two such entries are for the 'Oodassee' (plate 229) and the 'Akalee', both considered to be outsiders to the Sikh faith, the former because of their austerity and the latter for their fanaticism: 'Oodassee. The word "Oodas" signifies unsettled, melancholy or sad and has been adopted by these devotees to distinguish their class or sect. What the Bairagees are to the Hindoo classes, the Oodassees are to the Sikhs.'[19] Of the Akali, it was noted, 'The Akalee is always armed to the teeth. His high conical turban like the rest of his dress of a blue colour is encircled by rings of sharp steel quoits, in the use of which he is very skilful . . . the Akalee is a truly grim and formidable looking person . . .'[20]

231. *Ranjit Singh's Tomb from the top of Ranjit Singh's
Palace*, Lahore, *c*.1860. Albumen print,
19.2 × 25 cm. 2469-1900.

Alongside the production of *The People of India* another official project was reinstated: the documentation of the architecture and antiquities of India. The use of photography to replace the draughtsman in this exercise was necessary to hasten the process and to reduce the cost. It was so important that from 1855 military cadets of the East India Company were taught photography as part of their training. It was envisaged that it would be used throughout India 'in cases where it may be considered desirable by the Government to obtain representations of objects of interest'.[21]

During the mid-1850s several projects were initiated by the Bombay and Madras Presidencies (areas controlled and later ruled by the British), and army officers such as Linnaeus Tripe and Colonel Biggs were sent out to photograph the main architectural sites in south and west India. However, financial constraints and a lack of systematic planning meant that the projects were rarely completed. Even with the appointment of a director of archaeology in 1861 little progress was made until 1867. In August that year the viceroy, Sir John Lawrence, asked the presidencies to obtain photographs of the monuments and other antiquities under their control in the interests of conservation and preservation. Again, it was seen as desirable to have two copies of each image sent to the India Office in London. In a *List of Photographs in the India Office, 1887*, the 'Punjab' section included Lahore and Amritsar, Chamba, Kangra and Delhi. The work of professional photographers – 'Bourne and Shepherd, Mr Craddock [plates 232 and 233] and Burke' – came to represent the Panjab. Between them they covered many of the main sites in Lahore, including the Hazari Bagh, the Jami Masjid, the Shalimar Gardens and Jahangir's tomb, as well as the Golden Temple in Amritsar.

232. *Marble Pavilion and Old Entrance to the Fort*, J. Craddock, *c*.1860. Albumen print, 23 × 28.9 cm. 79863.

The most famous of the commercial photographers was Samuel Bourne. His search for picturesque views drew him to the Himalayas on three separate trips between 1863, when he arrived in India, and 1870. He also photographed much of the Panjab during these visits, including Amritsar and Lahore in March 1864, and Muree, the hill station, in 1866. In the account of his travels serialised in the *British Journal of Photography*, a typical post-Mutiny hostility was clearly evident, betraying a positive dislike for the Indian climate and the people. He constantly compared the scenery to that of Britain and lamented the lack of appropriate lakes, foliage and ivy-clad ruins which he deemed necessary for a 'pleasing and enjoyable picture'. However, despite himself, he was forced on

233. *The Badshahi Masjid Gateway*, J. Craddock, Lahore, 1860s. Albumen print, 28 × 22 cm. 79865.

234. *Alexander Gardner,*
Bourne & Shepherd, 1864.
Albumen print, 26.8 × 23 cm.
52.979.

235. *The Raja of Nabha,*
Bourne & Shepherd, 1903.
Albumen print, 29.2 × 22.6 cm.
By permission of The British Library
(99/74).

several occasions to praise the beauty of the 'grand and impressive scenery' and the mountains as 'mysterious and sublime creations'. Bourne was using the wet collodian process where glass sheets replaced paper as the base for a negative. This enabled the photographer to produce a much sharper positive print but was also cumbersome: on his journey to Kashmir, Bourne required 42 men to carry 650 glass plates along with cameras and chemicals, and encountered problems with the effects of damp on exposed negatives and broken glass. Nevertheless, his photographs of the mountainous regions, Kashmir and the adjoining territories were of stunning quality and remain some of the most beautiful images taken in India.

The views of Bourne and his partner Charles Shepherd were made available for purchase through a catalogue produced in 1866.[22] Shepherd had established himself, with his previous partner A. Robertson, as a specialist in photographs of the north west and many of their images of 'native characters', such as the 'Oodassee' (plate 229), had been incorporated into *The People of India.* They were also available in Bourne & Shepherd's catalogue, to which were added photographs of people from a cross-section of society, including the princes of the Panjab in their sumptuous costumes adorned with opulent jewellery, and eccentric characters such as the adventurer Colonel Gardner with his tartan suit and matching turban (plate 234).

A rival to Bourne & Shepherd was the firm of W. Baker & Co. William Baker had set himself up as a photographer in Peshawar after leaving the army in 1861; John Burke joined him in October of that year and in 1862 they established a studio in Muree, followed by another in Rawalpindi. Their early photographs chart the rise of Peshawar and Muree as outposts of the British administration and document British life in cantonments and official residencies, with their churches and cemeteries. In 1867 the firm was appointed official photographer to the Government of the Punjab and photographed dignitaries and official functions. Although it is not clear whether they were officially commissioned to photograph monuments and antiquities, their 1872 catalogue contains images of the Golden Temple as well as a section on Lahore and the remoter regions of the Panjab. The firm became known as Baker & Burke in 1871, but the partnership lasted only until June 1872.[23]

John Burke continued to practise alone, opening a studio in Lahore in 1885 and photographing the rapidly developing infrastructure. The railways, colleges and town halls were all documented and served to demonstrate the great achievements of the Panjab administration. Burke is best known, however, for his striking group compositions of

Afghan and Pathan troops and encampments set against the rugged mountains, which he photographed while covering the Second Afghan War for the British in 1878.

Many other photographers, both army officers and professionals, were active in the Panjab at that time. James Craddock, for example, worked during the 1860s and 1870s and had studios in Peshawar, Simla and Lahore, but little is known about his career, although his work was included in the India Office *List* of 1887.

These photographs were seen by the widest possible audience through exhibitions and publications. Both the ethnographic and architectural photographs were displayed at the great international exhibitions from the 1850s to 1900 and, together, presented a documented and categorised record of the people and places of India. The Paris International Exhibition of 1867 was one of the largest and included in the display of some five hundred architectural photographs a set of Beato's images of the Golden Temple along with Bourne's prints of Lahore and Amritsar.

Publications with tipped-in photographs had for the most part been projects such as *The People of India* or other ethnographic works and books on monuments commissioned by the Archaeological Survey of India. By the 1870s the availability and use of photographs had become more common. In 1876 Francesca Wilson published her travelogue *Rambles in North India*, described by a reviewer as a handsome addition to the literature on India; embellished with 'beautifully executed photographs of places of note in India, it is a book without which no Indian library is complete'.[24] Its 12 large photographic illustrations included the Golden Temple, and Ranjit Singh's tomb taken by Saché, another rival to Bourne & Shepherd. The travelogue itself was a light-hearted account, but the Mutiny continued to maintain a firm grip on the Victorian mind, the front page proudly advertising 'incidents and descriptions of many scenes of the Mutiny'.

Photography in the nineteenth century developed through experimentation and exploration. Its effects were profound and wide ranging. Like the Mutiny, photography changed the way India was perceived. In many instances the photographs legitimised British rule, the scenes of damaged buildings and dead bodies confirming the 'degenerate' nature of the country and its people to a British public devastated by the effects of the rebellion. However, there was also a public who had been reading of the Panjab as a 'model province' under the governance of the British hero Sir John Lawrence. To them the photographs presented another view. The images of the 'akalees' and 'oodassees', the princes, sirdars and soldiers of the Sikhs, together with the stunning landscape and impressive architecture, confirmed the glory of the romantic, mysterious and exotic Panjab.

236. *Ranjit Singh's Tomb*, Bourne & Shepherd, Lahore, 1860s. Albumen print, 23.9 × 29.3 cm. IS 7:35-1998.

CATALOGUE OF EXHIBITION OBJECTS

SHOWN AT THE ARTS OF THE SIKH KINGDOMS EXHIBITION,
VICTORIA AND ALBERT MUSEUM, MARCH 25, 1999 TO JULY 25, 1999,
CURATED BY SUSAN STRONGE.
THE LIST WAS CORRECT AT THE TIME OF GOING TO PRESS
AND ANY INACCURACIES OR OMISSIONS ARE DUE TO LATE CHANGES
IN THE CONTENT OF THE EXHIBITION.

NB	Nicholas Barnard, V&A
PC	Pierre Cambon, Museé National des Arts asiatiques-Guimet, Paris
NC	Neil Carleton, V&A
RC	Rosemary Crill, V&A
JD	Jeevan Deol, St John's College, Cambridge
BNG	B. N. Goswamy, Emeritus Professor, Punjab University, Chandigarh
AJ	Amin Jaffer, V&A
NK	Narinder Kapany, Chair, Sikh Foundation of America
SK	Sat Kaur, Postgraduate student, Sorbonne, Paris
DK	Daljit Khare, National Museum of India, New Delhi
ASM	Amandeep Singh Madra, Independent researcher, London
ASM-C	A. S. Melikian-Chirvani, CNRS, Paris
SM	Simon Metcalf, V&A
GP	Graham Parlett, V&A
DP	Divia Patel, V&A
AP	Anamika Pathak, National Museum of India, New Delhi
TR	Thom Richardson, Royal Armouries, Leeds
RS	Rita Sharma, National Museum of India, New Delhi
KS	Kavita Singh, Independent researcher, New Delhi
CS-H	Christiane Sinnig-Haas, Musée Jean de la Fontaine, Château-Thierry
SS	Susan Stronge, V&A

THE SIKH RELIGION

PAINTINGS AND MANUSCRIPTS

1 Janam Sakhi (plate 27)

239 folios, 57 illustrations, 15 lines per page in Gurmukhi script with rubrications in red ink. Compiled by Daia Ram Abrol, illustrated by Alam Chand Raj. Probably Kapurthala, dated Bhado *sudi* 3, 1780 vs/AD 1733. H. 25 cm; W. 14 cm
British Library: MS Panj. B 40

This prose hagiography of Guru Nanak's life consists of 58 *sakhis*, or stories, written in the mixture of Panjabi and Hindi common at this period. The *sakhis* revolve round or culminate in the exegesis of a *sabad* (composition) of Guru Nanak. The manuscript was compiled by Daia Ram Abrol (known to have written at least one other manuscript in his lifetime) at the request of a patron named Sangu Mal, son of Dasvandhi. The early history of the manuscript is unknown, although it has been suggested on the basis of external evidence that it was written in the region of Lahore, Gujranwala or, most convincingly, Kapurthala. It seems to have been with a book dealer in Lahore at the start of the 20th century, then brought to London and sold to the India Office in 1907. The story illustrated concerns Guru Nanak's journey to the 'land of unbelievers' (*munafik des*), where cultivators depended on the raja to bring forth rain to irrigate their crops. When Guru Nanak arrived with Mardana and a group of ascetics, the raja lost his ability to call forth rain. On being asked to intervene, the Guru told a cultivator to repeat the Name of God and sow his seeds. All the cultivators of the area followed his example and had a bumper crop, whereupon they, and the raja, became Guru Nanak's disciples. In the painting, the Raja sits before Guru Nanak with folded hands while Mardana watches from the right and the raja's servant waves a *chauri* (whisk) over his head. [JD]

PUBLISHED: [text] McLeod, 1980; Piar Singh, 1989; [illustrations] Surjit Hans, ed., *B-40 Janamsakhi Guru Baba Nanak Paintings*, Amritsar, Guru Nanak Dev University, 1987.

2 Dasam Granth (plate 4)

687 folios, 3 paintings, 21 lines per page of Gurmukhi script with rubrications in red ink. Probably Lahore, *c*.1820–49. H. 35.4 cm; W. 33 cm.
British Museum: MS Or. 6298

The compilation of texts in Braj Hindi, Persian and Panjabi attributed to the tenth Guru, Gobind Singh, was put together in 1730 by Bhai Mani Singh. It consists of devotional works, a biography of the Guru, narrative tales, praises of weapons and legendary accounts of the gods and goddesses. During the 18th and 19th centuries the Dasam Granth was generally treated with the same reverence as the Adi Granth. This manuscript belonged to Diwan Mulraj, the governor of Multan, and was captured during the siege of the city of January 1849, along with a suit of armour and a sword. The manuscript is in a form and style linking it to a number of Adi Granth and Dasam Granth manuscripts presented to nobles as well as to Sikh and Hindu shrines. These were probably produced in workshops associated with or patronised by the court; the volumes travelled with individuals on tour, and at all times with army units on the field of battle. The first pages of this manuscript, and of similar Adi Granth and Dasam Granth manuscripts of the period, have illustrations arranged in the form of a lotus around a central portion of the text with floral decoration between the pictures. The left-hand folio has at the top Ganesh (the Hindu god of wisdom and remover of obstacles) with his consort on their mount, the rat, and pictures of the first five Gurus around the remainder of the circle; the right-hand folio has at the top Sarasvati (goddess of learning, speech and poetry, and tutelary deity of poets and writers) on her mount, the swan, with the last five Gurus around the rest of the circle. [JD]

3 Guru Nanak's visit to Bhai Lalo the carpenter (plate 29)

Gouache and gold on paper. Panjab, 19th century. H. 16.5 cm; W. 15.5 cm
Kapany Collection

This is one of a series of paintings loosely inserted into a *janam sakhi* and describes an incident during Guru Nanak's travels when he stayed with a humble carpenter called Lalo. The Guru refused the invitation of a wealthy local dignitary, Malak Bhago, to attend a sumptuous feast and was taken there by force. Asked why he had refused the invitation, Guru Nanak squeezed a piece of Lalo's bread and milk issued forth; when he did the same to food from the rich man's table blood flowed from it. One had been earned by honest labour, the other through exploitation. [SS and SK]

4 Guru Nanak (plate 28)

Gouache and gold on paper. Lucknow or Faizabad, *c*.1770. H. 16.87cm; W. 15.5 cm
Kapany Collection. Formerly in the collection of the Hon. Stephen Tennant (1906–1987)

In a gold cartouche above the painting is a Persian inscription: 'tasvir-e darvish nanak shahi' (a picture, or likeness of the darvish Nanak the king). [SS]

PUBLISHED: Toby Falk, Brendan Lynch and Indar Pasricha, *Images of India*, London, 1990, p. 9, pl. 7.

5 Panjab paintings of the Gurus

As the depictions of the Gurus were not observed portraits but idealised works, Panjabi painters drew on oral tradition and available sacred literature to establish what may be called 'iconographies', at least in the case of four of the great Gurus: Guru Nanak, the founder of the faith; Hargobind, the sixth Guru who laid claim as much to temporal as spiritual power and was thus often depicted with a royal falcon on his hand (5a); Harkishan, the eighth Guru who died young and was often represented as a boyish figure; and Guru Gobind Singh, shown as a commanding, majestic figure on horseback, a falcon resting on one gloved hand (5c). [BNG]

a Guru Hargobind Singh on a terrace with an attendant (plate 104)

Gouache and gold on paper. Punjab Plains, 1750. Page H. 25.5 cm; W. 18.5 cm; painting H. 10 cm; W. 7.25 cm
Kapany Collection

This is one of an important group acquired by the New York dealer, Subhash Kapoor, in different styles but with Panjabi themes and inscriptions on the back stating that they were sold for specified sums by one Brijnath to Khudabaksh between 1730 and 1751 (see chapter 6). On this painting there is a later Persian inscription identifying the Guru.

b Guru Har Rai, the seventh Guru (plate 30)

Gouache and gold on paper. By a member of the Seu-Nainsukh family. Panjab Hills, first quarter of the 19th century. H. 22 cm; W. 16 cm
Government Museum and Art Gallery, Chandigarh: F 45

The artist was trained in the workshop tradition of the renowned family descended from Seu and Nainsukh, originating in Guler but moving to new patrons in different hill courts or the Panjab plains. The subject is categorically 'Sikh', but reverence for the Gurus was not confined to members of the Sikh community, nor to the plains of the Panjab. Painters from this family worked for Sikh patrons at Lahore. With no clear 'iconography' available to him, the painter here renders Guru Har Rai as a figure of great dignity, simply dressed, walking with a staff in one hand and with an attendant holding over his head a large parasol indicating royalty. The head is surrounded by a finely delineated nimbus, symbol of both royal and spiritual status; his face is serene. Walking ahead of the Guru, but turning back to look at him, is a small dog, probably included because the animal is traditionally associated with the surroundings of 'men of God'. [BNG]

PUBLISHED: Anand, 1981, p. 74; Paul, 1985, p. 44 and fig. 16.

c Guru Gobind Singh (plate 31)
Gouache and gold on paper. Guler,
c.1830. H. 32.6 cm; W. 23.5 cm
Collection of Elvira and Gurshuran
Sidhu, previously in the collection of
the Maharaja of Tehri Garwal

This magnificent portrayal of the last
Guru on horseback depicts him as a
commanding, majestic figure with
attributes of royalty such as the halo
and parasol. Guru Gobind Singh
initiated the Khalsa on 30 March
1699 at Anandpur, when five Sikhs
took *amrit* (sweetened water stirred
with a double-edged sword) and
formed the nucleus of a new
fellowship whose members would be
identifiable as Sikhs by their names
(Singh for the men, meaning lion, and
Kaur for the women, meaning
princess), and by adopting five symbols
including uncut hair. Before he died,
Guru Gobind Singh ended the line of
personal Gurus by passing on the
spiritual succession to the Guru
Granth Sahib, the Holy Book of the
Sikhs.

PUBLISHED: Archer, 1966, fig.7 and
p.125.

6 The Golden Temple (plate 2)
Watercolour, gold and silver on paper.
Panjab, probably Amritsar, c.1840.
H. 25.1 cm; W. 27.5 cm
Kapany Collection

Pencil comments, in English, include
'entrance gate' at the right, an arrow
showing the way across the causeway
with 'way between they walk'. A
yellow-clad figure within the
Harmandir reads the Guru Granth
Sahib, holding the ceremonial *chauri* in
his hand. Although extremely stylised,
the painting may date from before
c.1840 as the marble *parkrama* is not
shown. [SS]

7 The Golden Temple (plate 45)
Watercolour on European paper (1854
watermark). Amritsar, c.1855–60.
H. 25.5 cm; W. 41.9 cm
The British Library, London: Add. Or.
486. Sent to the International
Exhibition in London, 1862

The Persian inscription notes that this
is 'shri darbar sahib' (i.e. the
Harmandir) in Amritsar, the 'holy
worshipping place of the Sikhs'. A
label on the back states that it was
'Drawn at Umritsar under the
direction of Lalla Chumba Mull' and

that it was sent to the [International]
Exhibition of 1862, although it did
not appear in the catalogue (Archer,
1972, p. 225). [SS]

PUBLISHED: M. Archer, 1972, no. 186,
p. 224; Singh, Poovaya-Smith and
Ponnapa, 1991, cat. 31, p. 81 and illus.
p. 55.

ARMS WITH RELIGIOUS INSCRIPTIONS

8 Quoit (plate 3)
Steel inlaid with gold inscriptions from
the Adi Granth. India (Maharashtra?),
late 18th or first half of the 19th
century. Diam. 21 cm
Metropolitan Museum of Art:
36.25.2878. Bequest of
George C. Stone, 1936

A detailed description of this quoit, or
chakkar, was given by La Rocca (1996),
with inscriptions read by Dr Gurinder
Singh Mann of the University of
California, Santa Barbara, both of
whom gave permission for them to be
reproduced here. The gold Gurmukhi
inscription, in a script of the late 18th
or the 19th century, is a quotation
from the Adi Granth: 'Lord is
protector of our forehead / Lord is the
protector of our hands and body /
Lord protects our soul and body / The
compassionate Lord is the saviour of
all / The remover of fear and
suffering / Nanak seeks shelter with
the Lord / Who loves his devotees and
protects the helpless' (pp. 1358–9).
There is also an anonymous 18th-
century quotation from the same
book, in praise of the first and last
Gurus: 'Guru Nanak and Guru
Gobind Singh / were the perfect
Gurus / Their boundless light is
situated / in the city of Abchal
Nagar'. Finally there is a phrase used
in the Khalsa initiation ceremony:
'Victory belongs to God'.

PUBLISHED: La Rocca, 1966, pl. 25, cat.
65, p. 47.

9 Quoit
Steel inlaid with gold. Amritsar, late
18th or first half of the 19th century.
Diam. 22 cm
Metropolitan Museum of Art:
36.25.2876. Bequest of
George C. Stone, 1936

The Gurmukhi inscription, read by
Dr Mann, translates: 'One God

[attained with] the grace of the true
Guru / The Darbar Sahib /
Amritsar'.

UNPUBLISHED.

SIKH COINS

The emerging Sikh states followed the
pattern of the Mughal and Afghan
Durrani rulers in their coins, but broke
radically with tradition by issuing
them in the names of Guru Nanak
and Guru Gobind Singh rather than
in the name of the ruler. A very few
gold coins were issued with weights
ranging from 9.5 to 12 gm., and rare
specimens of double gold *mohurs* are
also found, all struck at Amritsar or
Lahore. Amritsar was the place where
the annual Sarbat Khalsa met and was
therefore the nucleus of political
power: as such it was mentioned as the
mint town on many coins, even if
these were struck at other mints. Such
coins contain the Gobindshahi couplet
(see p. 63) and a standard year (VS
1884–5/AD 1827–8), with the actual
year and place of issue on the reverse.
All the regular issues of *mohurs* and
rupees bear a Gobindshahi or
Nanakshahi couplet in Persian (see
Herrli, 1993, pp. 32-9); these would
have been circulated in the north-west
of India, local languages and scripts
being used on copper coins. [RS]

**10 Gold coin (*mohur*) (plates 61
and 62)**
Amritsar mint, dated VS 1885/
AD 1828 and VS 1893/AD 1836.
Diam. 2.1 cm
British Museum: 1912. 7.9. 209.
Bleazby Collection

The Gobindshahi couplet, in Persian,
is on the obverse with the date 1885;
the inscription on the reverse gives
Amritsar as the mint town, and the
actual date of issue (93, i.e. VS1893).
[RS]

**11 Gold coin (double *mohur*)
(plates 61 and 62)**
Amritsar mint, VS 1883/AD 1826.
Diam. 3.2 cm
British Museum: 1874.10.1. Guthrie
Collection

The Gobindshahi couplet on the
obverse, the inscription on the reverse
giving the mint town as Amritsar and
the date VS 1883. [RS]

**12 Special rupee issue depicting
Guru Nanak and Ranjit Singh
(plates 61 and 62)**
Silver. Dated VS 1885 and VS
[18]93/AD 1837. Diam 2.3 cm
British Museum: 1936.10-17.1

The obverse depicts Guru Nanak
seated, nimbate, with Ranjit Singh on
his right holding a flower; below them
is the date 1885 (AD 1829). On the
reverse is the Gobindshahi couplet in
Persian, which may be translated
'Abundance, Power and Victory [and]
assistance without delay, are the gifts
of Nanak and Guru Gobind Singh'.
These rare coins were thought to be
medals because of the depiction of
Guru Nanak, but the date suggests
that they may have been struck for
presentation at the marriage of
Naunihal Singh on 8 March 1837.
The design may have been inspired by
Baron Hugel's suggestion to Ranjit
Singh that he should be depicted, with
folded hands, before Guru Nanak
(Herrli, 1993). [RS]

SIKH TOKENS

The tradition of religious tokens, or
'tankas', is traceable to the 16th
century and the earliest examples in
gold belong to the Vijayanagar
kingdom. They were originally offered
to Hindu temples all over India, but by
the 19th century their use had spread
to other religions, including Sikhism
and Islam. The different types of Sikh
tokens include one depicting Guru
Nanak and his companions Bala and
Mardana, with Guru Gobind Singh
on the reverse holding a falcon, and
including the inscription 'Sat Katar'
(True Lord); these are found in silver,
bullion or brass and some are dated VS
1804/AD 1747. A second, similar, type
lacks the inscription. A third, in silver
or gold, has the same representations
of Guru Nanak, Bala and Mardana
on the obverse but includes a
Gurmukhi inscription on the reverse
which may be translated 'The One All
Prevailing: Truth is His Name, the
Creator-Being, without fear, without
enmity, the Timeless Being, without
birth, self-existent and revealed by the
grace of Guru (God). That Master is
ever true, His Name is Truth. The
One who has created this creation is
true and will be true for all times
(Japuji-Guru Nanak).' (Sahib Kaur,

Sikh Thought, Vasant Vihar, New Delhi, 1990). [RS]

13 Gold token depicting Guru Nanak with devotees Bala and Mardana (plate 59)
Diam. 2 cm
National Museum of India: 65.497

14 Silver token depicting Guru Nanak with Bala and Mardana
Diam. 2.7 cm
British Museum: 1922.4.24.4348.
R. B. Whitehead Collection

PHOTOGRAPHS

15 The Golden Temple (plate 47)
Albumen print. Captain
W. G. Stretton. Amritsar, *c*.1870s.
H. 17.7 cm; W. 26.8 cm
2466-1906
Given by R. Taylor

During the Prince of Wales's 1876 visit to India, he spent a day in Amritsar and visited the Harmandir. The *Times of India* described the scene: 'The Temple is profusely adorned with gold and on its walls are passages from the sacred writings. The domes are all gold, both inside and outside and the latter covered with lamps of all colours whose reflections mingled in the pool below created a scene as delicate as it was beautiful. Illuminated fish of extraordinary size glided on the gently heaving bosom of the glittering lake and there were also several boats and barges brilliantly illuminated floating on the surface' (weekly edn, 31 Jan. 1867, p. 4). Little is known about Captain Stretton except that he ran commercial studios in Bombay and Calcutta in the 1870s, and his photographs of cotton cultivation in Western India were in the 1873 Vienna Universal exhibition.
[DP, with thanks to John Falconer for information on Captain Stretton]

16 'Golden gate of Entrance – Near View' (plate 225)
Albumen print. Felice Beato. Amritsar, *c*.1858–60. Neg. no. U7. H. 24.6 cm; W. 28.5 cm
80092

Beato seems to be the only photographer who took 'near views' of the Harmandir, and they demonstrate his skill in capturing architectural details with clarity and depth. The

architectural historian, James Fergusson, felt that Europe could learn from India's attention to architectural decoration, having recognised at an early stage the importance of photography for recording India's monuments. Fergusson was responsible for the inclusion of some 500 photographs in the 1867 Paris Universal Exhibition, shown in the Fine Arts Division of the British Section under the heading 'History of Labour', to 'best illustrate the progress of industry in the British dominions' (*Paris Universal Exhibition, 1867*, British Section, Fine Arts Division London). Fergusson wrote the first comprehensive history of Indian architecture (J. Fergusson, *Illustrations of various styles of Indian Architecture*, London, 1870) and used woodcuts and lithographs taken from photographs, and later the photographs themselves, to illustrate his books. [DP]

17 'Golden Gate and Entrance to the Temple' (plate 224)
Albumen print. Felice Beato. Amritsar, *c*.1858–60. Neg. no. U6. H. 25 cm; W. 28.5 cm
80088

This is a view from the Harmandir of the causeway leading towards the entrance gate.

18 'View through the Piazza (marble), with Golden Lamps leading to the Sikh Temple' (plate 48)
Albumen print. Felice Beato. Amritsar, *c*.1858–60. Neg. no. U13. H. 23.7 cm; W. 28.5 cm
80094

19 'Baba Atal's Temple – The Sacred Temple – East View' (plate 33)
Albumen print. Felice Beato. Amritsar, *c*.1858–60. Neg. no. U2. H. 23.2 cm; W. 27.9 cm
80093

20 'The Akal Boonga – The Sacred Temple – North View'
Albumen print. Felice Beato. Amritsar, *c*.1858–60. Neg. no. U1. H. 20 cm; W. 28.4 cm
80096

After the Indian army 'mutinied' in 1857 Felice Beato travelled through India photographing the sites connected with it. Although there had

been incidents in Amritsar, it was not a 'Mutiny' site such as Lucknow and Delhi. In all, Beato took eleven photographs of the Harmandir from different viewpoints. In the bottom right hand corner of this print is Beato's negative number U1, which corresponds to Hering's catalogue advertising the sale of his work. It has been suggested that the numbers were put onto the negatives after Beato had left India and that these prints are therefore of a later date. Ten of the 17 views of Amritsar offered for sale were displayed in the Paris Universal Exhibition of 1867; the V&A has 11 of the 17 views, three of which were displayed in Paris and retain their original 1867 mounts marked with their 1867 catalogue numbers.

PUBLISHED: Hering, H., *Paris Universal Exhibition, 1867*, British Section, Fine Arts Division. (London) p.35. [DP with thanks to Mark Haworth-Booth, Sophie Gordon and Victoria Hamilton.]

21 'Interior – The Sikh Temple – Marble Mosaic' (plate 49)
Albumen print. Felice Beato. Amritsar, *c*.1858–60. H. 28 cm; W. 23.7 cm
80091

The inscription above the doorway of the Harmandir reads 'The great Guru in His wisdom looked upon Maharaja Ranjit Singh as his chief servitor and Sikh, and in his benevolence, bestowed on him the privilege of serving the temple' (P. Singh, 1988, p. 103). This image was used by Fergusson in *Illustrations of Various Styles of Indian Architecture*. He wrote 'It shows great splendour, but a marked decline in taste from the temples erected in India proper, either contemporaneously, or at an earlier date' (pl. 15). Francesca Wilson gave the more popular opinion when she referred to it as one of the 'great sights of the Punjab . . . it is so unique, so unlike anything but itself that nobody should be within 200 miles of it and not visit it' (Wilson, 1876, chap. 2). The photograph corresponds to Beato's negative number U8 though the number itself does not appear on the print. [DP]

22 'Street – Inside Sacred Tank Area' (plate 222)
Albumen print. Felice Beato. Amritsar, *c*.1858–60. Neg. no. U10. H. 28.4 cm; W. 23.7 cm
80089

This view of the area near the entrance to the Harmandir shows the side of the gateway, with a group of people seeking shade underneath Guru Arjun Dev's tree, the Lachi Ber. It was displayed in the 1867 Paris Universal Exhibition and retains its original mount. [DP]

23 'The Great Square, Amritsar' (plate 34)
Albumen print. Photographer unknown. Amritsar, *c*.1880s.
H. 20.9 cm; W. 27.8 cm
British Library: Photo 50/2 (55)

In this photograph, the eye is led towards the Akal Takht. The first Akal Takht ('Throne of the Almighty'), was built by Guru Hargobind opposite the entrance to the causeway of the Harmandir and was originally an earthen embankment with a raised brick platform (P. Singh, 1988, p. 57). It was intended to provide a seat of authority to deal with worldly matters, which would then allow the Harmandir to retain its spiritual supremacy. Here, the Guru would meet those who came to see him for guidance, and representatives of the Sikhs could assemble to make decisions about the Sikh nation as a whole. The Akal Takht was destroyed by the Afghans in 1762, but rebuilt in 1774. In the 19th century it became the five-storeyed building embellished with gold seen in this photograph, but was irreparably damaged in 1984 during 'Operation Blue Star'. It was again rebuilt, and the courtyard remains the gathering place for all important events including celebrations of the birthdays of the Gurus. [DP]

71 Parashurama leads Krishna and Balarama towards Mount Gomanta (plate 116)
Gouache and gold on paper. Ascribed to Purkhu of Kangra. Folio from a *Harivamsa* series of *c*.1800–1815.
H. 35.2 cm; W. 47.6 cm
Government Museum and Art Gallery, Chandigarh: 3171

Purkhu, who worked for the royal house of Kangra and later established contact with the Sikh chiefs in the Panjab plains, chooses an episode from the text which is not often painted. Krishna and Balarama flee from a determined enemy and seek the help of the warrior sage Parashurama, who advises them to bide their time and take refuge in the safety of the Gomanta mountain. The sage and the two brothers are in the bottom right-hand corner, identified by *devanagari* inscriptions, but the rest of the painting is occupied by the mountain, a place where wondrous things happen and semi-divine figures dwell, unmindful of the grinding world of mortals. Small vignettes of life are fitted into spaces between peaks and lotus-filled valleys. The mountain is brilliantly conceived, the richness of the colouring and exuberance of the human, animal and bird life compensating for the rendering of figures in a slightly summary fashion. [BNG]

PUBLISHED: Goswamy and Fischer, 1992, cat. 164.

72 Wedding procession of Prince Anirudh Chand of Kangra (plate 115)
Gouache and gold on paper. Ascribed to Purkhu of Kangra, *c*.1800–1805.
H. 35 cm; W. 48 cm
Government Museum and Art Gallery, Chandigarh: 353

The painting is celebratory, saturated with colour and filled with the air of princely festivity that characterises the paintings done by Purkhu and other members of his family for Sansar Chand, the great ruler of Kangra, much of whose power was first eroded and then supplanted by Maharaja Ranjit Singh. Prince Anirudh Chand was the heir-apparent to the throne of Kangra and this wedding procession is evidently on its way to the bride's home. The prince, barely fifteen years of age, rides in a palanquin of the

kind favoured for princely bridegrooms in the hills, the top pole of which bears a Persian inscription identifying him: *Sri Maharaj Kunwar Anirudh Chand ji*. His father, seen towards the bottom of the painting, is the most magnificently dressed personage in the procession, with his turban jewels and scarlet attire. Other figures - members of the family or the most important guests - are also identified through inscriptions, many of which are now rubbed. The focus of the painting is the young bridegroom, clad in a gold *jama*, heavily bejewelled, the chaplet of flowers, pearl strings and gold pieces meant to cover the face here pushed to the side. [BNG]

PUBLISHED: Randhawa, 1961, fig. 22; Goswamy and Fischer, 1992, cat. 163.

73 Rama's court with his brothers Hanuman, Jamavanta and others in attendance (plate 103)
Painting on cotton. From a Mankot workshop (?), second half of the 18th century. H. approx. 125 cm; W. approx. 185 cm
Sheesh Mahal Museum and Medal Gallery, Patiala

As Rama holds court in Ayodhya, musicians play, retainers bustle about and elephants bow in homage. Only the architectural setting is reserved by the painter of this finely painted textile for the women of the royal household. Stylistically, the elements are mixed, recalling both Mankot and Chamba, but the work evidently reached the Panjab plains, possibly exercising some influence there. [BNG]

74 A Sikh ruler shooting wild boar from a platform (plate 112)
Gouache and gold on paper. Pahari, possibly Nurpur, *c*.1820–30.
H. 27.3 cm; W. 36.6 cm
Kapany Collection

The figures in this painting, tantalisingly anonymous, are predominantly Sikhs but include a number of Hindus, wearing the same style of turban but with clearly depicted cut hair. Matchlock muskets of similar type are illustrated in plates 158 and 159. [SS]

75 A Sikh sardar sits outside an armoury with a child (plate 153)
Gouache and gold on paper. Pahari, *c*.1840. H. 31.5 cm; W. 25.5 cm
Chester Beatty Library, Dublin: MS 58.25

This enigmatic scene seems to depict a ruler, who is offering a turban jewel, an emblem of royalty, to a boy (?his heir). The setting may be the royal storehouse, or *toshkhana*, where the money, jewels, and precious Kashmir shawls surrounding them are being issued or taken in, a clerk at right keeping account of the proceedings. The catalogues of the auctions which dispersed the Lahore *toshkhana* in 1850–51 (see p. 87) show the typical range of material stored, from weapons and armour to jewels and luxury fabric. [SS]

PUBLISHED: Leach, 1995, vol. II, cat. 11.128 (illus. p. 1093).

76 School scene
Gouache on paper. Panjab, *c*.1800–1810. H. 28.1 cm; W. 21.6 cm
IS 20-1952. From the collection of P. C. Manuk and Miss G. M. Coles

This narrative painting incorporates two distinct scenes. The foreground depicts a courtyard in which a teacher blesses a child, his father or guardian sitting behind him, and seven other pupils nearby. An eighth is being punished by having to stand in the *kukkar*, or 'cockerel' position: looping his arms around his legs, he bends to hold his ears. A book being read by one of the pupils is in Arabic script, but this does not seem to be a religious school as the variety of headgear worn suggests different communities. The second scene, at upper right, shows the same courtyard in abbreviated form, the teacher watching as the pupil and his guardian walk away. [KS]

77 A Sikh youth dallying with his consort (plate 122)
Gouache on paper. Kangra style, *c*.1840. H. 18 cm; W. 13.8 cm
Chester Beatty Library, Dublin: MS 58.15.

PUBLISHED: Leach, 1995, vol. II, cat. 11.127, pp. 1094–5.

TEXTILES

78 Coverlet (*rumal*) (plate 147)
Cotton embroidered with floss silk. Himachal Pradesh, probably Chamba, late 18th century. L. 95 cm; W. 95 cm
AEDTA, Paris: 2633

The fine embroideries done in Chamba and other hill states are closely comparable to local miniature painting styles and were probably designed and drawn by artists to be embroidered by professional embroiderers. While the themes of the designs are often religious or mythical, with stories of Krishna especially popular, hunting and courtly subjects are also found. This piece is unusually lively in its treatment of animals and humans, and is exceptionally finely embroidered, with both sides equally finished. [RC]

79 Coverlet (*rumal*)
Cotton embroidered with floss silk. Himachal Pradesh, probably Chamba, late 18th or early 19th century.
H. 68 cm; W. 124 cm
IS 2096-1883

Coverlets from the Panjab hill states were often made for use at weddings, and marriage rituals and celebrations are consequently popular subjects for their designs. This depicts the marriage of Krishna and Rukmini, with Krishna appearing beside the marriage *mandapa* (canopy) and again at the top of the scene. Rukmini, at the head of a procession of ladies, enters the *mandapa* on the other side of the ritual fire where the multi-headed god Brahma is seated above his goose vehicle. Vishnu and Shiva are also present, together with their vehicles Garuda and Nandi, and Ganesh is at the centre of the scene. The style of this embroidery, and particularly the group of seated musicians, relates to Pahari paintings. A *rumal* in Baroda Museum shows a very similar wedding scene, and it has been suggested that it could have been made for a wedding between a prince of Chamba and a princess of Jammu in 1783 AD (see Goetz (1945-6). This may have been made at the same time. [RC]

PUBLISHED: Guy and Swallow (eds.), 1990, pl. 129.

METALWORK

80 Punch dagger (*katar*) (plate 156)

Steel, chiselled and pierced with traces of silver and gold overlay. Panjab Hills, early 19th century. L. 32 cm.
L. blade 20.9 cm
Royal Armouries, Leeds: XXVID. 62

The blade is chiselled with a different scene on either side, both of which were once overlaid with gold to emphasise jewellery, details of textiles and facial features. On one side, Krishna sits on a hexagonal *takht*, or throne, playing his flute to the three milkmaids (*gopis*) next to him, and a fourth below. Two cows seem to smile at the god as they look up at him. On the other side, Krishna sits on his throne with the monkey-god Hanuman approaching from the left; on the right are a lion and two ladies, one of whom kneels before Krishna. These motifs relate stylistically to those on Chamba *rumals*, particularly in details such as the throne, and Krishna's three-pointed crown. The inner surfaces of the side-bars of the hilt are decorated with motifs including a crane, pavilions, temples and palm trees, all overlaid with silver; the outer surfaces bear the avatars of Vishnu. [SS]

UNPUBLISHED.

81 Punch dagger (*katar*) (plate 157)

Steel, chiselled and pierced with traces of gold overlay. Panjab Hills (?); late 18th or early 19th century (?).
L. 41.8 cm. L. blade 22.5 cm
Royal Armouries, Leeds: XXVID. 85

The decoration chiselled on this dagger derives from the Iranian tradition. On one side of the blade Rustam, one of the heroes of Iran's great literary work, Ferdowsi's 10th-century *Shah Nama*, or Book of Kings, fights a lion, clutching a buckler which has four circular bosses and a cresent moon at the top. To the left, a lion attacks an elephant. On the other side, Rustam is again shown, but has changed his *jama* and boots for a tight top edged with gold, and narrow trousers. The hilt is decorated with flower heads, undulating lines and chevrons, all overlaid with gold. [SS]

UNPUBLISHED.

THE COURT OF MAHARAJA RANJIT SINGH

THE TREASURY

82 The Golden Throne of Maharaja Ranjit Singh (plate 91)

Sheets of gold worked in repoussé, chased and engraved, over a wooden core. Made by Hafez Muhammad Multani. Lahore, *c*.1820–30.
H. approx. 93 cm
2518 (IS)

Hafez Muhammad Multani, a leading goldsmith of the Lahore court, is mentioned twice in Dr John Login's inventories made at Annexation in 1849, which incorporated detailed information from the treasurer, Misr Makraj. They note that Hafez Muhammad made the throne, and that a saddle-drum decorated by him was still in the *toshkhana*. Lord Dalhousie was unsure if the East India Company would want the throne: 'It is set apart as an object which the court [of the East India Company] would probably desire to preserve, but as it is bulky, I shall not forward it until I received orders to do so' (BL: P/19/22, India Political Consultations, 20–27 Dec. 1850, no. 109). The Company did wish to preserve it: in 1853 the throne travelled to Calcutta, where Dalhousie had it copied in wood before it was shipped to London for the Indian Museum. In 1879, the throne moved to the South Kensington Museum (later named the V&A), where it has remained ever since. [SS]

PUBLISHED: in all general guides to the Indian section; specifically discussed in Skelton et al., 1982, cat. 571, p. 168; Guy and Swallow (eds.), 1990, p. 191.

83 Seal ring of Maharaja Ranjit Singh (plate 81)

Inscribed emerald set in gold. Amritsar or Lahore, dated VS 1869/ AD 1812–13. Emerald: H. 2.2 cm; W. 1.4 cm. Bezel: H. 2.2 cm
Kapany Collection

The ring's velvet-lined case has two brass plaques, the first inscribed: RING OF RANJIT SINGH THE LION OF PUNJAB

'kal sahai ranjit singh 1809' 'With the help of the Eternal One Ranjit Singh 1809 this ring has sealed many death warrants' and the second: 'Given to Sir David Salomons by Robert T Lattey Esq.' Robert Lattey was presumably connected with the firm of Lattey Bros., organiser of the series of auctions in Lahore in 1850 and 1851 that disposed of the 'confiscated property' of the Sikh kingdom. Some of the catalogues were later privately reprinted by Maharaja Dalip Singh as part of his campaign against the British Government, but no ring of Ranjit Singh is specifically mentioned in this incomplete series. The Gurmukhi inscription actually reads 'akal sahai [God is Great, or Victory to God], ranjit singh 1869 [AD 1812]'. [SS/NK]

84 The 'Timur Ruby' (plates 64 amd 93)

Inscribed spinel of 352.5 carats, and three smaller spinels, on a necklace of gold and diamonds made by Garrard of London in 1853
Lent by Her Majesty the Queen.
Given to Queen Victoria by the Honourable East India Company in 1851

The beautiful rose-pink gemstone usually referred to as a ruby is the gemmologically distinct spinel, and was probably mined in Badakhshan. The Persian inscriptions testify to its having been owned by the Mughal emperors Jahangir, Shah Jahan, Aurangzeb and Farrukhsiyar, as well as the Iranian ruler Nadir Shah, and Ahmad Shah, the Durrani ruler of Afghanistan. The dates on it range from 1612 to 1771. There is no mention of Timur, the great Central Asian ruler and ancestor of the Mughal emperors whose erroneous association with this stone, followed without exception by western jewellery historians, is based on a study which misinterpreted the longest inscription. This took the title 'Lord of the Conjunction' to mean Timur. The study also assumed that all references

PHOTOGRAPHS

175 'Maharajah Duleep Singh' (plate 179)
Salted paper print by the Prince of Wales, July 1856; carbon copy print by Hughes and Mullins, 1889.
H. 25.3 cm; W. 17.5 cm
Windsor Castle, Royal Photograph Collection: Photographic portraits vol. 1/59 (1853–1857), p. 104

The Prince of Wales was 14 when he visited Dalip Singh at the Roehampton residence of the Logins on 7 June 1856 and took this photograph; at the same time, Dalip Singh, who was a few years older, took a photograph of the prince. They may well have been experimenting with the camera under the influence of Prince Albert who, like Queen Victoria, displayed a genuine enthusiasm for photography. They became Patrons of the Photographic Society when it was set up in 1853, collected prints, and were taught to use the camera, probably by Dr Becker. By 1855 Windsor Castle had its own portable photographic portrait room and darkroom.   [DP with thanks to Frances Dimond]

176 'Duleep Singh on the lower terrace at Osborne' (plate 180)
Salted paper print by Dr Becker, 1854. Carbon copy print by Hughes & Mullins, 1889. H. 17.4 cm; W. 25.4 cm
Windsor Castle, The Royal Photograph Collection: *Photographic Portraits*, vol. 1/59 (1853–7) p. 40.

Shortly after his arrival in England, Dalip Singh was invited by Queen Victoria to visit her at Osborne House. He spent four days there in August, 1854, during which time the queen and the young princes became very fond of him. The photographer Dr Becker was the German secretary and librarian to Prince Albert and a founder member of the Photographic Society of London. He introduced photography to the royal family and bought photographic equipment for them. He was an enthusiastic amateur and took photographs of the young princes dressed in Indian costumes that were probably given to them by Dalip Singh.   [DP]

PUBLISHED: Dimond and Taylor, 1987, p. 112; Alexander and Arnand, 1980, pl. 11.

177 Royal shooting party (plate 185)
Albumen print. J. W. Clarke.
8 Dec.1876, Elveden Hall.
H. 20.3 cm; W. 27.9 cm
Windsor Castle, The Royal Photograph Collection

When Dalip Singh acquired Elveden Hall in 1863 it already had a good reputation for partridge shooting and by 1867 he had made it one of the best sporting estates in the country. The maharaja, rated the fourth best shot in England, held regular shooting parties and his guests usually included the Prince of Wales and other members of the aristocracy. The maharaja is seen here seated on the ground with his two sons, Frederick on the left and Victor Albert on the right. Seated from left to right are the Duke of Atholl, Earl de Grey and the Marquis of Bowmont, with the Prince of Wales and the Maharani Bamba, and others, sitting on chairs. The maharaja must have used the local photographic company 'Imperial J. W. Clarke' of Bury St Edmunds whenever the need arose, and J. W. Clarke took other photographs of shooting parties, as well as cartes-de-visite of him and his family.   [DP, with thanks to Frances Dimond for identifying the individuals in the photograph]

178 Page of *cartes-de-visite*: 'The Maharaja Duleep Singh'; 'Maharanee Bamba, wife of the Maharaja Duleep Singh'; 'Bamba, daughter of the Maharaja Duleep Singh'; 'Catherine, daughter of the Maharaja Duleep Singh' (plate 186)
J. W. Clarke, London, 1877.
Image size H. 10.5 cm; W. 6.4 cm
Windsor Castle, The Royal Photograph Collection: *Photographic Portraits*, vol. 71.

The *carte-de-visite* was first popularised in Paris by André Adolphe Disderi and was introduced to England in the late 1850s. In 1860 J. E. Mayall, one of the best portrait photographers of the time, issued his 'Royal Album' of *cartes* and started a craze for nobility and celebrities to have their photographs taken. This page taken from an album assembled by Queen Victoria shows Dalip Singh and his family in western dress. The photographs reflect their assimilation into English society. Dalip

Singh became an English landowner in 1863 when he acquired Elveden Hall to which he brought his new wife Bamba to live in 1864. He mixed with English nobility, became a member of the most fashionable clubs in London and was nominated to stand for a seat in the House of Commons. By 1873 he is said to have worn western dress 'on all but the grandest of occasions'   [DP]

PUBLISHED: Alexander and Anand, 1980, pl. 29.

179 Page of *cartes-de-visite*: 'Dhuleep Singh, Maharajah di Lahore' by Mayall; 'Maharanee Dhuleep Singh' by Claudet; 'Maharajah de Putteala' by Bourne and Shepherd; 'Begum de Bopal' by Bourne and Shepherd (plate 184)
Each image H. 9 cm; W. 5.3 cm
2831 to 2834-1934. Given by Miss O. Pasqui

The introduction of *cartes-de-visite* in the 1850s enabled the public to own photographs of royalty and celebrities, and during the 1860s millions of the royal family in particular were sold. Queen Victoria herself was responsible for 'cartomania' or 'cardomania', the craze for collecting and arranging *cartes* in albums (O. Mathews, 1974). In India, Samuel Bourne found that the 'carte-de-visite is as popular as in England' when he arrived in Calcutta in 1863 (Bourne, 1863, p. 269). This page is from a two-volume album set, one containing photographs of royalty from around the world and the other European aristocracy. The non-European album included photographs of nobility in their national costumes. The *cartes* of Dalip Singh with his turban and jewels, and his wife in the dress she wore on her first visit to Windsor in November 1865 when Queen Victoria described her as 'beautifully dressed in Indian stuffs, covered with splendid jewels and pearls' (Alexander and Anand, 1980, p. 113) were probably favoured by this collector for their exoticism.   [DP]

180 'Maharajah Duleep Singh' (plate 183)
Albumen print. Horne, Thornthwaite & Wood. London, *c*.1854. H. 14 cm; W. 11 cm
Ph. 192-1982

Dalip Singh converted to Christianity in 1851 and rid himself of one of the distinguishing features of his discarded Sikh faith: his long hair. He is said to have presented his cut hair to Mrs Login, the wife of his guardian (Alexander and Anand, 1980, p. 31). This photograph was taken shortly after his arrival in England in 1854 and is unusual in showing him in western dress as well as shorn hair. Fallon Horne was an important portraitist and the firm enjoyed the patronage of Queen Victoria, enlarging transparencies from her own negatives and supplying the royal family with cameras and chemicals. The firm was one of many that began to operate in the early 1850s, the popularity of studio photography being such that by 1857 there were 155 firms in London alone.   [DP, with thanks to Mark Haworth-Booth and Frances Dimond]

THE CONTINUING TRADITIONS 1849–1900

PAINTINGS AND BOOK ILLUSTRATION

181 Maharaja Karam Singh of Patiala (r. 1813–45) and his son, Narinder (plate 188)

Gouache and gold on paper. Patiala, c.1840. Page: H. 27.6 cm; W. 20 cm. Painting: H. 18.4 cm; W. 12.5 cm
Kapany Collection

The Gurmukhi inscription gives Karam Singh's name and title; the identical clothes of both figures suggest the boy is his son. Patiala was an important cultural centre from its foundation in 1752 by Baba Ala Singh (1691–1765); its impressive fort, Qila Mubarak, with its carved wooden doorways (plate 196) and painted interiors, still stands and was begun in 1763. Raja Karam Singh built shrines in honour of the Gurus, making endowments for their maintenance, and reconstructed the old Saifabad Fort outside Patiala, renaming it Bahadurgah after Guru Tegh Bahadur. His son further developed the town, adding buildings such as the Motibagh Palace which followed the design of the renowned Shalimar Gardens in Lahore, and the Shish Mahal Palace. [SS]

PUBLISHED: Sotheby's London, 28 April 1981, lot. 130; Topsfield, 1986, pp. 49–50, pl. 29.

182 Eight Sikhs, courtiers and servants of the Raja of Patiala (plate 198)

Watercolour on paper. By a Delhi artist. Delhi or Patiala, probably c.1817. H. 22.1 cm; W. 30.61 cm

James Baillie Fraser (1783–1856) joined his brother William (1784–1835) in India in 1815 and was almost immediately inspired to try and draw the scenery and people he saw. The lapsed amateur artist was frustrated by his inability to draw figures, and instructed an Indian artist to do this for him. A larger project developed, involving both brothers and lasting from 1815 to 1820, in which the best local artists were employed to record scenes around Delhi, and the village of Rania in Haryana, where William's Indian family lived. When his official duties took him to Patiala in 1817, during Karam Singh's reign, he took the opportunity to have portraits of the royal servants made. [SS]

PUBLISHED: Falk, 1988, no. 6, p. 6 (illus. p. 10) and p. 4; Bailey, 1991, cat. 86, pp. 85–6.

183 The Guru Granth Sahib carried in procession before Maharaja Narinder Singh (r. 1845–62) (plate 200b; details plates 187 and 200a)

Gouache and gold on paper. Patiala, c.1850. H. approx. 100 cm; W. approx 110 cm
Sheesh Mahal, Museum and Medal Gallery Patiala

Maharaja Narinder Singh's artistic patronage ensured that the cultural life of Patiala flourished during his reign. This extraordinary processional scene provides a glimpse of a school of painting that is almost unkown, even to historians of Indian art (see chap. 10).

PUBLISHED: S.P. Srivastava, 1991, pl.128.

184 Lady watching the moon go by (plate 192)

Gouache and gold on paper. Folio possibly from a Rasikapriya series. Kapurthala(?), c.1850. H. 28.5 cm; W. 23 cm
Government Museum and Art Gallery, Chandigarh: 1772

The devanagari inscription on the top border almost certainly belongs to a verse from some rhetorical text in Hindi, possibly Keshadeva's classic, the Rasikapriya. The context is not easily established from this fragment, but the nayika, a love-lorn virahini, may be addressing Chandra, the moon-god, as he traverses the heavens in his antelope-driven chariot. Her two female companions remark upon her distracted state. There is an atmosphere of quietness produced by the star-studded night and the still, unpopulated architecture. The group of trees below are silent witnesses to the exchange between the nayika and the moon-god. The painting comes from a series done in the Panjab plains and is believed to have been in the Kapurthala royal collection. There are echoes of the style of the Seu-Nainsukh family of Pahari master painters in the facial types of the women, their stance, and the architecture, but there is some stiffness in the work. The painting is nevertheless affecting, the unlikely encounter and the still atmosphere giving it a distinctly poetic feeling. [BNG]

PUBLISHED: Paul, 1985.

185 A tree springs to life (plate 191)

Gouache and gold on paper. Folio possibly from a Rasikapriya series. Kapurthala(?), c.1850. H. 23.7 cm; W. 17.3 cm
Government Museum and Art Gallery, Chandigarh: 1777

The setting is sylvan, with tall trees at the back and a stream flowing through a range of low, undulating rocks at the bottom, and three attractive young women in its midst. There is no indication of the text on which the work is based, but it seems that the lakshanas (the characteristic or cognitive attributes) of a nayika are being discussed by the two women on the right. The reference is perhaps to the wonderful and ancient myth in which a dried-up tree springs into life at the mere touch of a perfect woman. Since the striking of the trunk of such a tree with the foot is specifically mentioned in early descriptions, it may be that the painter has rendered a young and lissom nayika doing precisely that. The tree, placed perfectly at the heart of the painting, stands out from all the vegetation around it, laden with rich, brilliantly coloured blossoms as if by a magical suddenness. The other flowering shoots in the work do not grow on the trees: they are flowering creepers winding around their trunks. This tree, enlivened by the nayika's touch, is the only one which flowers on its own. The painting belongs to the same series as cat. 184, and is said to have come from the Kapurthala royal collection. [BNG]

PUBLISHED: Paul, 1985.

186 Salhotar, or Kitab-e asp namah, a treatise on farriery (plate 203)

Illustrations by Kishan Singh. Kapurthala, AH 1268/AD 1851–2. 42 folios, 17 paintings, 15 lines per page in nasta'liq script with headings, captions and key words in red ink. H. 32.5 cm; W. 20.5 cm
British Library, London: Or. 6704

The treatise on the classification, care and diseases of horses was translated into Persian from Sanskrit by Khwajah 'Abdullah Khan during the reign of Shah Jahan (1628–56). Descended from a famous Muslim holy man of the Naqshbandi order, 'Abdullah Khan came to India during the reign of Akbar (1556–1605) and held high rank under Jahangir and Shah Jahan. The author states that his copy of the Sanskrit text was part of the spoils won after the defeat of Rana Amar Singh of Mewar in 1613, and was translated for him by a group of pandits. This copy was made in the princely state of Kapurthala in 1851–2 during Maharaja Randhir Singh's reign (r. 1852–70). The illustrations of stallions and their grooms are by Kishan Singh, a Kapurthala painter related to the famous Amritsar artist Kehar Singh, and the younger brother of the Amritsar painter Bishan Singh (for two of his paintings, not attributed in the catalogue, see Canby, 1998, pp. 185–6). Various members of his family were known for their miniature and mural painting, and some were employed at the Golden Temple complex. Kishan Singh may have been in Maharaja Sher Singh's service and exhibited an album of watercolours at the 1864 Lahore exhibition of arts and crafts. [JD]

PUBLISHED: Titley, 1977, p. 2; Losty, 1982, cat. 139, p. 154.

187 A study of a hawk (plate 199)

Ink and watercolour on paper. By Kapur Singh. Panjab, third quarter of the 19th century. H. 21.9 cm; W. 18.2 cm.
Government Museum and Art Gallery, Chandigarh: L-80

The hawk sits on a little perch, leather thongs securing its legs to the base. Its details are well observed: its body is erect, its eyes sharp, alertness runs through its entire frame. Attached to the leather thongs are small brass bells that would sound at the slightest movement. The bird of prey is obviously trained, ready to take wing the moment it is released. Kapur Singh, who was active in the Panjab plains, had obviously seen European works and studied the European technique of watercolour paintings, but also seems to have had other models in mind, like the work of the great Mughal painters of fauna and, closer to home, some of the Pahari masters. This drawing stands out from the many he made of birds and animals for, even if it lacks the penetration of the Mughal master Mansur, it is a sympathetic work, rendered with sharpness and a keen, fluent line. [BNG]

PUBLISHED: Paul, 1985, p. 97 and fig. 29.

188 Sikh ladies riding in a covered carriage (plate 41)

Watercolour and gold on paper. By Kapur Singh. Probably Amritsar, dated vs 1931/AD 1874. Page: H. 46.5 cm; W. 59.6 cm. Painting: H. 36.9 cm; W. 49.8 cm
British Museum, London: 1997-6-16-01. Formerly in the collection of Lord Hobhouse (1819–1904)

The deceptively simple painting provides a wealth of detail of Panjabi life. The focus of the scene is the group of ladies and a child, passing a Hindu temple and a couple visiting a holy man in the background, riding on a cart pulled by bullocks, the dust rising around them. They all wear gold jewellery, including the little boy, and the weight of the multiple pearl earrings the ladies wear makes the tops of their ears curve over. Shade is provided by scarlet canopies supported by turned wooden poles, their bright colours probably produced by an application of lac rather than paint, as this is one of the traditional crafts of the Panjab. The inscription above the painting, written in gold Gurmukhi script, records that the painter Kapur Singh, son of Kishan Singh, worked in the Ahluwalia quarter of Amritsar. [SS]

PUBLISHED: Sotheby's, London, *The Indian Sale*, Thursday 8 May 1997, lot 202.

189 Maharaja Sangat Singh, ruler of Jind (plate 25)

Gouache on paper. Panjab plains, late 19th century. H. 26.8 cm; W. 19.2 cm
Government Museum and Art Gallery, Chandigarh: 3687

Written on the border of the painting in Gurmukhi script are four lines of Hindi verse which translate: 'Beautiful is the turban which adorns his head, dyed in saffron, of the colour of Basant [yellow]; and equally beautiful, of the Basanti-yellow colour, is the *dukul* shawl draped around his form; appropriate and beautiful is the hawk that this princely son of Jit Singh, adorned also in the Basanti-yellow colour; it would seem as if everything around his auspicious self has turned Basanti-yellow in this wonderful season of Basant'. The work comes from the relatively small Sikh court of Jind in the 'cis-Sutlej' region, and has a distinctive flavour of its own. There is no attempt to establish any great sign of estate or grandeur: the painter places his patron against a plain ground, with the emphasis on the way he is dressed. Everything is drenched in the colour of the spring season, to which the verses, apparently composed for the occasion by the court poet, draw insistent attention. The ruler cuts a handsome figure, but the impression the painting makes is the result of its sumptuous colouring rather than sharp observation or any penetration of character. The work is difficult to ascribe to any well-known painters' workshop and may have been done by a local painter familiar with the work of the neighbouring areas of Patiala or Kapurthala. [BNG]

PUBLISHED: Paul, 1985, p. 68.

190 Raja Jaswant Singh of Nabha (r. 1783–1840) (plate 26)

Gouache and gold on paper with applied beetle-wings. Nabha (?), dated vs 1907/AD 1850. H. 15.7 cm; W. 10.7 cm
British Library, London: Add. Or. 2601

Jaswant Singh succeeded his father when he was eight and was under the guardianship of his stepmother, Mai Deso, assuming full responsibility on her death in 1790 (H. Singh, vol. II, p. 360). The Persian inscription has been read as 'Raja Jaswant Singh deceased ruler of Nabha, dated month of Sahawan, Samvat 1907 [AD 1850]' (Singh, Poovaya-Smith and Ponnapa, 1991, p. 80).

PUBLISHED: Singh, Poovaya-Smith and Ponnapa, 1991, cat. 22.

191 Raja Devinder Singh of Nabha (r. 1840–46) (plate 197)

Gouache and gold on paper with applied beetle-wings. Probably Nabha, c.1840–46. Page: H. 25.2 cm; W. 20.2 cm. Painting: H. 18 cm; W.13 cm
British Library, London: Add. Or. 2602

The dark green of the vegetation provides a dramatic background for the raja, who sits in his golden chair in a crimson robe flecked with gold against the white architecture of his palace. The style of the painting is similar to some of the works signed by Imam Bakhsh. [SS]

PUBLISHED:

192 Raja Jai Singh of Guler (r. 1878–84) with Prince Raghunath Singh and others (plate 132)

Gouache and gold on paper. Muhammad Baksh of Guler. Guler, late 19th century. H. 25.3 cm; W. 31.3 cm
Government Museum and Art Gallery, Chandigarh: 4.201

This painting done at Guler, the home of some of the greatest artists the Pahari area had produced, demonstrates that Pahari painting had finally succumbed to outside influences. There is nothing Pahari about this work: the line does not 'sing'; the colouring is strong and dissonant; the surface approximates the appearance of oil colours even though the medium is opaque watercolour; the grouping has no rhythm. Even the figures do not appear Pahari, everyone being dressed in 'Sikh' fashion, with voluminous turbans covering the ears, heavy Kashmiri *choga* coats, and loose *dopattas* draped around the neck. If the figures were not clearly identified as belonging to Guler, this might even be thought to be a Sikh court, were it not for the presence of the *huqqa* which the raja smokes, which would be inconceivable in a Sikh setting. The painter was probably an itinerant artist, familiar with European work and perhaps called in specifically to create a 'European-style' record of the ruler, the heir-apparent, and some of the important men at the much-diminished court at Guler. However conventionalised and theatrical-looking, his attempt here, perhaps even his commission, was to produce a sumptuous work, full of glitter and fading gold. [BNG]

PUBLISHED: Randhawa, 1953, fig. 17; Archer, 1960, col. pl. 99; Archer, 1973, vol. I, p. 169, illus. vol. II, p. 122; Paul, 1985, p.75.

193 Design for a wall painting

Gouache on paper. Probably Lahore; c.1880. H. 100 cm; W. 69 cm
IS 3-1998

Under John Lockwood Kipling's direction, the students of the Mayo School of Arts in Lahore copied fresco designs on mosque interiors in the city (Baqir, 1993, p. 352). The close relation to this design (one of a group of four probably acquired by Caspar Purdon Clarke during his purchasing trip to India for the South Kensington Museum in 1881–2), to architectural decoration in Amritsar (Kang, 1977), 30 miles away, suggests Lahore was not the sole source of inspiration. The drawing is labelled (wrongly) 'The Golden Temple, Amritsar' in the hand of Caspar Stanley Clarke (Purdon Clarke's son, and successor as head of the Indian Department). [SS]

UNPUBLISHED.

194 Two designs for shawls (plates 133a and b)

Ink and gouache on paper. Kashmir, c.1880. H. 57.6 cm; W. 25.7 cm and 25.2 cm
06600&A (IS)

These highly stylised *buta* or 'Paisley' patterns show how far the Kashmir shawl had evolved under European influence from the simple floral designs of the late 17th century, and would probably have been intended for a shawl combining woven and embroidered elements. [RC]

PUBLISHED: Irwin, 1973, fig. 5 (wrongly identified as IM 32-1924).

TEXTILES

195 Shawl
Embroidered pashmina. Kashmir,
c.1870. L 229 cm; W. 198 cm
IS 31-1970.
Given by Mrs Estelle Fuller

This extraordinary shawl is
embroidered with a map of Srinagar,
the Kashmiri capital, and includes the
river Jhelum running through the
heart of the city, Lake Dal to the
north, the main mosques, streets,
bazaars and bridges, and the pleasure
gardens edging the lake. The stylised
plan is filled with people, trees and
animals, as well as the pleasure boats
on Lake Dal, one of which carries the
maharaja, probably Ranbir Singh,
Gulab Singh's third son (r.1857–85).
The Superintendent of the Jammu
Treasury reported that Ranbir Singh
commissioned two shawls depicting
maps of Kashmir in 1870 (Crill, 1993,
p. 94) and it is very likely that this is
one of them. Another comparable
shawl, perhaps the companion to this
one, is in the Sardar Pratap Singh
Museum in Srinagar. The two other
known map shawls are in the British
Royal Collection and the National
Gallery of Australia, Canberra. [RC]
PUBLISHED: Irwin, 1973, pls. 42–4;
Crill, 1993.

196 Shawl (plate 134)
Pashmina. Kashmir, c.1870.
L. 350 cm; W. 144 cm
IS 119-1958. Given by the Dowager
Marchioness of Reading, GBE

The exaggerated and flamboyant
pattern and colours of this shawl are
typical of the late 19th-century pieces
made for the western market in
response to European, mainly French,
taste. Since the period of General
Allard's activities (around 1835),
European agents had supplied new
export designs to the Kashmiri shawl
weavers. One of these, Mr R.
Chapman, the agent for the French
company Oulman, reported 'At first . .
. much difficulty was experienced in
persuading the native designers to
alter or amend their patterns. They
were attached to their old style . . . but
now [c.1870] this difficulty has been
overcome and the weavers are willing
to adopt hints, in fact they now seldom
begin to work till the pattern has been
inspected or approved by the agent for

whom they work' (Baden-Powell,
1872, p. 44). The brilliant colours
were produced by artificial dyes, which
reached Kashmir about the mid-19th
century and were rapidly adopted by
the local dyers. [RC]
UNPUBLISHED.

197 Three robes (choga) for men:

**a Pashmina, embroidered with
gold-wrapped thread**
Kashmir or Lahore, c.1850–70.
L, 135 cm
IPN 2618

**b Pashmina embroidered with
wool (plate 142)**
Kashmir, c.1850–70. L. 135 cm
IS 1-1880

**c Cotton embroidered with
gold-wrapped thread**
Afghanistan, late 19th century.
L. 127 cm
1018-1898

Loose-fitting robes like these were
worn by men throughout much of
northern India during the later 19th
century and into the 20th. The shawlcloth and the style of the embroidery
identify the first two as Kashmiri, or
alternatively from a centre such as
Lahore or Amritsar, where embroidery
of this type was also carried out on a
large scale. The third, also with
embroidery of similar style, was said
on acquisition to be from Afghanistan.
The choga has its origins in Turkish
Central Asia, where it is usually found
in a padded form, a usage reflected in
the Turkish word choqal, meaning a
coat of mail or a padded coat worn for
protection. [RC]
PUBLISHED: 203a: Gupta, 1996, pl. 95,
p. 152.

**198 Man's wrapped garment
(lungi) (plate 145)**
Silk with gold-wrapped thread.
Multan, c.1855. L 300 cm; W. 155 cm
0782 (IS)

Silk lengths with gold borders were
worn in a variety of ways in Panjab
and north-west India during the 19th
century, and were seen as turbans,
waist-sashes and draped round the
upper body. Yellow silk is known to
have been a favourite material of
Ranjit Singh and his successors, and
this example may have been used at
one of the Sikh courts. [RC]
UNPUBLISHED.

**199 Group of silk fragments
(plate 128: 7913 (IS); plate 146:
7247A (IS))**
Silk, some with gold-wrapped thread.
Panjab, mid-19th century
7247A (IS), 7244A (IS), 7637 (IS),
7913 (IS), 7258C (IS), 8100B (IS),
7792 (IS), 7910 (IS), 7265A (IS)

Silk fabrics, both plain and with
elaborate woven patterns, were
produced at several centres in the
Panjab, notably Amritsar, Lahore,
Patiala, Multan, Bahawalpur and
Jallandhar. These textiles were used
for luxurious garments, turbans and
furnishings. [RC]
UNPUBLISHED.

**200 Length of gold-printed
fabric**
Cotton stamped with gold. Panjab or
Rajasthan, mid-19th century.
L. 76 cm; W. 76 cm
6171 (IS)

Plain muslins with gold-stamped
patterns are frequently seen in
depictions of Sikh courtiers, used for
the inner robes (jama) worn under a
heavier choga, for trousers and as light
waistcloths. The gold patterns were
produced either by gold leaf stamped
on to an adhesive on the cotton cloth,
by ground gold mixed with gum arabic
printed directly on to the cloth or, in
the cheapest method, gold or other
metallic dust sprinkled on to adhesive
stamped on the cloth. This method is
still popular in north India today. [RC]
UNPUBLISHED.

**201 Two shawls (phulkari)
for women**

a (plate 148)
Cotton embroidered with floss silk.
Panjab, early 20th century. L. 264 cm;
W. 140 cm
AEDTA, Paris, no. 148

b (plate 149)
Cotton embroidered with floss silk.
Panjab, early 20th century. L. 264 cm;
W. 127 cm
AEDTA, Paris, no. 1558

While often considered to be the work
of rural Jat women in Panjab, phulkaris
were worn by Hindu, Muslim and
Sikh women at several levels of society.
Finely embroidered examples like
these may either have been made by
women for use in their own family or
commissioned from professional

female embroiderers by affluent urban
families, many of whom had
embroiderers employed in their
household. Densely embroidered
phulkaris are called baghs (gardens), and
were particularly associated with
weddings and other family
ceremonies. [RC]
PUBLISHED: 207a: Bérinstain, 1991,
p. 19; 207b: Bérinstain, 1991, p. 24.

METALWORK AND JEWELLERY

**202 Pair of perfume holders
(plate 23)**
Gold, cast, chased and engraved.
Panjab, c.1875. H. 13.1 cm;
diam. of base 5.3 cm
Presented by the Raja of Kapurthala
to the Prince of Wales. The Royal
Collection: 11317.1&2

The Prince of Wales travelled the
length of the Indian subcontinent,
including the Panjab, during his tour
of 1875–6, immediately before Queen
Victoria was proclaimed Empress of
India.
PUBLISHED: Clarke, 1898, p.16, nos.
247 and 248; illus. pl. between pp. 14
and 15.

203 Watch and chains (plate 21)
Demihunter watch by H. Grandjean
& Co., 18-carat gold, enamelled and
set with diamonds; the gold key set
with an emerald; the gold chains set
with diamonds and emeralds.
Watch: diam. 5.6 cm. H. 8 cm.
Chains: L approx. 67 cm
Presented by Mahinder Singh, GCSI,
Maharaja of Patiala (r. 1870–6), to the
Prince of Wales in 1876. The Royal
Collection: 11476-8

The enamelled portrait on the back of
the watch depicts the maharaja
wearing the Grand Cross of the Star
of India, copied exactly from the
photograph by Bourne & Shepherd
taken some time in the 1860s (see cat.
178) The lid of the watch is engraved
on the back 'Chatelain Montandon &
Cie. Watchmakers and jewellers to
H H the Maharajah of Patiala GCSI';
and the back of the case has an
engraved inscription noting it is
'warranted by C Marcks & Co.
Bombay and Poona'. [SS, with thanks
to Sat Kaur for identifying the source
of the portrait]

PUBLISHED: Clarke, 1898, nos. 111 and 112, illus. ('Case E') between pp. 6–7; Singh, Poovaya-Smith and Ponnapa, 1991, cat. 82 p. 90, illus. p. 58.

204   Address casket (plate 24)
Gold, set with diamonds, rubies and emeralds, lined with purple velvet embroidered with gold and silver wrapped thread. Amritsar, c.1876.
H. 8.3 cm; W. 32 cm; depth 12.3 cm
Presented by the city of Amritsar to HRH Albert Edward, Prince of Wales, in 1876. The Royal Collection: 11230

Three inscriptions on the lid repeat the English 'A[lbert]. E[dward]., Amritsar, 1876' in Arabic and Gurmukhi scripts, with the same date according to the Islamic and Vikramsamvat calendars. The lining is heavily worked in *zardozi* (gold embroidery); Amritsar was one of many centres specialising in this (Gupta, 1996). The casket was made for an illuminated address recording in Urdu and English the loyalty of Amritsar's inhabitants to Queen Victoria (English text in full in Singh, Poovaya-Smith and Ponnapa, 1991, p. 89). On his return to England, the prince arranged for all the Indian gifts to be displayed at the South Kensington Museum, and in 1877 at the Bethnal Green Museum. After travelling to Paris, Edinburgh, Glasgow, Aberdeen and York, the collection was installed at Marlborough House and Sandringham (Clarke and Birdwood, 1891). [SS]

PUBLISHED: Clarke, 1898, no. 253, p. 16; illus. pl. between pp. 14–15 ('Case L'); Singh, Poovaya-Smith, Ponnapa, 1991, cat. 79, p. 89).

205   Inscribed spinel of the Raja of Nabha (r. 1877–1911) (plate 22)
L. 4.6 cm; max W. 2.4 cm; wt. 123 carats
Presented to Edward VII by Raja (later Maharaja) Sir Hira Singh of Nabha. The Royal Collection: 11526

At the end of 1901 the Raja of Nabha asked James Dunlop Smith, the political agent of the Phulkian States and Bhahawalpur, to examine the 'ruby' he wished to present to Edward VII for his coronation as king-emperor. Dunlop Smith reported 'His Highness feels that, as a badge of the

Moghul Empire which is now under His Majesty's sway, it can properly belong to the Emperor of India' (Stronge, 1996, p. 10). Dunlop Smith later discovered the spinel had been taken by the Sikhs in 1763 when they defeated Zain Khan of Sirhind and divided his treasury between them, and had come into the possession of Raja Hamir Singh of Nabha. It stayed in Nabha until 1901. The Persian inscriptions record its previous illustrious owners: 'King Jahangir [son of] King Akbar AD 1608–9' (*jahangir shah-i akbar shah 1017* [AH]); Shah Jahan, 'Lord of the Second Conjunction' in 1628 or 1629 (*saheb qiran sani 1038* [AH]); and Aurangzeb, 'alamgir shahi 1070' [i.e. belonging to Aurangzeb, AD 1659–60]. The maharaja was one of Nabha's ablest rulers and, in addition to supporting the Khalsa College at Amritsar and establishing the Khalsa printing press in Lahore, was also the patron of M. A. Macauliffe, then writing his six-volume work, *The Sikh Religion* (H. Singh, vol. II, p. 276). [SS]

UNPUBLISHED.

206   Casket (plate 97)
Blued steel inlaid with gold. Sialkot, c.1880. H. 27.3 cm; max. diam. 20.3 cm
2411-1883 (IS). Bought by Caspar Purdon Clarke in India in 1881–2 for £19 5s.

The casket was designed by a student of the Mayo School of Art and made at Sialkot, a traditional centre of *kuftkari*, the overlaying of steel with gold. [SS]

UNPUBLISHED

ARMS AND ARMOUR

207   Sword and scabbard
Watered steel blade overlaid with gold; silver-gilt hilt inlaid with diamonds and set with rubies on the pommel; wooden scabbard covered with black velvet and embroidered with seed pearls, and with silver-gilt mounts set with diamonds. Probably Patiala, c.1875. L. approx. 87.5 cm; blade L. 7.3 cm; hilt L. 17.3 cm; scabbard L. 79 cm
The Royal Collection: 11303

The Maharaja of Patiala presented this sword to the Prince of Wales in

1876. The single-edged, curving sword has deeply-cut indentations on the back of the blade which at one point form the top of the head of a *makara* (mythical water beast); gold, overlaid on to the flat of the blade, gives emphasis to this detail.

PUBLISHED: Clarke, 1898, p. 16, no. 237 and illus. between pp. 14–15 ('Case L').

208   Punch dagger (*katar*) (plate 194)
Steel, chiselled and overlaid with gold. Patiala, possibly 18th century.
H. approx. 35 cm
Qila Mubarak Museum, Patiala: 73/13

The finely watered blade with armour-piercing point has a deeply chiselled sunflower on both sides, overlaid in gold, which is similar to motifs carved in wood or plaster in the Qila Mubarak, the fort founded in Patiala in 1763. [SS]

209   Saddle pommel
Silver, chased and partly gilt. Lahore, probably second quarter of 19th century.
H. 25 cm; W. 13.1 cm
05040 (IS)

The pommel entered the Indian Museum in 1855 as a piece from Lahore. [SS]

UNPUBLISHED.

EUROPEAN PAINTINGS, DRAWINGS AND PRINTED BOOKS

210   Camp scene in a rocky gorge in Kashmir (plate 204)
Pastel on paper. By George Landseer. Kashmir, 1860. Page: H. 51 cm; W. 71 cm. Painting: H. 25 cm; W. 35.2 cm
41-1881 2/3. Given by Mrs George Landseer

George Landseer (1834–78) was the nephew of Sir Edwin Landseer and natural son of the wife of the engraver Thomas Landseer. He set out for India in 1859 and appears to have stayed there for fifteen years, travelling all over the subcontinent. Much of his time was spent making portraits in oils of the Indian princes in Rajasthan and south India, which helped finance his

travels, but these cannot now be traced. This drawing depicts a rocky gorge below a distant hill fort, with a British couple resting under a canopy while a servant fills water-pots, and horses and mules are unloaded; hill porters with their baskets have brought chickens, ducks and fruit. The picture was probably done during Lord Canning's tour of the hills in the hot weather of 1860. [GP]

UNPUBLISHED.

211   'Akal Boonga, at the Golden Temple. Umritser. Punjaub.' (plate 46)
Pencil and watercolour on tinted paper. William Simpson. Sketched March 1860, finished 1864. H. 28 cm; W. 44 cm
1141-1869

In 1859 the publishers Day & Son commissioned William Simpson (1823–99) to visit India and make drawings for a book illustrating in particular the areas that had become well known in England during the Indian Mutiny of 1857. Simpson travelled over a much wider area, not only in Upper India but in the Himalayas and central, southern and western India. During these journeys he made rapid pencil drawings in his sketchbooks, many of which were heightened with touches of colour in preparation for working up finished watercolours which could be used for chromolithographs. After his return to England, however, Day & Son went into liquidation and 250 of Simpson's watercolours were sold off in 1869 as bankrupt stock. 'Here was the reward of my seven years' work', he wrote. 'This was the big disaster of my life.' [GP]

PUBLISHED: M. Archer, 1986, pl. 34.

212   The Akalis' tower at Amritsar (plate 51)
Watercolour on paper mounted on card. By William Carpenter, c.1854.
H. 24.5 cm, W. 17 cm
IS 40-1882

William Carpenter (1819–99) was born in London, the son of the artist and miniaturist Margaret Sarah Carpenter (née Geddes) and William Hookham Carpenter, Keeper of Prints and Drawings at the British Museum. He first visited India in 1850 to paint portraits and make studies of

Indian life and scenery, and appears to have remained there continuously until the outbreak of the 'Mutiny' caused him to return to England in 1857. For the next two years, his Indian scenes were reproduced in the *Illustrated London News* and were among the first to be depicted in colour in that magazine. An exhibition of his Indian subjects was held at the South Kensington Museum in 1881. [GP]

UNPUBLISHED.

213 Maharaja Gulab Singh of Jammu and Kashmir (plate 212)
Watercolour on paper mounted on card. William Carpenter. Kashmir, *c*.1855. H. 24.5 cm; W. 28 cm
IS 153-1882

This drawing was one of 134 bought from the artist by the South Kensington Museum in 1880 and depicts the maharaja with his grandson and an attendant. [GP]

PUBLISHED: Archer, 1966, p. 148 and fig. 53.

214 Carpet-weavers (plate 130)
Charcoal, ink and water-colour on paper. John Lockwood Kipling. Amritsar, 1870. H. 26.2 cm; W. 35.6 cm
0929: 33 (IS)

John Lockwood Kipling (1837–1911) was a potter in Staffordshire before studying art at South Kensington. In 1865 (the year his son, Rudyard, was born), he went to India to become Architectural Sculptor at the Bombay School of Art. From 1875 to 1893 he was Principal of the Mayo School of Art, and Curator of the Central Museum, in Lahore. He was fascinated by the vast range of skills to be seen in India and made a large number·of detailed drawings documenting them. This scene was probably drawn in Amritsar gaol, which became a major centre of carpet weaving in Panjab during the late 19th century, when the commercial carpet-weaving industry was in decline. Kipling includes in the scene tools such as the beater for compacting the wefts (on the left of the left-hand weaver), a short knife with a curled blade for cutting off excess wool when the knots are tied on the warps, and the large scissors used to trim the pile when the rug is complete (both behind the right-hand weaver).
[RC/GP]

215 *Original Sketches in the Punjaub* (plate 219)
By A Lady. Lithography by Dickinson Bros., London, 1854. H. 28 cm; W. 37.5 cm
F 18 (39)

The 'Lady', the wife of an 'Officer in the Queen's Service' according to the preface to the book, remains anonymous. The artist noted of her original drawings, which are confined to Lahore and Amritsar, 'No attempt has been made to draw pictures as they *ought* to be; the desire has been to convey to an English eye some notion of the bright, vivid colouring of Indian scenes – the strange, and often uncouth attitudes of the natives, – and their costume, as far as the scale of these sketches will admit of exactness. Nothing is more unreal than the heavy, brassy sky, the usual accompaniment of an Indian sketch. The great heat, on the contrary, takes away colour from the atmosphere, and makes it almost white, leaving the houses, and gay clothing of the natives, all the brighter for the contrast' (Preface). [SS]

PUBLISHED: Aijazuddin, 1991, pp. 151–3 (includes one original sketch, pl. 90).

FURNITURE AND WOODWORK

216 *Sarinda* (plate 42)
Wood inlaid with ivory. Hoshiapur, 19th century. L 67 cm; W. 28 cm; D 27 cm
IM 67-1911. Given by Mrs R. Irvine

The *sarinda* is a form of *sarangi* especially popular in Bengal and Afghanistan. It has four gut strings, and a number of sympathetic wires (*tarb*) made of brass. The hollow body is of wood inlaid with ivory, the belly half covered with parchment chamfered or pared away – the chief characteristic of this kind of instrument. The *sarinda* is held with the left hand and rests against the performer's body with the neck at the top resting on the left shoulder. The bow is held in the right hand with an underhand grip similar to that used by an Elizabethan viol-player. According to the *Ramayana*, the great Hindu epic, this kind of instrument was invented by Ravana, the monster-king of (Sri)

Lanka. An almost identical *sarinda* is in the Golden Temple Museum in Amritsar. [GP]

217 Box
Shisham wood (*Dalbergia sissoo*), inlaid with wood and ivory. Hoshiarpur, *c*.1881–2. H. 21 cm; W. 39.5 cm; D. 29.7 cm
IS 1610-1883. Acquired for the South Kensington Museum by Caspar Purdon Clarke in India in 1881–2 for £2 8*s*.

This is one of the stock products of Hoshiarpur, the principal centre of ivory and brass inlaying in the Panjab. Hoshiarpur work was characterised by dense and minute floral designs, often around a central bulb or plant, within geometric borders, usually of diaper ornament, quatrefoils and crosses. As on this box, brass bands were frequently applied on the corners of Hoshiarpur cabinet-ware, both as a reinforcing device (taken from British campaign furniture) and as an efficient method of concealing joints. The carcases were usually of locally grown shisham (sold at up to Rs 1.8.0 per cubic foot in the 1880s), inlaid with ivory scraps imported from comb and bangle makers in Amritsar and Jalandhar. Hoshiarpur wares were widely exported from the 1880s onwards, mainly to Britain and America through dealers such as Liberty & Co. and Proctor & Co. [AJ]

218 Armchair
Wood, painted and varnished, with caned seat and silk cushion. Kashmir, *c*.1871. H. 88.4 cm, W. 62 cm, D. 64 cm
1598-1871. Bought from the International Exhibition of 1871 for £12 10*s*.

The chair is decorated on both back and front with a floral pattern, *hazara* or 'thousand' flowers, on a gold ground. The application of Kashmiri painted and lacquered decoration to full-scale Western furniture forms such as chairs and tables does not seem to have occurred until the second half of the 19th century, and was not well received by contemporary critics. In their eyes, such ornament, originally intended for small papier-mâché articles such as pencases, was inappropriate for Western furniture both on aesthetic and practical grounds (the decoration was prone to

rub off). The design of this chair illustrates how in British India furniture forms continued to be manufactured well after they had ceased to be fashionable in Britain. This chair, with its scrolling arms and sabre legs, is based on a prototype of the 1820s, but was not manufactured until 1871. [AJ]

PHOTOGRAPHS

219 'Gateway of the Ram Bagh – The Cutcherry inside' (plate 12)
Albumen print, negative number U 16. Felice Beato. Amritsar, *c*.1858–60. H. 23 cm; W. 28.7 cm
80087

The Ram Bagh, in the north-east of the city, was laid out by order of Ranjit Singh and, like the Shalimar gardens in Lahore, was intended to provide a haven of tranquillity. The gateway, with its two imposing octagonal towers, was known as a *bunga* and was one of several built during Ranjit Singh's reign for the use of Sikh chiefs visiting Amritsar. It was common for watercolourists and photographers to place a 'native' in front of the building being recorded to provide a sense of scale. [DP]

220 'Babatul Temple, Umritsar. Flying-foxes in trees' (plate 52)
Albumen print. Neg. no. 410. Bourne & Shepherd. Amritsar, *c*.1863–4. H. 23 cm; W. 28.5 cm
52,899

The octagonal tower of Baba Atal, the tallest building in Amritsar, was built as a shrine to Atal Rai, the son of Guru Hargobind. According to popular legend, he performed a miracle which restored a close friend to life. Guru Hargobind saw this as defying the law of nature, and his son therefore offered to give his own life for breaking that law. Atal Rai died after going into a meditative trance and although only a child he was given the title 'Baba', to denote his wisdom. The building was started in 1778 on the south side of the Harmandir complex, and was completed by the end of the century (Kang, in Marg 1977, p.39). Its nine storeys represent the nine years of Baba Atal's life. The photographer Samuel Bourne always sought the most picturesque view, and the charming quality of this photograph, which includes a tree with flying foxes, contrasts with Felice Beato's photograph of a few years earlier where Beato 'focused in' on the tower and its architectural details. Both images were displayed in the Paris International Exhibition of 1867. [DP]

221 Hazuri Bagh and the Fort, Lahore (plate 228)
Albumen print. Bourne & Shepherd, neg. no. 425. Lahore, c.1863–4. H. 23.5 cm; W. 29 cm
52907

Following the conventions of the 'picturesque' set by 18th-century watercolour artists, Samuel Bourne often chose to take distant views of architecture set in landscape, rather than photographs of architectural details. He believed in photography as an art form and commented on the forthcoming exhibition of *Raw Materials, Manufactures and Fine Arts of the Punjab* to be held in January 1864; 'I am happy to tell you that unlike the treatment that photography received last year at the hands of the commissioners in London, it is here classified as one of the *fine arts* . . . Are we then more enlightened, or simply more just and unprejudiced, in this land of rising British enterprise, than the would-be patron of art in professedly free but somewhat clique-ridden England?' (Bourne, 15 Feb. 1864, p. 70). A sum of 100 rupees was given by the Bengal Photographic Society for the best series of six landscapes to Charles Waterloo Hutchinson, an engineer based in Lahore (*Bengal Journal*, vol. II, no. 6, Dec. 1863, p. 60; I am grateful to Sophie Gordon for this reference). [DP]

222 'View from Palace in Fort, Lahore'
Albumen print. Bourne & Shepherd; neg. no. 416. Lahore, c.1863–4. H. 22.1 cm; W. 29.1 cm
52,901

This impressive view was taken from the Shish Mahal of Lahore Fort. Rising over the landscape and dominating the scene is the Badshahi Mosque, its imposing gateway facing the marble pavilion in the Hazuri Bagh just visible on the left. In the

foreground, an assortment of artillery lies in one corner of the Shish Mahal's marble court. Overlooking the graceful curved roof of the Naulakha pavilion nearby is Ranjit Singh's tomb. Samuel Bourne was in Lahore for several months before leaving in March 1864. He intended to write about the city for the *British Journal of Photography*, but circumstances prevented this (Bourne, 1864, p. 70). He took more than twelve photographs of Lahore, four of which (including this one) were exhibited in Paris at the Universal Exhibition of 1867. This image was also shown at the 1873 Vienna Universal Exhibition. [DP]

223 Ranjit Singh's tomb from the top of Ranjit Singh's palace (plate 231)
Albumen print. Photographer unknown, Lahore, c.1860–70. H. 19.2 cm; W. 25 cm
2469-1900

This photograph was taken from a slightly different view to that chosen by Bourne (52,901), enabling the photographer to focus on the tomb of Ranjit Singh and include a number of carts positioned in the courtyard, giving a sense of activity rarely seen in early photographs. The fuzziness surrounding the carts would probably have been caused by people or livestock moving around the well. [DP]

224 'Marble pavilion and old entrance to the fort' (plate 232)
Albumen print. James Craddock. Lahore, c.1860–70. H. 23 cm; W. 28.9 cm
79,863

The marble pavilion, in the tree-lined terraces of the Hazuri Bagh, was built by Ranjit Singh in 1818 to provide a cool garden retreat where he could take refuge from the heat. The European gentleman in the pavilion is likely to be James Craddock, who had a tendency to include himself in some of his photographs. [DP]

225 The Badashahi Masjid gateway (plate 233)
Albumen print. James Craddock. Lahore, c.1860–70. H. 28 cm; W. 22 cm
79865

The magnificent gateway leads into the great courtyard of the Badshahi

Mosque which dominates Lahore. The mosque was built by the Mughal emperor Aurangzeb (r. 1658–1707); the marble tablet above the doorway has the Kalima as well as a Persian inscriptions recording the date of completion of the mosque, AH1084/AD 1674. During the Anglo-Sikh Wars it was used to store ammunition but was given back into Muslim hands in 1856, after which it became the repository of relics associated with the Prophet Muhammad. Dr John McCosh took the earliest photograph of the mosque in 1849, capturing the soldiers stationed outside, although the inadequacy of his photographic equipment probably prevented him from taking a view of the steps. Twenty years later, with the advancement of technology and experience, Craddock was able to show the grand scale of the scene. [DP]

226 A Sikh, from *The Costumes and People of India* (plate 230)
Albumen print. Captain W. W. Hooper and Surgeon G. Western. South India, c.1860. H. 18.6 cm; W. 12.2 cm
0932:5 (IS)

Hooper and Western took a group of photographs of the 'native types' of South India, among them this striking photograph of an Akali Sikh. The photography of 'native types' began as early as 1848–9 with John McCosh's calotypes of Sikhs and Madras men, and in 1856 the *Indian Amateurs Photographic Album* became the first publication to use a series of such photographs to depict the 'Costumes and Characters of Western India'. Individuals were shown in costumes or with objects identifying their caste or trade group, and illustrated racial differences as well as regional variations in dress. This photograph was mounted on a page with eight others under the title 'The Costumes of the People of India', and was probably part of a set of 'forty-five photographs of native heads' displayed in the London International Exhibition in 1871 (*London International Exhibition. Indian Department Catalogue*, London, 1871, p. 73). They were part of a much larger section of photographs in that exhibition. [DP]

227 Three Sikh native officers (plate 227)
Albumen print. Felice Beato. Lucknow, March 1858. H. 21 cm; W. 15.2 cm
British Library: Photo 27 (20)

During the visit of the Prince of Wales to India in 1876, many newspaper articles reflected on the Indian 'Mutiny' of 1857. The *Times of India* (weekly edn, 31 Jan. 1876, p. 14) published a long article on Sikh loyalty, and the *London Illustrated News* (26 Feb. 1867, pp. 209–10) reported on a group of 'native soldiers distinguished for their service', with qualities of 'fidelity, bravery and ability in military duties'. Included in this group was Major Maun Singh, the senior native officer of Hodson's Horse, seen here on the left. On the right is Jai Singh, of whom General Sir Henry Dermont Daly wrote 'he deserves of me the best character I can give, a stern strict officer held in much regard by those under him...he may be thoroughly relied upon. I have never had the slightest reason to doubt his truth' (*Memoirs of General Sir Henry Dermont Daly*, London, 1905, p. 71). The identity of these men was noted, the seated figure being 'Goormuck Singh'. It is likely that Beato knew the well-established reputation of these men when he took the photograph. DP (with thanks to Parmjit Singh for the references to the *London Illustrated News* and General Daly's memoirs).

228 Colonel Alexander Haughton Campbell Gardner (plate 234)
Albumen print, neg. no. 808. Bourne & Shepherd. Srinagar, 1864. H. 26.8 cm; W. 23 cm
52,979

According to Colonel Gardner's memoirs he was born in America in 1785 of Scottish and Spanish parentage and had many adventures travelling through the Middle East, Central Asia and Afghanistan, including marriage to an Afghan beauty, before he arrived in the Panjab (Pearse, 1989). However, much of this has been disputed, especially by subsequent travellers, and records suggest that he may have been an Irish deserter who arrived at Ranjit Singh's court in 1831. He commanded the artillery in Gulab Singh's forces in 1842 but was dismissed in 1846 and ordered to leave Lahore (S. Jones, 'Introduction to "A Sketch on Kaffiristan & the Kaffirs . . ."', *Afghanistan Journal*, p. 47). In 1864 he was living in Srinagar and a Captain Segrave noted that he had 'a most peculiar and striking appearance, clothed head to foot in the 79th tartan, but fashioned by a native tailor. Even his *pagri* [turban] was of tartan, and it was adorned with the egret's plume, only allowed to persons of rank. I imagine he lived entirely in native fashion: he was said to be wealthy and the owner of many villages' (Pearse, 1989, p. 281). Samuel Bourne was in Srinagar between July and September 1864 and must have photographed him before continuing his journey through Kashmir. He also photographed Gardner in full native dress surrounded by a group of Dogra soldiers (Bourne neg. no. 599). Gardner died in Jammu in 1877 and was buried in Sialkot cemetery. [DP]

229   The Raja of Nabha (plate 235)

Albumen print. Bourne & Shepherd. Delhi, 1903. H. 29.2 cm; W. 22.6 cm
British Library, Photo 99 (74)

Sardar Hira Singh became Raja of Nabha on 10 August 1877 and was said to have shown 'unswerving loyalty and friendship to the sovereign power', a loyalty similar to that shown by his predecessor, Raja Bharpur Singh during the Mutiny of 1857 (Griffin and Massey, 1910, pp. 411–14 and H. Singh, ed., vol. II, p. 276). Hira Singh sent 200 cavalry and 500 infantry to serve in the Afghan war of 1879–80 and was awarded the Grand Cross of the Star of India in 1879. At the Delhi Coronation Durbar in January 1903 he was invested with the Grand Cross of the India Empire and was ranked fourth among the chiefs of the Panjab. [DP]

230   Ranjit Singh's tomb (plate 236)

Albumen print mounted in an album, negative no. 417a. Bourne & Shepherd. Lahore, *c*.1863–4.
H. 23.9 cm; W. 29.3 cm
IS 7:35-1998

When Dr John McCosh took the earliest known photograph of the tomb in 1849, it had been a small print, capturing the dome of the tomb in a deep purple tone. In this

photograph taken over ten years later, technological advances allowed Bourne to take a full view of the tomb with the added interest of people in the foreground, an example of the care he took in framing his shots. [DP]

231   The Golden Temple

Albumen print mounted in an album. Bourne & Shepherd. Amritsar, *c*.1863–4. H. 23.9 cm; W. 29.3 cm
IS 7:36-1998

Notes

CHAPTER 4

1 Bhagat Singh (1990), p. 346 ff. See p. 347: the court language of the Lahore Durbar and in most of the other states was Persian. On the education system, see pp. 348–9.

2 A detailed analysis of the analogies in the metaphysics and ethics of Sikhism and Sufism has yet to be undertaken. This should include a close study of the quotations from the Koran and from the Sufi writers in the Guru Granth Sahib.

3 Harbans Singh (ed.) *The Encyclopaedia of Sikhism* (Patiala, 1996, vol.2), makes the point, but is not quite accurate when defining the *langar* within the East Iranian tradition or providing a linguistic commentary. *Langar* does not mean almshouse, nor a public kitchen kept by a great man.

4 Borhan Tabrizi, *Borhan-e Qaté*, ed. Mohammad 'Abbasi (Tehran 1344/1965), p.1042: *langar: ja'i ra niz guyand ke har ruz dar anja be mardom ta'am ra dahand va li-haza khanqahra* [the Sufi communal residence] *ham langar mi-guyand*, 'a place where food is distributed to people every day and this is why a *khanqah* is also called a langar'.

5 Kohli (1928). I am very grateful to Parmjit Singh for lending me this book. For a quotation from Sa'adi, see p. 246. Three consecutive couplets on p. 302 celebrate the first three Persian poets in that order. A verse in Arabic by Hafez is quoted on p. 9, but not identified as such – it is too obvious to an eastern audience.

6 Bhagat Singh (1990), p.333 and Kohli (1928), p.xv.

7 *Ibid.*, pp.194–5.

8 As noted by Kohli (1928), the remarkable editor of the *Zafar-Nama*, English introduction pp. xiv–xv. See, for example, p.9.

9 Herrli (1993), p. 32.

10 *Ibid.*, p. 36 in which the Persian text is transcribed in fully satisfactory form. Its versified form (*Ramal* metre) is not recognised by Herrli and the omission of 'u' ('and'), which appears to surprise him, is common in monetary inscriptions as in metalwork. The correct form and rendition into English was published by Major James Browne, *History of the Origin and Progress of the Sikhs* (London, 1788). See excerpts in Ganda Singh, ed., *Early European Accounts of the Sikhs/Indian Studies* (Calcutta reprint, 1962), p.15.

11 This is the interpretation offered in an oral communication by Jeevan Deol, a PhD student of Sikh history at Cambridge University.

12 Archer (1966), fig. 1. On p.19 Archer cryptically notes that 'it is significant that Guru Nanak is portrayed along with Guru Govind Singh – the last Guru confronting the first', but makes no mention of the Persian couplet discussed here.

13 Herrli (1993), p. 39. The first hemistich strictly follows the *Ramal* metre according to Persian metrics. The second one does not. The name Gobind scans only if the consonantic group 'nd' is reduced to 'n' by eliding the *dal*. Jeevan Deol tentatively suggested, when consulted, that the sign which would transcribe the group 'nd' in the Gurmukhi script would receive a 'mute' value and this solution was adapted to the Persian. Specialists in Panjabi poetry and the possible influence of its metrics on the Persian verse may offer alternative explanations.

14 Herrli (1993), p. 38, no. III.

15 *Ibid.*, p. 16.

16 Ferdowsi, *Shah-Name: Le Livre des Rois par Abou'l kasim Ferdousi*, ed. and tr. Jules Mohl (Paris, 1976; 7 volumes), vol. I, p. 54, l. 83: 'when emperor Jamshid, demented by power, requests to be worshipped,

thereby turning away from God: For Jamshid, daylight turned into obscurity – That glory [*farr*] that illuminates the world declined'. Two lines down that light is characterised as 'Divine glory'.

17 For example, Amina Okada (1992), frontispiece, standing portrait of Jahangir; fig. 27, p.29, portrait of Jahangir holding the portrait of Akbar according to a librarian's inscription; fig. 215, p.179, Shah Jahan. The glory emanates from the emperor's head and from his name 'Shah Jahan', also framed by a halo of glory over his head.

18 On the parasol (*chatr*) as a symbol of royalty in literature see Ferdowsi, *Shah-Name* (Jules Mohl, ed. 1976) vol. I, p. 134, l. 236; vol II, p. 38, l. 404 (Afrasiyab pledges to reward whoever defeats Rostam with a kingdom, the parasol, and his own daughter's hand), etc. The symbolism continues from the tenth to the nineteenth century in literature as in art.

19 The mural painting is described by Bhagat Singh (1990), p. 355. The miniature is reproduced in Archer (1966), fig. 7.

20 Archer (1966), fig. 3.

21 Christie's South Kensington, *Oriental Ceramics and Works of Art* (London, 23 July, 1998) lot 207, p. 21. Text described as the '*Tarikh-i Nadir* by Muhammad Mihdi Astrabadi b. Muhammad Nasir' without reference to the edition of the *Tarikh-e Naderi*.

22 Mirza Mehdi Khan Astarabadi, *Tarikh-e Jahangosha-ye Naderi* (Tehran 1368/1989) from a manuscript dated Sha'ban 1272AH (April 1856) where the book is stated to be 'known as' the *Tarikh-e Naderi*. The text displays variants, some perhaps due to negligence and others due to a different, apparently East Iranian manuscript tradition (e.g. instead of

arabized name forms, the original Persian forms are preferred).

23 A.S. Melikian-Chirvani, 'L'école de Chiraz et les origines de la peinture moghole', in Ralph Pinder-Wilson (ed.) *Paintings from Islamic Lands* (London, 1969), pp. 124–41. See fig. 82, p. 126.

24 Thomas W. Lentz and Glenn D. Lowry, *Timur and the Princely Vision* (Los Angeles, 1989), p. 26, cat. 3.

25 Kohli (1928), introduction p. iv. All biographical data relating to Diwan Amar Nath are from the editor's introduction.

26 Kohli (1928), pp. 231–36. The author of the *Zafar-Nama*, Amar, Nath, specifies that he completed it at the age of thirteen (p.231).

27 Kohli (1928), pp. 272–86.

28 'Abdi Beg Shirazi, *Dowhat ul-Azhar*, ed. 'Ali Mina-i Tabrizi and Abu'l Fazl Rahim (ov), (Moscow 1974).

29 Kohli (1928), p. 306 l. 2: *Mikunam aghaz-i Zafar-Nama-ra/Gardesh-i aflake daham khama-ra* ('I make it the beginning of the *Zafar-Nama/* I give my quill a walk around heaven'). Sita Ram Kohli writes that the title would have been followed by Ranjit Singh's name, but produces no evidence to support this view.

30 Sharaf al-Din 'Ali Yazdi, *Zafar Nama*, ed. Mohammad 'Abassi (Tehran 1336/1957), 2 vols.

31 Kohli (1928), English introduction, pp. xiv–xv.

32 Kohli (1928), p. 307: *Shah-i jahandar, falak-iqtidar-Khusraw-i Jam-hishmat-i vala tabar.*

33 Okada (1992), frontispiece.

34 Kohli (1928), p. 308 l. 3: *Teghzan-u safdar-u Feroz-i Jang - Shah-i Jahan Rajah Ranjit-e Singh.*

35 Kohli (1928), p. 303, lines 2–3: *Amad sarhange ki: bardare gam/show soy-i dargah-i falak ihtisham/Shah-i Jahan chon ba-tu yadavarast/Manzilat az charkh-i barin bartarast.*

36 Archer (1966), fig. 11. Mentioned

p. 20 where the vessels are correctly identified as wine cups.

37 On the identification of the North Hindustan school, see A.S. Melikian-Chirvani, 'The Iranian Style in North Hindustan Metalwork', in Françoise 'Nalini' Delvoye, ed., *Confluence of Cultures. French Contributions to Indo-Persian Studies* (New Delhi/Tehran, 1994), pp. 54–81, 22 figs.

38 On the eighteenth-century leader Kapur Singh, see Grewal (1990), p. 89. For the artist Kapur Singh, see Percy Brown, *Indian Painting*, (Calcutta, 1917), p. 62.

39 The revivalist style in arms was identified in A.S. Melikian-Chirvani, 'The tabarzins of Lotf 'ali' in Elgood (1979), pp. 129–32. See fig. 142–3 (a downright copy of an Iranian master's work with a fake signature); fig. 146 (an axe-head made in the early 19th century at Lahore). A.S. Melikian-Chirvani, *Islamic Metalwork from the Iranian World 8–18th centuries* (London, 1982), pp. 340–2, pl. 158 p. 341 and fig. 172, p. 342. For a revivalist wine boat or *kashti-e mey*, see A.S. Melikian-Chirvani, 'From the Royal Wine Boat to the Beggar's Bowl', *Islamic Art* (Genova/New York), vol.iv, 1990–91, fig.69–73, pp.100–102 and text p.38.

40 A.S. Melikian-Chirvani (1994), pp. 61–2, fig. 6 (overall view), 7 (detail showing patron's name and date).

41 This important tray inscribed to the name of a courtier of Jahangir could not be included in the exhibition but is to be published at a future date by this writer.

Chapter 5

1 Suri (1961) pp. 326–30.
2 *Ibid.*, p. 345.
3 *Ibid.*, pp. 342, 346.
4 Fane (1842), vol. I, p. 120.
5 *Ibid.*, p. 132.
6 See Sher Singh (1966), chap. 1, for weapons manufacture at Lahore and relations between the 'Sikligars', or arms-makers, and the Sikhs in the seventeenth century.
7 Akbar (1974), pp.15, 298 and 302.
8 Asher (1992), p.316. For Ranjit

Singh's renovations of Mughal monuments see, for example, Bhagat Singh, (1990) p.368.
9 Bhagat Singh, (1990), p.367.
10 Very little has been written on the secular architecture of Ranjit Singh's reign; see e.g. Anand (1981), pp. 43–4 for a brief note.
11 Brown (1968), p.114.
12 This term, seemingly a corruption of the Persian *takhtkhane*, or place where bedding, vessels etc. were kept, is used in the Persian text of Sohan Lal Suri's account of the daily life of Ranjit Singh's court, *Umdat ut-Tavarikh*. The 'tosha-khana' became a special department attached to the Foreign Secretariat of the British Government of India (Yule 1886, p.713) and is the term used in Login's inventory of Sikh Crown Property after the 1849 annexation.
13 Suri (1961), pp.496–7.
14 *Ibid.*, pp. 590–1.
15 *Ibid.*, p.347.
16 *Ibid.*, p.123.
17 A copy of the inventory is in the British Library (OIOC): L/P&S/5/202. See also Stronge in Brown (1999). It was noted that the throne was 'made to order' by this goldsmith (P199/22 [p.4]) and another reference (P/199/22 [p.2a]) notes that he made a drum for Ranjit Singh in the *toshkhana*.
18 See Balfour (1987) pp.15–22, for a comprehensive and judicious review of the conflicting accounts of the stone's history.
19 Lockhart (1976), p 152.
20 Login (1890), p. 196.
21 Hugel (1845), p. 303.
22 Stronge (1996). The discovery of the real 'Timur Ruby' was announced by Manuel Keene, Curator of Islamic Art at the Dar al Athar al Islamyya, in the Benjamin Zucker Lecture on Mughal Art given at the V&A in 1997. Its publication is forthcoming.
23 Suri (1961), p. 513.
24 Fane (1842), pp.165–6.
25 British Library (OIOC): L/P&S/5/202.
26 See Balfour (1987), p. 27. Haworth (1980), illustrates Chubb's case between pp. 120–1, see also pp.140–3.

27 See Stronge in Brown (1999).
28 British Library: 'List of Arms and Armour Selected by the Most Noble the GG of India from the late Lahore Durbar Toshakhana for Her Majesty Queen Victoria', P/199/22, no. 111.
29 *Ibid.*
30 Fane, (1842), pp. 163–4.

Chapter 6

1 Foster (1968), pp. 161 ff.
2 This group of paintings, once in the collection of the art dealer Subhash Kapoor of New York, has been dispersed. Many of the paintings, done in what may be termed the 'provincial Mughal' manner, carried inscriptions in the hand of a later owner, giving the sum paid for the work.
3 Archer's distinguished work (1966) established this connection almost entirely on the basis of the visual evidence then available. Since then other materials have come to light, many of them supporting his conclusions.
4 See nos. 4, 27 and 36 in Goswamy (1987).
5 This splendid, unusually large drawing was first published in Goswamy (1968). For a better and more detailed reproduction see Goswamy (1972) pls. lxxiv–lxxvi.
6 The painting bearing the number 250 is in the Chandigarh Museum. The personages in it are identified in a long inscription on the back. A variant is in the V&A (IS 128-1955). An early 'Assembly of the Sikhs', now in the Boston Museum of Fine Arts (Coomaraswamy, (1916), pl. lxxvi) also shows a Pahari prince (at bottom right) who may well be Mian Man Chand, younger brother of Maharaja Sansar Chand of Kangra.
7 Archer (1966), p. 31.
8 These documents remain among the most valuable sources of their kind in the history of Indian art. Comprising a group of twenty *parwanas*, or orders, and letters, nearly all of them in Persian, they were first published in Goswamy (1975).

9 This five-line note by Purkhu to his elder brother, Buddhu, is written on the back of a leaf on which are three painted portrait sketches (illustrated in Goswamy and Fischer (1992), p. 372).
10 Deviditta, son of Gursahai and great-grandson of Nainsukh of Guler, seems to have come from Basohli, where this branch of the family had settled, to Lahore. An entry in one of the records kept by a priest mentions him living at Lahore in 'the [quarter called] Macchihatta, the street of Kahaniaya Kapur, the house of Bulaki Misar', in VS 1913/AD 1856. See Goswamy, (1968).
11 Barr (1844), pp. 39–40.
12 Archer (1966), p. 31.
13 Baron Charles Hugel, who met Ranjit Singh during his stay in Lahore, remarks: 'the maharaja did not seem to comprehend how an art so little esteemed by himself could possibly occupy the time of a great white man'. Hugel (1845), p. 250. See, however, Goswamy (1984).
14 Suri (1961), pp. 192–3.
15 See Goswamy (1984), for a detailed discussion.
16 See Goswamy, (1975) for documents issued in favour of painters by the Sandhanwalia chiefs and Maharaja Sher Singh.
17 Imam Bakhsh was responsible for a fine series of drawings of horses, now dispersed, which included one depicting Napoleon Bonaparte astride a horse. One or two drawings from the series are in the Himachal Pradesh State Museum, Shimla. His French patrons took some of his other work back with them to France.
18 Lt. Barr found the perspective of the scenes painted on the walls of General Allard's house in the Anarkali, Lahore 'most ridiculous...at the siege of Moultan, the cannons are turned up on end to enable the gunners to load them, the figures overtop the fortifications and the cavalry seems to be manouvering in the air'. Barr (1844), pp.69–70.
19 For the work of itinerant Kashmiri painters and scribes active in the Panjab plains in the nineteenth

century, and responsible for vast numbers of surviving calligraphed texts, see K. Goswamy (1998).

20 This set seems to have been very extensive, each portrait showing a prominent figure at the Lahore court seated under an arch and resting against a bolster, or some other conventional setting.

21 These painted sketches are in many collections, such as the V&A, Chandigarh Museum and Lahore Museum. Most carry brief captions identifying the person portrayed and place the figure against an uncoloured ground, primed in white broadly in the space used for the portrait.

22 Archer (1966), contains an especially evocative account of this period of painting in the Panjab.

23 There are repeated references in Suri (1961), to pilgrimages to Haridwar by Sikh chiefs and nobles. There is an air of routineness in these descriptions, as for example in an entry in 1832: 'Bhai Ram Singh presented to the Maharaja *parshad* from Gangaji with some garments and an elephant'.

24 For example, the Maharaja's orders to Dewan Moti Ram to distribute pashmina worth 10,000 rupees to the Brahmins. Suri (1961), during the events of 1832.

25 These panels on the Sheesh Mahal walls, with the usual renderings of the lover and the beloved as Krishna and Radha, are obviously based on a Pahari miniature series on the same theme, formerly in the collection of the Maharaja of Tehri-Garhwal.

26 This is the series, by painters in the first generation after Nainsukh, published by M. S. Randhawa (1963).

27 Dispersed leaves from different series with this theme, with an obvious Panjabi flavour, are in many collections, though complete series are rare.

28 The set of 'portraits' of the great Gurus, formerly in the collection of Wazir Kartar Singh of Bassa Waziran in Nurpur, or the extensive series of drawings of the *Janamsakhi* in the Chandigarh Museum, are cases in point.

CHAPTER 7

1 Osborne (1840), p.72.
2 Fane (1842), vol.I, p.134.
3 Eden (1978), p.227.
4 Fane (1842), vol.II, p.2.
5 Login (1890), p.163
6 *Ibid.*
7 Eden (1978), p.206; Pemble (1985), p.193; Fane (1842), p.132.
8 Eden (1978), pp. 213–4.
9 Osborne (1840), p.71
10 Eden (1978), p.199.
11 Osborne (1840), p.63.
12 Pemble (1985), p.217.
13 Login (1890), p.181.
14 Osborne (1840), pp.76–8
15 Grier (1905), p.336.
16 Levi-Strauss (1986), pp.18–27.
17 Moorcroft, Eur. Mss. G.28 (no.45), quoted in Irwin, (1973), p.13.
18 Welch (1978), p.125.
19 Eden (1978), p.197.
20 *Ibid.*
21 Crill (1993).
22 Paul (1982).
23 Vigne (1842), p.124.
24 Watt (1903), p.301.
25 Guy and Swallow (1990), pl.129.
26 Hall (1996), pp.83–97.
27 Acc. No. 59.92.
28 Irwin and Hall (1973), p.148; Nabholz-Kartaschoff, (1986), p.192.
29 Archer (1970): Guler 46; Chamba 14, 19.
30 Goetz (1945–6), pp. 35–42; Koezuka (ed.), (1993), no.107.

CHAPTER 8

1 Letter addressed 'Camp, Ramnaggar, 25 November 1848', published in the *Illustrated London News*, 27 January 1849.
2 Osborne (1840), pp.102–3.
3 *Ibid.*, pp.102–3.

CHAPTER 9

1 John Login selected some of these 'boyish arms and armour' for the Prince of Wales, though they may never have been presented to him. See Login (1890), p.220.
2 The Sikh War was terminated by the Treaty of Lahore, which was followed two days later by further articles, and a year later by the Treaty of Byrowal, each stage marking a further consolidation of British power.

3 The British Resident's young team of administrators provoked Afghans against their Sikh governors in Bannu and Hazara. As the men on the spot they were encouraged to expect unquestioning support from the Resident, and particularly under John Lawrence and Frederick Currie, behaved in a very high-handed way.

4 See Ganda Singh, *Maharajah Duleep Singh Correspondence*, Department of Punjab Historical Studies, Punjabi University, Patiala, 1972.

5 See Alexander and Anand (1980), pp. 7–8.

6 Dalhousie was to find pretexts for annexing Awadh, Jhansi, Sattara, Nagpur and Coorg, and terminated pensions to the Peshwa, the Nawab of Arcot, the Raja of Tanjore, and others.

7 For a good description of Fatehgarh at this time, see Andrew Ward, *Our Bones are Scattered*, p. 87 ff.

8 As the widow of Dalip's brother Maharaja Sher Singh, she was by Sikh custom a possible bride for Dalip Singh, but against Dalhousie's wishes.

9 If this story had been true it is difficult to understand the Khalsa accepting Dalip Singh as Ranjit Singh's heir, when Sher Singh's legitimate son Shahzadeh Shah Deo Singh was still alive, as well as two older illegitimate sons, Kasmira and Peshora Singh.

10 I am grateful to Susan Stronge for this reference. The letter was shown to her by Fakir Saif ad-Din Bokhari, and translated by Dr Anjum Rehmani, Director of the Lahore Museum.

11 Owing to the importance of the conversion, Bhajan Lal had to write a detailed report to Dalhousie designed to show that no undue influence had been involved.

12 This was a period when there was fierce internal debate amongst Hindus as reflected in the career of Raja Ram Mohun Roy and the rise of the Brahmo Samaj, in which leading thinkers left and then rejoined Hinduism. Dalip Singh's concerns were the burning issues of the day.

13 As well as Azimullah Khan, agent for the Peshwa (and later a leading figure in the Mutiny) relatives and agents of most of Dalhousie's deposed rulers went to London, as well as the far-from-deposed dictator of Nepal, Jang Bahadur Rana.

14 Sketches illustrated in Alexander and Anand (1980), pl.12–15.

15 Alexander and Anand (1980), pp. 47–8.

16 Nevertheless, he faced a whispering campaign that he had never clearly condemned the Mutiny, and that his life-long love of falconry betrayed a cruel Eastern nature, as opposed to a healthy love of hunting. His estates at Fatehgarh were ruined. It is not known whether he was aware of the brutal suppression of potential mutinies in the Panjab. It is possible that the Queen's strong support for Canning's moderate policy towards the defeated Indians was influenced by the close personal friendships she had formed with Dalip Singh and others.

17 That he took the trip, and showed her so much affection despite the advice of the Queen, suggests that he had never been convinced by the attempts of Dalhousie and Login to turn him against her.

18 Alexander and Anand (1980), p. 192.

19 His financial position was very complicated: he was entitled by treaty to a pension of 400,000 rupees a year, administered for him during his minority by the India Office which also made deductions to pay pensions to his old servants. As they died, the money did not revert to Dalip Singh, nor did he receive the income from his family estates. Former Sikh officials of his own government received higher pensions than he did and still received rents from their personal estates.

20 In fact, the investigation proved that he had been generous in supporting Lady Login and the widow of his equerry, Oliphant, and

other old English servants. He settled the debts of his old friend Tommy Scott, and supported charity work in Elveden, but was hardly wastefully extravagant given his position in society.

21 Alexander and Anand (1980), p. 197.

22 *Ibid.*, pp. 150–5.

23 *Ibid.*, p. 247.

24 It was believed that Hira Singh, raja of Nabha and leader of the Cis-Sutlej Sikhs, was ready to join. Thakur Singh set himself up in the French-Indian town of Pondicherry where British agents reported that soldiers on leave from Sikh regiments were coming to swear allegiance to Dalip Singh on behalf of their comrades. Some 40,000 Sikh and Rajput soldiers had sworn in this way. The Namdhari Sikhs believed that their dead leader, Baba Ram Singh, would rise from the dead and join Dalip Singh in Moscow. Forty of them were blown from cannons by a British officer. Some of Dalip's followers led by Benarsi Das Faqir were caught attacking the Meerut police station.

25 The nature of Dalip Slngh's Fenian contacts is puzzling. It is not clear whether or not this is the Casey involved in the Phoenix Park assassination and later shot as an informer.

26 These plans were sufficiently well known to form the basis of a short story by Kipling, 'The Mutiny of the Mavericks', and generally to form the background to *Kim*.

27 In Paris, Dalip Singh was to marry the Englishwoman Ada Wetherill who had accompanied him to Russia and by whom he had two daughters. There is some suspicion that she too might have been in the pay of British intelligence.

28 Alexander and Anand (1980), p. 293.

29 *Ibid.*, p. 54.

CHAPTER 11

1 Even though it is now dated, Lepel Griffin's *Rajas of the Punjab* (first published 1873; reprint, Patiala,

1970), still succeeds in presenting a connected and evocative account of the 'Phulkian' group of states.

2 Khalifa Muhammad Hussain's history of Patiala in Urdu, *Tarikh-i-Patiala*, R.P. Srivastava's collection of essays (1990), and S.P. Srivastava (1991), all contain useful information on the period.

3 The case of Nainsukh's grandson, Deviditta, is of great interest. Having moved from Basohli to Lahore at a date unknown, his circumstances seem to have changed between 1856 and 1866. The continued availability of patronage at the princely state of Patiala when Lahore had gone into decline must have been a factor. See Goswamy (1968).

4 This information comes, once again, from the pilgrimage records kept by the priests at Haridwar. See Goswamy (1980), pp.56 ff. for a brief discussion.

5 These frescoes are discussed in detail in Karuna Goswamy, 'Frescoes in the Sheesh Mahal, Patiala', *Roopalekha*, vol.xxxviii, nos. 1–2. See also Kanwarjit Kang's doctoral dissertation, *Mural Paintings in 19th century Punjab*, Chandigarh, 1978.

6 'Mistri' Ude Ram Jaipuria appears to have moved to Patiala in the reign of Maharaja Karam Singh. Most of his work, however, seems to have been done under Maharaja Narinder Singh. See S.P. Srivastava, (1991), pp. 20–21.

7 There are several entries relating to this Rajasthani group of craftsmen settled at Patiala in the records of Pandit Gopal Toombria at Haridwar.

8 This painting is now in the Himachal Pradesh State Museum, Shimla. R.P. Srivastava (1990), has recorded very useful information from the family to which Basharat Ullah and Muhammad Sharif belonged and which is now settled in Lahore.

9 The two brothers, Khalifa Muhammad Hassan and Khalifa Muhammad Hussain, were sons of Mir Sadat Ali who served as a tutor in Urdu and Persian to Maharaja Narinder Singh. Names of other Muslim administrators and

counsellors coming from Lucknow are also remembered with respect. See S.P. Srivastava (1991), pp. 6–7.

10 No detailed study of the work of these artists has yet been made. However, there is a notice and brief discussion in Randhawa (1971); Aryan (1975); and R.P. Srivastava (1990), p.204.

11 A large number of these drawings and sketches, some of them very finely done, were once in the collection of Shri Ramjidas of Patiala, descendant of one of these Rajasthani families in Patiala. Most of the works bore small descriptive captions in Rajasthani *devanagari*, identifying the person portrayed.

12 This painting is now in the collection of the Sarabhai Foundation, Ahmadabad (Acc. No. KA-18)

13 The drawing is now in a private collection.

CHAPTER 12

1 Wurgart (1983), pp. 11–16.

2 McCosh (1856).

3 Lady Login (1890), pp. 178–9. The daguerreotype was the earliest photographic process and could only produce a single image on a copper plate; it is unlikely that McCosh actually used this process.

4 The album is the largest single collection of his work and is now in the National Army Museum, London (6204/3).

5 McCosh (1856), p.191.

6 Written on the flyleaf of his album in 1859.

7 Hering, H.

8 Mason (1974), p. 212, 307.

9 *Ibid.*, p.379.

10 Illustrated in Christie's *Photographs* sale, London, 20 October (1993), p. 30.

11 Mason (1974), p.315.

12 Thomas (1985).

13 *The Englishman*, 31 March 1859: 'Report of the meeting of the Photographic Society of Bengal'. I am very grateful to Sophie Gordon for this reference.

14 Sampson (1992), p.337. Bourne mentions seeing Beato's print of

Delhi in his article in the *British Journal of Photography*, 1863, p.345.

15 *Nepal Residency Reports*, p. 489.

16 *Ibid.*

17 Pinney (1990), pp. 252–64.

18 Watson and Kay (1868–75).

19 Watson and Kay, vol. 4 (1869), photograph 196.

20 *Ibid.*, photograph 225.

21 British Library (OIOC): E/4/829 India and Bengal Despatches, 7 February, 1855, ff.623–5, quoted in Desmond (1982), p.112.

22 Bourne & Shepherd (1866).

23 Khan (1997), pp.236–43.

24 *The Times of India*, weekly edition (1867), p.13.

GLOSSARY

Adi Granth 'First [ie primal] Book'. One of the names for the holy book of the Sikhs, compiled and edited by Guru Arjan Dev, the fifth Guru, in 1604. Since 1704, when guruship was conferred on it, it has also been called **Guru Granth Sahib**.

AH 'Anno Hegira', the Islamic era

Akal Bunga 'Pavilion of the Timeless One [God]'; the place of the sixth Guru, Hargobind at **Amritsar**, opposite the entrance to the **Golden Temple**.

Akal Takht 'Throne of the Timeless One'. The building on the west side of the pool of the **Darbar Sahib** at **Amritsar** was established as a seat of temporal authority in 1609 by Guru Arjan. Severely damaged during Operation Blue Star in 1984, it has since been rebuilt.

Akali/Akalee/Ukalee Devotee of Akal, the Timeless One (God); also known as **nihangs**.

Akbar Nama 'Book of Akbar'. The history of the reign of the Mughal emperor written by Abu'l Fazl between 1590 and 1602.

Akhand Path Continuous recitation of the **Guru Granth** by a series of readers.

Amrit Lit. 'nectar'. The sugared water used in the initiation ceremony of the **Khalsa** which has been stirred by the double-edged sword (**khanda**), while certain scriptural passages have been recited.

Amritdhari One who has been initiated into the **Khalsa** according to prescribed rules, and who follows vows taken at the ceremony known as Amrit **Pahul**.

Amritsar Lit. 'pool of nectar'. Founded by Guru Ram Das in 1577, and the location of the **Harmandir**.

Ardas Petition of a servant to a superior. Used as the name of the

formal Sikh prayer which begins or ends almost every ritual.

Baisakh Second month of the North Indian calendar used in Panjab.

Baisakhi Festival taking place on the first day of the solar month of **Baisakh**; the time of the spring harvest festival, and New Year. Sikhs now usually celebrate **Baisakhi** on 13 April as the anniversary of the **Khalsa**, though in 1699 this fell on 30 March.

Bedi The Hindu subcaste to which Guru Nanak belonged.

Bhagavata Purana The 'Ancient Story of the Blessed One': the Hindu scripture written in Sanskrit extolling Vishnu as Supreme Lord of the Universe, including the cycles concerned with Krishna and the incarnations of Vishnu.

Bhai 'Brother'; also a title conferred on men of acknowledged learning or piety as a term of respect.

Brahmin Highest level of the Hindu caste system.

Bunga Dwelling place; a structure attached to a Sikh temple for the use of pilgrims; the mansions erected by **sardars** around the **Harmandir** at **Amritsar** as residences and for defensive purposes; also the high peak in which a **Nihang**, or **Akali**, finishes his turban.

Chakkar/chakra Circle or wheel; a large sized ring or quoit; one of the arms worn by **Nihangs** on their turbans.

Choga Man's robe.

Cis-Sutlej The land across the river Sutlej.

Cuerda seca Lit. 'dry cord'. The technique of outlining elements of the design on glazed tiles with a mixture of manganese and a greasy substance to prevent the different colours intermingling during firing.

Daftar Persian, 'office, register, volume'.

Dal Army

Darbar/Durbar Court, or royal audience. In Anglo-Indian usage it became Durbar, meaning the audiences held by the Governor General or Viceroy.

Darbar Sahib 'Divine Court'. Synonym for the **Harmandir**, or **Golden Temple**.

Darshani Deohari/Darshani Deorhi Entrance gate of the **Golden Temple** at **Amritsar**.

Dasam Granth 'Tenth Book': the sacred book of material attributed to Guru Gobind Singh, the tenth Guru, and compiled by Bhai Mani Singh, one of his devoted followers, by 1734. It includes the **Zafar-nama**.

Daswand/Daswandh Tithes (one tenth of the income) paid by true Sikhs for the Guru's fund fixed by Guru Arjan; a votive offering made by the Sikhs for charitable purposes.

Deg tegh fateh 'Cauldron, sword, victory': motto of the 18th-century **Khalsa**

Devanagari Script of classical Sanskrit and modern Hindi.

Devi The supreme Goddess, of whom all other godesses are manifestations.

Dharam/dharma The moral law, the one ultimate reality; code of conduct in life that sustains the soul.

Dharamsala The abode of **dharma**; early name for a Sikh place of worship, replaced by **Gurdwara** in the time of Guru Hargobind.

Divali/Diwali The major Hindu festival observed on the last day of the dark half of the lunar month of *Kartika* (October–November). Its name derives from the Sanskrit 'dipavali', a row of lights. Sikhs celebrate two

historical events which took place at Divali: the laying of the foundation stone of the **Golden Temple** in 1577, and the release of Guru Hargobind from imprisonment in 1619.

Faqir/fakir Poor man, mendicant; loosely used to designate **Sufis** and also non-Muslim renunciants.

Fath-Nama Persian, 'Book of Victory or Conquest'. A traditional genre in Persian literature.

Fauj-i-Ain Persian for 'army'. Strong professional infantry and cavalry of Ranjit Singh's army, trained by former Napoleonic generals.

Five Ks *see* **Panj Kakke**

Ghorchurra From Panjabi 'ghora', meaning horse, and 'churr', meaning mounted. Part of the irregular forces of Ranjit Singh's army, they were Sikh landowners who defended their own lands, paying taxes to Lahore and collecting taxes on behalf of the Lahore durbar.

Gita Govinda 'Song of the Cowherd', the poetical work written in Sanskrit by Jayadeva describing the love of Radha and Krishna.

Golden Temple *see* **Harmandir**.

Granth Collection of writings, anthology, book, volume; especially used of the Sikh scriptures.

Granthi Reader or reciter of the Holy **Granth** of the Sikhs

Gurdwara Lit. a door (*dwara*) to the Guru or enlightenment. Often incorrectly described as the Sikh 'temple', though any suitable building or room may be a **gurdwara** as the only requirement is that it should contain a copy of the **Guru Granth Sahib** which must be treated with due respect.

Gurmukhi 'The word, from the mouth of the Guru'. The written form of Panjabi used in the Sikh scriptures and one of the three scripts in which Panjabi may otherwise be written (the others being Arabic and **devanagari**).

Guru Religious teacher, a spiritual preceptor or a guide, usually a person, and in Sikhism referring to the Ten Gurus through whom the word of God was revealed. It is also to be understood as the divine inner voice. The Sikh scripture is sometimes called the eleventh Guru.

Guru Granth Sahib The 'Book of the Lord Guru', also called the **Adi Granth**, the sacred scripture of the Sikhs. It is installed in all **gurdwaras** and is the focus of all ceremonial and ritual occasions. Ritually it is treated like a living **Guru** in many respects, taken in procession in the morning from its resting place to be installed under a canopy with an attendant holding a chauri over it. Sikhs prostrate themselves on entering its presence, and at night it is ceremonially returned to its resting place.

Harmandir The 'Temple of God' at Amritsar, also called the **Darbar Sahib** and the **Golden Temple**, is the principal Sikh holy monument. The third Guru, Amar Das, conceived the idea of a building which would be the focus of Sikhism and his son, Ram Das, began work on it in 1577. The first structure was completed in 1601, and in 1604 the newly compiled **Adi Granth** was placed within it. It has four doorways which symbolise its openness to all people, regardless of caste, and stands in the middle of an artificial pool, linked by a causeway to a marble walkway (**parkama**), which runs along the four sides of the lake. The structure erected by Jassa Singh Ahluwalia in 1764 was embellished by Maharaja Ranjit Singh and given marble walls and its characteristic golden dome, which was recently restored.

Hindustan 'Land of the Hindus'. The Persian name for the northern part of the Indian subcontinent, including present-day Pakistan and parts of Afghanistan.

Holi The Hindu festival of colours.

Hukam God's will, God's command; order, authority (legal or executive), rule, law, direction, decree, demand.

Huqqa Water pipe for smoking tobacco

Ik Oankar/Ikk Oan Kar/Ek-Ong-Kar First sentence of the **Guru Granth Sahib** which gives the quintessential Sikh formula: 'There is one being'. This is one of the two most used Sikh symbols (the other being the **khanda**) and is formed from the figure 1 and the word 'oankar'. It corresponds to the word Om in Hinduism.

Jagir Assignment of land or land revenue; an estate or holding.

Janamsakhi Stories (**sakhi**) from the life (**janam**) of Guru Nanak.

Japji Lit. 'meditation'. Traditionally regarded as the first of Guru Nanak's compositions. Guru Arjan placed it at the beginning of the **Adi Granth**.

Jaratkari Art of inlaying coloured stones in marble in set patterns; inlaying of coloured cut-stone in marble. The type of work can be seen on the outer walls of the Central Shrine in the Golden Temple.

Kanhaiya/Kanahya One of the twelve **misls** of the Sikh confederacy.

Kaur Lit. 'princess'. The title given to female Sikhs as a surname.

Kes/kesh Uncut hair.

Khalsa From Arabic, *khalis* (feminine *khalisa*), meaning pure or unsullied. In the Panjab context also describes the lands directly under government management. In Sikhism it has different nuances of meaning. It is used to describe the community of Sikhs initiated into the Khalsa, and more specifically to describe the new initiatory rites introduced by Guru Gobind Singh on 30 March 1699, on **Baisakhi**. During the 18th century the volunteer force organised by Sikhs was known as the Khalsa army (Dal Khalsa); the government of Maharaja Ranjit Singh was called Sarkar-i Khalsa.

Khanda Double-edged sword; also the name of an emblem of Sikhism which has a khanda at the centre within a **chakkar** and is supported by two swords at right and left.

Khil'at Robe of honour, often accompanied by jewellery and other items, presented by a superior on ceremonial occasions as a mark of distinction.

Kirtan Devotional music, the singing of hymns from the **Guru Granth Sahib**.

Koh-i-nur Persian, 'mountain of light'. The diamond formerly owned by the Mughal emperors, Nadir Shah of Iran, the Afghan Durrani dynasty, and the Sikh Maharajas from Ranjit Singh to Dalip Singh. Became part of the British Crown Jewels after the annexation of the Panjab in 1849.

Kshatriya The second, warrior level of the Hindu caste system.

Kuftkari/koftgari The decoration of iron and steel by hammering gold or silver into engraved lines, or gold or silver wires across a hatched surface. The practitioner is called a *kuftkar*.

Langar From the Persian word meaning 'anchor'. In Sikhism it is the communal refectory found in every **gurdwara** where food is served to all, regardless of caste or creed.

Lungi Cloth which is wrapped around the waist as a lower garment or used as a turban.

Maharaja Title meaning the 'great king'.

Maharani Wife of a **maharaja**.

Misl From the Arabic meaning 'like'. A military cohort of **Khalsa** Sikhs in the mid-18th century.

Misldar Head of a **misl**.

Mohur Gold coin, from the Persian *mohr* (seal).

Naqqash Designer or pattern-maker.

Nasta'liq 'Hanging' style of cursive Arabic script used in Iranian calligraphy.

Nayaka A hero (fem: *nayika*).

Nihang From the Persian *nahang* (crocodile). One who has nothing and is free from anxiety and care; a Sikh of the **Akali** class. Nihangs wear a blue uniform and often live together in camps.

Pahari 'Of the hills'. Particularly used to describe the paintings of the courts of the Panjab Hills.

Pahul Rite of Sikh initiation, generally called *Khande ki pahul*, with the two-edged sword according to the ceremony adopted by Guru Gobind Singh at the time of the creation of the **Khalsa** at Anandpur Sahib in March, 1699.

Palki The structure in which the Guru Granth Sahib is installed. Resembles a litter (*palanquin*, a word to which palki is related).

Pan Leaves of the betel plant wrapped round chopped areca nuts, spices and lime, and chewed as a digestive and mild stimulant; also used to mark the end of a formal visit.

Pandan Box in which **pan** is kept.

Panjab Persian, 'five rivers'. The land now divided between India and Pakistan, encompassing the river basins of the Indus, Jhelum, Chenab, Ravi and Sutlej.

Panjabi Language of the Panjab which can be written in three alphabets: **Gurmukhi**, *Urdu*, and **Devanagari**.

Panj Kakke/the Five K's The five external symbols which must be worn by all members of the **Khalsa**, both male and female, all beginning with the initial letter 'k' (*kakka*): *Kesh/kes*, uncut hair; *kangha*, comb; *kirpan*, sword; *kara*, plain steel bangle; and *kachha/kacch* a pair of shorts, worn as an undergarment by women and by males (including those who have adopted western dress).

Panj Piare The five 'chosen ones', who were given the first **pahul** by Guru Gobind Singh on the famous Baisakhi day of 1699 at Anandpur Sahib.

Panth Derived from Sanskrit, meaning 'path' or 'way', but now used to describe groups following a particular religious way; also used to designate the Sikh community.

Parkarma/parikarma The circumambulatory path around a holy place or site (or, in Hinduism, the deity).

Pashmina From the Persian 'pashm', meaning wool. The soft hair of the Himalayan goat used to make Kashmir shawls and formerly used in the highest quality Mughal carpets.

Patka Man's sash. Also a piece of cloth which fits tightly over the **kesh**, often worn by boys or sports players.

Phulkari 'Flower work'. Floss silk embroidered on cotton in the Panjab and used for women's shawls and garments.

Phulkian States Nabha, Jind and notably Patiala, tracing their origin to Phul (d.1652) who had met Guru Har Rai during his travels and received his blessing. They grew as a result of the Phulkian **misl**, an 18th-century Sikh ruling clan to the south of the river Sutlej.

Pietra dura Inlay of semi-precious stones into hardstone.

Purana Some popular ancient holy scriptures of the Hindus. There are eighteen Puranas, including the *Bhagavata Purana*. They do not enjoy the same status as the Vedas and Upanishads.

Qanat Panel of a tent; portable screens supported by a wood or bamboo framework.

Qila/qilla/kila Arabic *qal'a*, a fortified place.

Rag/raga Indian melodic organisation, a series of five or more notes upon which a melody is based. Derived from 'rang', or colour, indicating that the music is intended to evoke certain feelings. Ragas are personified as male, the female melodies being called *raginis*. All the hymns of the **Adi Granth** (with the exception of the **Japji**) are set to specific **rags**.

Ragamala Lit. 'garland of melodies'. The last poetical composition in the **Adi Granth**, a collection of **ragas** found in Indian music of the early 17th century; collection of illustrations inspired by classical melodies, each personifying a characteristic of love or heroic behaviour.

Raja King

Rani Queen

Ramayana 'The story of Rama'. The Sanskrit epic relating to the deeds of Rama and his wife Sita, traditionally attributed to the sage Valmiki. It is often reinterpreted by vernacular poets and dramatists.

Rasamanjari 'Posy of delights'. Sanskrit poetical text by Bhanudatta describing the types of lovers and their behaviour.

Rasikapriya 'The lovers' breviary'. Hindi poem by Keshavadasa describing and classifying the heroes and heroines of poetry.

Rumal Persian, 'covering a surface, or the face'. Piece of cloth used as a covering for trays, a handkerchief or, among Sikhs, the Guru Granth.

Sahib From the Arabic, 'owner, possessor, master'.

Sakhi Lit. 'testimony'. Used in a general sense to mean 'story', as in **Janam Sakhi**.

Samadh Mausoleum, tomb

Samvat *see* **VS**.

Sarbat Khalsa The assemblies of the **misldars** and **jathedars**, the entire **Khalsa**.

Sardar From the Persian, 'chieftain, a headman'; leader of a **misl**; the term is now commonly used as title of address for all Sikh men.

Sarkar khalsaji **Khalsa** state.

Sati The practice of immolating a widow on the funeral pyre of her husband, denounced by the Sikh Gurus.

Sepoy From *sipahi*, Persian for 'footsoldier'.

Seva/sewa Service, especially but not only dedicated to the Sikh community.

Shabad The Word of God revealed to those whose compositions are contained in the Sikh scriptures; also used to describe the hymns themselves.

Shah Persian, 'king'.

Shamiana Persian, cloth canopy or tent used at large public gatherings.

Shish mahal/Sheesh Mahal Persian, 'place of mirrors'. Building or a palace whose interior is decorated with small mirrors embedded into the plaster walls.

Shishya From Sanskrit, meaning a disciple or follower.

Shi'a or **Shi'ite** Muslims who hold Ali, the cousin and son-in-law of the Prophet Muhammad as his successor and the 'Friend of God'.

Shikaste 'Broken' style of Iranian calligraphy.

Sikh Panjabi word meaning 'disciple'.

Singh 'Lion'. Title given to all Sikh men as a surname, particulary after **pahul**. Singh is also the surname found among Rajasthani Kshatryas.

Singh Sabha Movement comprising several local Sikh societies dedicated to religious, social and educational reforms amongst the Sikhs. The first Singh Sabha was founded at Amritsar in 1873.

Sodhi/Sodhee Sub-caste of the *Khatris*. Seven Sikh Gurus, from Guru Ram Das to Guru Gobind Singh belonged to this caste. The *Sodhis* (the descendants of the Gurus) were held in great esteem by the Sikh masses and were given large **jagirs** and other privileges by the Sikh rulers.

Spinel Gemstone similar to, but gemmologically distinct from, ruby. Prized above all precious stones in areas under Iranian cultural influence.

Suba/subah Province of the Mughal empire.

Sudra The fourth in Hindu caste hierarchy.

Sufi Muslim mystics.

Sukarchakia One of the twelve **misls**, to which Maharaja Ranjit Singh belonged.

Takht Persian 'throne'; seat of royal or spiritual authority.

'Timur Ruby' Spinel of 352.5 carats erroneously thought to have belonged to Timur-i Leng, the Mongol ruler of Central Asia. Inscribed with the names or titles of Mughal, Iranian and Afghan rulers and owned by Ranjit Singh, it is now in the British Crown Jewels.

Toshkhana/toshakhana Storehouse, chamber, in which objects of value or curiosity not in daily use are kept.

Turban One of the most distinctive features of Sikhism, though not one of the five Ks (**Panj Kakke**). All pictures of the Gurus show them with turbans, though traditionally turbans were systematically adopted at the time of Guru Gobind Singh as an outward sign of Sikhism.

Udasi (**Oodassee**) Order of ascetics claiming as their founder Sri Chand, the elder son of Guru Nanak.

Umdat ut-Tavarikh 'Pillar of History', the Persian-language chronicle of the reign of Maharaja Ranjit Singh by Sohan Lal Suri.

Vaishya The third in Hindu caste hierarchy.

VS 'Vikrama samvat', or 'Valorous year': the era beginning in the reign of Vikramaditya, *c*. 57 BC.

Zafar-Nama 'Book of Triumphs'. One of the Persian-language chronicles of Ranjit Singh's reign; also refers specifically to the letter written in Persian by Guru Gobind Singh to the emperor Aurangzeb, denouncing him as a tyrant and laying down the Sikh doctrine of resistance to oppression by physical force. This is contained in the **Dasam Granth**.

Zardozi Persian, 'gold embroidery'. Embroidery worked in gold or silver threads and often embellished with sequins.

BIBLIOGRAPHY

Aijazuddin, F. S. *Pahari paintings and Sikh portraits in the Lahore Museum* (London, Sotheby Parke Bernet 1977)

Aijazuddin, F. S. *Sikh portraits by European artists* (London, Sotheby Parke Bernet 1979)

Aijazuddin, F. S. *Lahore, illustrated views of the 19th century* (Lahore, Vanguard Books Ltd. 1991)

Akbar, Muhammad. *The Punjab under the Mughals* (Delhi, Idarah-i Adabiyat-i 1974)

Alexander, Michael and Anand, Sushila. *Queen Victoria's Maharajah: Duleep Singh 1838–93* (London, Weidenfeld and Nicolson 1980)

Ames, Frank. *The Kashmir shawl and its Indo-French influence* (Suffolk, The Antique Collectors Club Ltd. 1986)

Anand, Mulk Raj. 'Painting under the Sikhs', in *Marg* (Bombay, Marg Publications 1954) vol.7, no.2, pp.23–31

Anand, Mulk Raj. [Golden Temple issue], in *Marg* (Bombay, Marg Publications 1977) vol.30, no.3, pp.1–74

Anand, Mulk Raj (ed). *Maharaja Ranjit Singh as patron of the arts* (Bombay, Marg Publications 1981).

Archer, Mildred. *British drawings in the India Office Library* (London, HMSO 1969) 2 vols

Archer, Mildred. *Company drawings in the India Office Library* (London, HMSO 1972)

Archer, Mildred. *Visions of India: The sketchbooks of William Simpson 1859–62* (India, Alfalak/Scorpion Publishing Ltd. 1986)

Archer, W.G. *Indian miniatures* (London, 1960)

Archer, W. G. *Paintings of the Sikhs* (London, HMSO 1966)

Archer, W. G. *Indian paintings from the Punjab Hills: a survey and history of Pahari miniature painting* (London and New York, Sotheby Parke Bernet 1973) 2 vols.

Arjan Dass, Malik. *An Indian guerilla war. The Sikh people's war 1699–1768* (New Delhi, Wiley Eastern Ltd. 1975)

Aryan, K. C. *Punjab painting* (Patiala, 1975)

Asher, Catherine B. *Architecture of Mughal India* (Cambridge, Cambridge University Press, 1992) The New Cambridge History of India I:4

Ashton, Sir Leigh (ed.). *The art of India and Pakistan* (London, Faber & Faber Ltd. 1947)

Baden-Powell, B.H. 'Hand-book of the manufactures and arts of the Punjab' in the *Hand-book of the economic products of the Punjab* (Lahore, Punjab Printing Company 1872) vol.2

Balfour, Ian. *Famous diamonds* (London, William Collins Sons & Co. Ltd. 1987)

Banerjee, P. *The life of Krishna in Indian art* (New Delhi, National Museum 1978)

Barr, W. *March from Delhi to Peshawur, and from thence to Cabul* (London, 1844)

Barthorp, M. 'The 24th's other battle, soldiers of the Queen' in the *Journal of the Victorian Military Society* (1993) issue 72, March 1993

Bautze, Joachim K. *Interaction of Cultures. Indian and western painting 1780–1910* (Alexandria, Art Services International 1998)

Bayly, C. A. (ed.). *The Raj. India and the British 1600–1947* (London, National Portrait Gallery Publications 1990)

Bérinstain, V. *Phulkari, embroidered flowers from Punjab* (Paris, A.E.D.T.A. 1991)

Bhai Vir Singh (ed.) *Varan Bhai Gurdaas* [Panjabi text], (Amritsar, Khalsa Samachar, 1951)

Blackmore, H. L. *The Armouries of the Tower of London* (London, HMSO 1976)

Bourne, Samuel. *British Journal of Photography* (London, Henry Greenwood and Co. 1863, 64, 66, 67, 69, 70)

Brown, Kerry (ed.) *Sikh art and literature* (London, Routledge 1999)

Brown, Percy. *Indian architecture (Islamic Period)* (Bombay, Taraporevala Sons & Co. Private Ltd., 5th edition 1968)

Bruce, G. *Six battles for India: the Anglo-Sikh Wars, 1845–6, 1848–9* (London, Arthur Barker Ltd. 1969)

Canby, Sheila. *Poets, princes and paladins* (London, British Museum Publications 1997)

Chhabra, Gurbux Singh. 'Ranjit Singh's military administration' in *The Sikh Review* (February 1959) pp.31–42

Clarke, C. Purdon and Birdwood, George. *Indian art at Marlborough House* (1898)

Clarke, C. Purdon and Clarke, C. Stanley. *Arms and armour at Sandringham* (London, W. Griggs & Sons Ltd. 1910)

Cole, W.O. and Sambhi, Piara Singh. *The Sikhs, their beliefs and practices* (London, Routledge & Kegan Paul 1978)

Cole, W.O. and Sambhi, Piara Singh. *A popular dictionary of Sikhism* (London, Curzon Press & The Riverdale Company 1990)

Cook, Col. H. C. B. *The Sikh Wars; The British Army in the Punjab 1845–49* (London, Leo Cooper Ltd. 1975)

Coomaraswamy, A.K. *Catalogue of paintings in the Boston Museum of Fine Arts* (Boston, Museum of Fine Arts 1916)

Crawford, E.R. 'The Sikh Wars 1845–9' in Bond, B. *Victorian Military Campaigns* (London, Hutchinson & Co. 1967)

Crill, Rosemary. 'Embroidered topography', in *Hali* (London, Hali Publications Ltd. 1993) No.67, pp.90–95

Cunningham, Captain J. D. A. *History of the Sikhs, from the origins of the nation to the battles of the Sutlej* (London, John Murray 1849)

Desmond, Ray. *The India Museum, 1801–79* (London, India Office Library and Records, HMSO 1982)

Dimond, F. and Taylor, R. *Crown and Camera* (London, Viking 1987)

Dunbar, Janet. *Golden Interlude, The Edens in India 1836–42* (London, John Murray Ltd. 1988; 1st edition 1955)

Eden, Emily. *Up the country. Letters from India* (London, Curzon Press 1978; 1st edition 1844)

Egerton, W. *An illustrated handbook of Indian arms* (London, 1880)

Elgood, Robert. *Firearms of the Islamic world in the Tareq Rajab Museum, Kuwait* (London, I. B. Tauris 1995)

Elgood, Robert (ed.). *Islamic arms and armour* (London, Scolar Press 1979)

Falconer, John. 'Photography in nineteenth-century India', in *The Raj, India and the British 1600–1947* (London, National Portrait Gallery 1990), pp.264–77

Falk, Toby. *The British in India* (London, Kyburg Limited 1988)

Fane, H. E. *Five years in India* (London, Henry Colburn 1842) 2 vols

Fauja Singh Bajwa. *The military system of the Sikhs during the period 1799–1849* (Delhi, Motilal Banarssidas 1964)

Featherstone, Donald. *Victorian colonial warfare: India* (London, Blandford 1992)

Fox, Richard G. *Lions of the Punjab; culture in the making* (Berkeley, University of California Press 1990)

Gernsheim, H. *The History of Photography* (London, Oxford University Press 1955)

Gluckman, Dale C. 'Wrapped in paradise: a brief early history of the Kashmir shawl and its decoration' in *Orientations* (April 1997), vol.28, no.4, pp.78–83

Goetz, H. 'An early Basohli-Chamba rumal: the wedding of Raja Jit Singh of Chamba and Rani Sarada Devi of Jammu 1783', in *Bulletin of the Baroda State Museum and Picture Gallery* (Baroda 1945–46) vol.3, pt.1, pp.35–42

Goswamy, B. N. 'Pahari painting: the family as the basis of style', in *Marg* (Bombay, Marg Publications 1968) vol.21 no.4, pp.17–62

Goswamy, B. N. 'Sikh painting: an analysis of some aspects of patronage', in *Oriental Art* (Surrey, The Oriental Art Magazine Ltd. 1969) vol.15 no.1, pp.44–50

Goswamy, B. N. *Painters at the Sikh Court: a study based on twenty documents* (Wiesbaden, Franz Steiner Verlag GMBH 1975)

Goswamy, B. N. 'Painting at Patiala', in *Pushpanjali* (Bombay, M. L. Bhuwania 1980) vol.4, pp.56–60

Goswamy, B. N. 'A matter of taste; some notes on the context of painting in Sikh Panjab' in *Maharaja Ranjit Singh as Patron of the Arts* (Bombay, Marg Publications 1981) pp.61–88

Goswamy, B. N. *Rasa – les neuf visages de l'art indien* (Paris, Ministère des Relations Exterieures & Association Française d'Action Artistique 1986a)

Goswamy, B. N. *Essence of Indian art* (San Francisco, Asian Art Museum of San Francisco 1986b)

Goswamy, B. N. and Fischer Eberhard. *Pahari Masters – court painters of Northern India* (Zurich, Artibus Asiae Publishers and the Museum Rietberg 1992)

Goswamy, Karuna. 'Frescoes in the Sheesh Mahal at Patiala' in *Roopa-Lekha* (New Delhi, All India Fine Arts and Crafts Society n.d.) vol. 38 no.1–2, pp.120–7

Goswamy, Karuna. *Kashmiri painting: assimilation and diffusion; production and patronage* (Shimla, Indian Institute of Advanced Studues 1998)

Grewal, J. S. 'The Sikhs of the Punjab' in *The New Cambridge History of India* (Cambridge, Cambridge University Press 1990) vol.2.3

Grier, S. C. *The letters of Warren Hastings to his wife* (London, William Blackwood & Sons 1905)

Griffin, Lepel. *Rajas of the Punjab* (Patiala, 1873; reprint 1970)

Griffin, L. and Massy, C. F. *Chiefs and families of note in the Panjab* (Lahore 1910)

Gupta, Charu Smita. *Zardozi, glittering gold embroidery* (New Delhi, Abhinav Publications 1996)

Guy, John and Swallow, Deborah (eds). *Arts of India 1550–1900* (London, V&A Publications 1990)

Guy, Alan J. and Boyden, Peter B. (eds). *Soldiers of the Raj, the Indian Army 1600–1947* (London, National Army Museum 1997)

Haider, S. Z. *Islamic arms and armour of Muslim India* (Lahore, Bahadur Publishers 1991)

Hall, M. 'The Victoria & Albert Museum's Mahabharata hanging', in *South Asian Studies* (1996) vol.12

Head, R. *Catalogue of paintings, drawings, engravings and busts in the collection of the Royal Asiatic Society* (London, Royal Asiatic Society 1991)

Heathcote, T. A. *The Afghan Wars 1839–1919* (London, Osprey 1980)

Hendley, Thomas Holbein. *Damascening on steel or iron, as practised in India* (London, W. Griggs & Sons Ltd. 1892)

Hering, H. *Photographic views and panoramas* (London, Hering n.d.)

Herrli, Hans. The Coins of the Sikhs (Nagpur, Indian Society 1993)

Hewitt, J. *Official catalogue of the Tower Armouries* (London, 1859)

Howarth, Stephen. *The Koh-i-Noor diamond: the history and the legend* (London, Quartet Books 1980)

Hugel, C. *Travels in Kashmir and the Panjab* (London, 1845)

Irwin, J. *The Kashmir shawl* (London, HMSO 1973) no.29

Irwin, J. *Treasures of Indian art at the Victoria and Albert Museum* (Edinburgh, Charles Skilton Ltd. 1978)

Irwin, J. and Hall, M. *Indian embroideries* (Ahmedabad, Calico Musem of Textiles and S. R. Bastikar 1973) vol.2

Israel, Nigel B. '"The unkindest cut of all" – recutting the Koh-i-Nur', in *Journal of Gemology* (London, the Gemmological Association 1992) 23–3, p.176

Kang, Kanwarjit Singh. *Punjab art and culture* (Delhi, Atma Ram & Sons 1988)

Kaur, Madanjit. *The Golden Temple: past and present* (Amritsar, Guru Nanak Dev University Press 1983)

Khalid Anis Ahmed. *Intercultural encounter in Mughal miniatures (Mughal-Christian miniatures)* (Lahore, National College of Arts Publications 1995)

Khan, Omar. 'John Burke: photo-artist of the Raj', in *History of Photography* (London and Washington DC, Taylor and Francis 1997) vol.21 no.3, pp.236–43

Khandalavala, K. *Pahari miniature painting* (Bombay, 1958)

Khilnani, N.M. *British power in the Punjab 1839–58* (Bombay, 1972)

Knight, I. *Queen Victoria's enemies (3); India* (London, Osprey 1990)

Koezuka, T. (ed.) *The art of the Indian courts: miniature paintings and decorative arts from the Indian collection at the Victoria and Albert Museum* (Osaka, 1993)

Kohli, Sita Ram (ed.) *Zafarnama-i-Ranjit Singh* (Lahore 1928)

Lafont, Jean-Marie. *French administrators of Maharaja Ranjit Singh* (New Delhi, National Book Shop 1986)

Lafont, Jean-Marie et al. *Le Songe d'un habitant du Mogol et autres fables (de Jean de la Fontaine) illustrées par Imam Bakhsh Lahori* (Paris, RMN and Imprimerie Nationale 1989)

LaRocca, Donald J. *The Gods of War: sacred imagery and the decoration of arms and armor* (New York, the Metropolitan Museum of Art 1996)

Lawrence, Henry Montgomery L. *Adventures of an officer in the service of Runjeet Singh* (London, 1845)

Lawrence, John. *Lawrence of Lucknow, a story of love* (London, Hodder & Stoughton 1990)

Leach, Linda York. *Mughal and Other Indian Paintings from the Chester Beatty Library* (London, Scorpion Cavendish 1995) 2 vols.

Levi-Strauss, M. *The Romance of the Cashmere Shawl* (Ahmedabad, 1986)

Lobligeois, Mireille. 'Les miniatures indiennes de la collection Feuillet de Conches' in *Arts Asiatiques* (Paris 1992) vol. XLVII, pp.19–28

Lockhart, C. *Nadir Shah* (Lahore 1976)

Login, Lady L. *Sir John Login and Duleep Singh* (London, William H. Allan and Co. 1890)

Losty, Jeremiah P. *The art of the book in India* (London, British Library 1982)

Mason, Philip. *A matter of honour* (London, Jonathan Cape 1974)

Mathews, O. *The album of carte-de-visite and cabinet portrait photographs, 1854–1917* (London, Reedminster Publications Ltd. 1974)

McCosh, John. *Advice to officers in India* (London, William H. Allan and Co. 1856)

McKenzie, Ray. '"The laboratory of mankind": John McCosh and the beginnings of photography in British India', in *History of Photography* (London and Washington DC, Taylor and Francis 1987) vol.11, no.2, pp.109–119

McLeod, W. H. *Guru Nanak and the Sikh Religion* (Delhi, Oxford University Press 1978; 1st edition 1968)

McLeod, W. H. (trans.) *The B-40 Janam-Sakhi* (Amritsar, Guru Nanak Dev University 1980)

McLeod, W. H. *Who is a Sikh?* (Oxford, Clarendon Press 1989)

McLeod, W. H. *Sikhism* (London, Penguin 1997)

Melikian-Chirvani, Assudullah Souren. *Islamic metalwork from the Iranian world 8th–18th Centuries* (London, HMSO 1982)

Menkes, Suzy. *The royal jewels* (London, Grafton Books 1985)

Murphy, Veronica. 'A note on some recently discovered Tipu shawl fragments in England and comparative material in the Bharat Kala Bhavan' in *Chhavi* (Benares, Bharat Kala Bhavan 1981) vol.2, pp.61–69

Nabholz-Kartaschoff, M.-L. *Golden sprays and scarlet flowers: traditional Indian textiles from the Museum of Ethnography, Basel, Switzerland* (Kyoto, Shikosha Publishing Co. Ltd. 1986)

Nadiem, Ihsan H. *Rohtas, formidable fort of Sher Shah* (Lahore, Sang-e-Meel Publications nd.)

Nesbitt, Eleanor. 'The body in Sikh tradition', in *Religion and the body*, edited by Sarah Coakley (Cambridge, Cambridge University Press 1997), pp. 289–305

Okada, Amina. *Imperial Mughal painters* (New York, Flammarion 1992)

Ondaatje, Michael. *The English Patient* (London, Vintage 1992)

Osborne, W. G. *The court and camp of Runjeet Singh* (London, Henry Colburn 1840)

Paul, Suwarcha. 'A dated Sikandar Nama shawl in the Chandigarh museum', in *Lalit Kala* (New Delhi, Lalit Kala Akademi 1982) no.20, pp.35–7

Paul, Suwarcha. *Sikh miniatures in Chandigarh Museum* (Chandigarh, Govt. Museum and Art Gallery 1985)

Pearse, Hugh (ed.). *Soldier and traveller, the memoirs of Alexander Gardner, Colonel of artillery in the service of Maharaja Ranjit Singh* (Edinburgh & London, William Blackwood 1898)

Pemble, J. *Miss Fane in India* (Gloucester, J. Pemble 1985)

Pinney, Christopher. 'Colonial anthropology' in *The Raj. India and the British 1600–1947* (London, National Portrait Gallery Publications 1990), pp.252–64

Prinsep, H. T. *Origin of the Sikh power in the Punjab and political life of Muha-raja Runjeet Singh* (Calcutta, G. H. Huttman, Military Orphan Press 1834)

Quraeshi, Samina. *Lahore – The city within* (Singapore, Concept Media Pte. Ltd. 1988)

Raghu Rai and Khushwant Singh. *The Sikhs* (Varanasi, Lustre Press Pvt. Ltd. 1984)

Rait, R.S. *Life and campaigns of Hugh, 1st Viscount Gough* (London, Archibald Constable & Co. Ltd. 1903)

Randhawa, M. S. 'Kangra Artists' in *Roopa-Lekha* (New Delhi, All India Fine Arts and Crafts Society 1956) vol.27, no.1, pp.4–10

Randhawa, M. S. 'Maharaja Sansar Chand – the patron of Kangra painting' in *Roopa-Lekha* (New Delhi, All India Fine Arts and Crafts Society 1961) vol.32, no.2, pp.1–30

Randhawa, M. S. 'Sikh Painting', in *Roopa-Lekha* (New Delhi, All India Fine Arts and Crafts Society 1971) vol.39, no.1, pp.21–32

Randhawa, M. S. 'Kehar Singh and Kapur Singh: Two Punjabi Artists of the 19th Century', in *Chhavi* (Benares, Bharat Kala Bhavan 1971) Golden Jubilee vol.1, pp.67–9

Riboud, K. et al. *Quelques aspects du châle cachemise* (Paris, A.E.D.T.A. 1987)

Robinson, H. R. *Oriental Armour* (London, 1967)

Sampson, Gary D. 'The success of Samuel Bourne in India', in *History of photography* (London and Washington DC, Taylor and Francis 1992) vol.16 no.4, pp.336–47

Se, S. *The military system of the Marathas* (Calcutta, 1928)

Seetal, Sohan Singh. *The Sikh misals and the Panjab States* (Ludhiana, Lahore Book Shop 1981)

Sher Singh. *The sikligars of Punjab* (New Delhi and Jullundur, Sterling Publishers Private Ltd. 1966)

Shiromani Gurdwara Prabandhak Committee: *Sabdarath Sri Guru Granth Sahibji* [Panjabi text], (Amritsar, 1969), vols.1–4

Singh, Bhagat. *Maharaja Ranjit Singh and his times* (New Delhi, Sehgal Publishers Service 1990)

Singh, Harbans. *The heritage of the Sikhs* (New Delhi, Manohar Publications 1983) 3 vols.

Singh, Harbans (ed.) *Encyclopaedia of Sikhism* (Patiala, Punjabi University 1992), vols.1–3

Singh, Khushwant. *A History of the Sikhs* (1st edition Princeton University Press 1963; 2nd Indian edition Delhi, Oxford University Press 1991)

Singh, Khushwant, Poovaya-Smith, Nima and Ponnapa, Kaveri. *Warm and rich and fearless, a brief survey of Sikh culture* (Bradford Art Galleries & Museums 1991)

Singh, Nikky-Guninder Kaur. *The feminine principle in the Sikh vision of the transcendent* (Cambridge, Cambridge University Press 1993)

Singh, Nikky-Guninder Kaur. *The name of my beloved: verses of the Sikh Gurus* (London, Harper Collins 1995)

Singh, Nripinder. *Sikh moral tradition* (New Delhi, Manohar Publications 1990)

Singh, Patwant. *The Golden Temple* (New Delhi, Time Books International 1988)

Singh, Piar. *B-40 Janamsakhi Sri Guru Nanak Dev ji*, [Panjabi] 2nd ed. (Amritsar, Guru Nanak Dev University 1989)

Skelton, R. et al. *The Indian heritage: court life and arts under Mughal rule* (London, V&A and Herbert Press 1982)

Skelton, R., et al. *Facets of Indian art: a symposium held at the Victoria and Albert Museum 26–28 April and 1 May 82* (London, V&A Publications 1986)

Smyth, Captain R. *Plans of ordnance captured by the army of the Sutledge...during the campaign of 1845–6, with elevations of gun carriages*, n.d. [1846]

Sotheby's: *Colstoun, Haddington, East Lothian, Monday 21st and Tuesday 22nd May 1990* (London, Sotheby's 1988)

Srivastava, R. P. *Punjab painting* (New Delhi, Abhinav Publications 1983)

Srivastava, R. P. *Art and archaeology of Punjab* (New Delhi, Sundeep Prakashan 1990)

Srivastava, S. P. *Art and cultural heritage of Patiala* (New Delhi, Sundeep Prakashan 1991)

Stronge, Susan, Smith, Nima and Harle, J. C. *A golden treasury. Jewellery from the Indian subcontinent* (London and Ahmedabad, V&A and Mapin Publishing Pvt. Ltd. 1989)

Stronge, Susan. 'Colonel Guthrie's collection. Jades of the Mughal era', in *Oriental Art* 1993, vol.39, no.4, pp.4–13

Stronge, Susan. 'The myth of the Timur Ruby', in *Jewellery Studies* (London, Society of Jewellery Historians 1996) vol.7 pp.5–12

Suri, V. S. (trans. by V. S. Suri), *Umdat ut-tawarikh Daftar III, parts I–V, Chronicle of the reign of Maharaja Ranjit Singh, by Lala Sohan Lal Suri, Vakil at the Court of Lahore* (New Delhi 1961)

Surjit, Hans. *B-40 Janamsakhi. Guru Baba Nanak Paintings* (Amritsar, Guru Nanak Dev University 1987)

Thomas, G. 'Indian Mutiny veterans: the Tytlers', in *History of Photography* (London and Washington DC, Taylor and Francis 1985) vol.9, no.4, pp.267–73

Titley, Norah. *Miniatures from Persian manuscripts. A catalogue and subject index of paintings from Persia, India and Turkey in the British Library and the British Museum* (London, British Museum Publications Ltd. 1977)

Topsfield, A. *Introduction to Indian court painting* (London, V&A Publications 1984)

Topsfield, A. *Paintings from the Rajput courts* (London, Pasricha Fine Arts 1968)

Twining, Lord. *A history of the crown jewels of Europe* (London, B. T. Batsford 1960)

Vigne, G. T. *Travels in Kashmir, Ladak, Iskardo, and the countries adjoining the mountain-course of the Indus and the Himalaya, North of the Panjab* (London 1842)

Viscount, H. A. Dillon. *Illustrated guide to the Armouries* (London, 1910)

Waldemar, Prince. *Zur Erinnerung der Reise des Prinzen Waldemar nach Indien in den Jahren 1844–46* (Berlin, 1853) 2 vols.

Walker, D. *Flowers underfoot. Indian carpets of the Mughal era* (New York, The Metropolitan Museum of Art 1997)

Watson, J. Forbes and Kaye, John William. *The people of India* (London, India Museum, William Allen and Co. 1868–75) 8 vols.

Watt, G. *Indian art at Delhi 1903* (Calcutta, Government Printing Press n. d.)

Welch, Stuart Cary. *Imperial Mughal painting* (London, Chatto & Windus, 1978)

Welch, Stuart Cary. *Room for wonder, Indian painting during the British period 1760–1880* (New York, The American Federation of Arts 1978)

Welch, Stuart Cary. *India, art and culture 1300–1900* (New York, The Metropolitan Museum of Art and Holt, Rinehart and Winston 1985)

Wurgart, Lewis D. *The imperial imagination: magic and myth in Kipling's India* (Middletown, Wesleyan University Press 1983)

Yule, Col. Henry and Coke Burnell, Arthur. *Hobson-Jobson: being a glossary of Anglo-Indian colloquial words and phrases and of kindred terms; etymological, historical, geographical, and discursive* (London, John Murray 1886)

Zulfiqar, Ahmad (ed.) *Notes on Punjab and Mughal India. Selections from the Journal of the Punjab Historical Society* (Lahore, Sang-e-meel publications 1988)

INDEX

AUTHOR PROFILES

SUSAN STRONGE, curator in the Indian and South-East Asian Department at the V&A, specialises in the courtly arts arts of northern India from the 16th to the 19th centuries.

KHUSHWANT SINGH is one of India's foremost novelists, historians and writers, whose *History of the Sikhs* is the starting point for any study of the subject, combining careful and methodical historical research with an extremely readable style.

NIKKY-GUNINDER KAUR SINGH is an associate professor of religious studies at Colby College in Maine. Her recent translation of devotional poetry of the Sikh Gurus, *The Name of My Beloved* (The International Sacred Literature Trust), has received wide acclaim.

PATWANT SINGH is another leading, highly respected Sikh writer. His many books include *The Golden Temple* (Times Books International, 1988), *The Sikhs* (John Murray, 1999).

A.S. MELIKIAN-CHIRVANI is a cultural historian and research director at the Paris National Centre for Scientific Research. He is the leading authority on the connection between the visual arts and literature in the Iranian world and the Persian-speaking courts of Islamic India.

B.N. GOSWAMY has devoted most of his life to the study of painting in the Panjab, carrying out seminal research on patronage at the Pahari courts and the movements of families of artists between them. He has a long association with the Museum Rietberg in Zurich which produced the landmark exhibition and book, *Pahari Masters*, in 1992.

ROSEMARY CRILL, deputy curator of the Indian and South-East Asian Department at the V&A, has published and lectured extensively on South Asian textiles. Her latest book is *Indian Ikat Textiles* (V&A Publications, 1998).

IAN KNIGHT is a well-known independent military historian whose work includes *Queen Victoria's Enemies: India* in the Men-at-Arms series (Osprey Military).

DAVID JONES, curator of Ipswich Museum, was commissioned by the Maharaja Duleep Singh Centenary Trust (UK) to carry out research on material connected with Dalip Singh in UK collections.

F.S. AIJAZUDDIN is a lineal descendant of Fakir Nuruddin, physician of Maharaja Ranjit Singh. He wrote the standard book, *Sikh Portraits by European Artists*, as well as volumes on European views of Lahore and Sikh and Pahari paintings in the Lahore Museum.

DIVIA PATEL is a curatorial assistant in the Indian and South-East Asian Department at the V&A with special responsibility for the important collection of photographs of Indian subjects.